THE PRINCE AND THE PRETENDER

BIOGRAPHY

Professor Youngson was Professor of Economics/Economic History at the University of Edinburgh from 1958 to 1974. Subsequently he was Director of the Research School of Social Sciences in Canberra, and on returning to this country, Chairman of the Royal Fine Art Commission for Scotland from 1983 to 1990. Among his other books are *The Making of Classical Edinburgh* and *Edinburgh and the Border Country*.

The Prince
&
The Pretender

TWO VIEWS OF THE '45

A J Youngson

MERCAT PRESS
EDINBURGH

First published 1985 by Croom Helm Ltd.
Reprinted 1996 by Mercat Press
53 South Bridge, Edinburgh EH1 1YS

ISBN 1873644 620

Printed and bound in Great Britain by
Athenæum Press Ltd., Gateshead, Tyne & Wear

CONTENTS

Acknowledgements   vii

Part I: Introduction   1

Part II: A History of the Rebellion   33

1. Global War   35
2. 'A Desperate Undertaking'   52
3. The Progress of the Rebels   71
4. Invasions One and Two   93
5. An Economical Victory   123

Part III: The Jacobite Rising   151

6. The House of Stuart   153
7. 'The Hour is Struck'   171
8. The Descent from the Highlands   188
9. Panic in London   206
10. Triumphs and Tragedy   228

Index   266

History is a pack of tricks we play upon the dead

Voltaire

ACKNOWLEDGEMENTS

This book is based on a study of both primary and secondary sources, many of the former and most of the latter easily accessible. I have been especially helped by two excellent recent works of scholarship, *France and the Jacobite Rising of 1745* by F.J. McLynn, and *The Butcher* by W.A. Speck. For valuable comments on the Introduction I am very much obliged to my friend Mr Jack Grainger. The errors of omission and commission which now appear in print are entirely my responsibility.

PART I

INTRODUCTION

INTRODUCTION

All perception is selection. This is another way of saying that our grasp of things is always incomplete; that there are facts before us which we fail to notice, influences that are manifest but to which we attach too little or no importance. Many of our failures, the imperfect success of many of our most earnest endeavours, are due to this cause. Selective perception affects what is done in politics, in business, in medical care, and perhaps in every sphere of life. It likewise affects what is said. The object of this book is to illustrate how this universal principle operates in the study of history.

The argument has almost nothing to do with the impossibility of our knowing everything. Certainly, the supply of information is never perfect; there are always gaps in what we know. Watching a golfing celebrity slice his drive far into the rough, we cannot be aware what vexatious thought suddenly crossed his mind, or what small blood-sucking insect at the crucial moment bit him in the back of the neck, thus causing him to play so badly. Partial knowledge is not only common, it is the rule; and its consequences can be very serious. The captain of the *Titanic* knew that there were icebergs in his area, but he did not know, and he had no means of knowing, that there was an iceberg dead ahead until he struck it in the darkness at twenty-two knots. Over 1,500 people died in that disaster, but it pales into insignificance in comparison with the consequences of other forms of not knowing. Consider the consequences of not knowing about the morbific properties of germs. Until 1676 no one had seen a microbe, although their existence here and there, or the existence of something like them, had been in a vague way suggested. Even when known about, the connection between microbes and disease was not in the least understood, and until the 1860s no proof was available that a large variety of minute organisms could enter and multiply in the body, causing fever and death. So people went on eating contaminated food and drinking water that was diluted sewage without in the least understanding what they were doing, with the result that such dreadful maladies as cholera and typhus continued to kill thousands of people in Britain every year, in some years, tens of thousands. Another aspect of unavoidable ignorance is that information takes time to travel. This is always important in war, and was especially important during the '45, for it meant — to take only one example — that Louis XV and his ministers, who supported Charles's campaign, learned of his successes and failures approximately two weeks after they took place. There could thus be no well-timed co-ordination of military activities. When Charles moved southward from Carlisle towards London, Louis might have struck a decisive blow; but by the time he learned of the Jacobite advance, Charles's army was retracing its steps to Scotland. Louis simply did not have the facts in time.

Some degree of ignorance is part of the human condition; not all the facts are to be had. But the point is, that we pick and choose among the facts that *are* to be had. Even familiar and elementary facts are observed incompletely and incorrectly. Asked to recall what is stamped on the two sides of a US one cent coin, fewer than 50 per cent of respondents in an extensive American test could remember even half the elements of the design; almost all stated (correctly) that a person is represented on one side, but there was no agreement as to whether this person is full-face, left profile, right profile, head and shoulders, or head only. The difficulties multiply when unique or unexpected events are in question. Eyewitness accounts are notoriously unreliable, especially if there is violence or danger involved. In describing a car accident, for example, half a dozen witnesses are most unlikely to agree about the sequence of events, and are almost certain to disagree about details. Even expert testimony cannot be relied on in such circumstances. Forty years ago, in the South Atlantic, the author used to fly a small seaplane which, having been launched from a catapult, returned after its flight to the mother ship and landed on the water alongside, to be recovered by a crane. Landing alongside was not easy and securing the attachment to the crane was even less easy, as the South Atlantic was never smooth and the ship did not stop; it was dangerous even to slow down. The ship carried two seaplanes and two crews. What was remarkable was that the account of the recovery given by the crew in the aircraft seldom coincided with that of the crew watching from the deck, although both understood exactly what was being done, knew what to expect, had an excellent view, and were giving matters their undivided attention. It is further the case that puzzling or disagreeable facts are apt to be suppressed or rationalised. In his well-known book *Remembering*, Sir Frederick Bartlett analysed the ways in which different people recalled a strange short story which was read to them entitled 'The War of the Ghosts'. As a North American Indian story, it contained several features alien to the European mind. When the story was recalled these features were usually omitted or westernised, and the slant of the story was consistently altered so as to fit in with the subject's own viewpoint, preferences and attitude. Thus even though the narrator had nothing to gain by providing a version that suited his or her own attitude, he (or she) invariably did so. In Bartlett's own words, 'The recall is then a construction made largely on the basis of this attitude, and its general effect is that of a justification of the attitude'.

Accuracy further diminishes with the lapse of time. In one elementary investigation, the question asked was what the weather had been like during the previous week, when it had snowed in the first few days and then cleared. Out of 56 respondents, only 7 reported snow. What is observed (correctly or otherwise) is only partly remembered, and to make matters still worse, when we recall an incident that took place five or ten years before, we are not neccessarily drawing on a five- or ten-year-old memory. That would be the case only if we had never recalled the event in the intervening years; if we have, then what we recall is not our original perception of the event but some later reconstruction of it. For example, one who escaped from Russia as a child in 1919 used to tell the story, years later, of his escape; how he and his parents boarded a train and travelled for several days, how the train was stopped by soldiers and everyone had to get out, how they waited in the snow, cold and fearful that their journey would not be resumed, how at last they were allowed back on board and finally crossed the border. When this story had become a part of history it was checked, and found to be correct in every particular but one; the escape had taken place in the summer; there could have been no snow on the ground. What we remember may thus be an amalgam of what we have experienced and what we later are told or imagine. And we are even capable, it seems, of remembering what never happened. Piaget, the famous Swiss psychologist, has left this reminiscence:

One of my first memories would date, if it were true, from my second year. I can still see, most clearly, the following scene, in which I believed until I was about fifteen. I was sitting in my pram, which my nurse was pushing in the Champs Elysées, when a man tried to kidnap me. I was held in by the strap fastened round me while my nurse bravely tried to stand between me and the thief. She received various scratches, and I can still see vaguely those on her face. Then a crowd gathered, a policeman with a short cloak and a white baton came up and the man took to his heels. I can still see the whole scene, and can even place it near the tube station. When I was about fifteen, my parents received a letter from my former nurse saying that she had been converted to the Salvation Army. She wanted to confess her past faults, and in particular to return the watch that she had been given on this occasion. She had made up the whole story, faking the scratches. I, therefore, must have heard, as a child, the account of this story, which my parents believed, and projected it into the past in the form of a visual memory.[1]

Yet recollection is the stuff of history! Letters, diaries, memoranda, reminiscences — these are what the historian relies on for a good deal of the time. It is no secret, of course, that the 'sources' do not all agree with one another — this is what makes history so interesting to write, and possibly makes it equally vexatious to read, because different historians tell different stories. Consider, for example, what is reported about Charles Edward at the battle of Culloden. There are a number of accounts given by persons who actually took part in the '45, and I have selected, more or less at random, those by Andrew Lumisden, Lord Elcho, MacDonell of Lochgarry and John Home. Lumisden, a young man of good education, was appointed private secretary to Charles when the latter reached Edinburgh, and accompanied him throughout the campaign. His version is as follows:

> The Prince, after riding along the lines to animate the men, placed himself about the center, that he might the more conveniently give his orders. The enemy's canon galled us much. One of the Prince's servants, who led a sumpter horse, was killed at his side . . . the Prince ordered to begin the attack . . . but the enemy . . . at last obliged us to quit the field . . . The Prince did all he could to rally his men, but to no purpose. He was therefore obliged to retire.[2]

Lord Elcho, who held high command in the army, was of much the same age as Lumisden, and he also joined Charles at Edinburgh. According to Elcho:

> The Prince who at the beginning of the Action was behind the

Irish piquetts [at the rear] guarded by Sixteen of Fitzjames's horse, turn'd about his horse and went off as soon as the left wing gave way, and never offer'd to rally any of the broken Corps.[3]

MacDonell of Lochgarry was a highland gentleman in the true celtic tradition, who joined Charles soon after he landed in Scotland, was a member of Charles's Council, and commanded the Glengarry clan during most of the campaign. He says that:

HRH being close to our line [the front line] in time of the action, and seeing at last such a total deroute of his army was obliged to retire. The horse he rode himself was shot under him, and one of his servants killed by his side with a cannon ball.[4]

Finally, what of Home's *History of the Rebellion*? This is a work which no student of the '45 can possibly ignore. Home was brought up and educated in Edinburgh, later became a minister in the Scots Kirk, and later still had to resign his parish because he wrote plays, three of which were performed with moderate but strictly ephemeral success. In middle life he was a minor figure in literary and political circles in London. His *History of the Rebellion* was not published until 1802. Unlike the other writers quoted above, Home was not present at the battle of Culloden, having fought against the Jacobites and been taken prisoner earlier in the campaign. His *History* is of great interest, however, not only because he played a part in many of the events he describes, but also because what he saw he 'committed to writing whilst the facts were recent', and subsequently, in his own words, took 'no small pains for many years, to procure authentic information of what I did not see, visiting every place which was the scene of any remarkable occurrence . . . accompanied and assisted by persons who had been present upon every occasion, and sometimes principally concerned'. Here is what Home tells us about Charles on the field of battle:

Charles placed himself on a small eminence behind the right of the second line, with Lord Balmerino's troop of Horseguards, and Colonel Shea's troop of Fitz-James's horse . . . When Charles saw the Highlanders repulsed and flying, which he had never seen before, he advanced, it is said, to go down and rally them. But the earnest entreaties of his tutor, Sir Thomas

Sheridan, and others, who assured him that it was impossible, prevailed upon him to leave the field.

Home then supplies the following footnote:

> The persons who attended Charles on the day of battle did not agree exactly in their accounts of what passed; most of them (some of whom are still alive) gave the same account that is given above. But the cornet who carried the standard of the second troop of horse guards, has left a paper, signed with his name, in which he says, that the entreaties of Sir Thomas Sheridan and his other friends would have been in vain, if General Sullivan had not laid hold of the bridle of Charles's horse and turned him about. To witness this, says the cornet, I summon mine eyes.[5]

What are we to believe? There is clearly a good deal of choice. Was Charles close to the front line or at the rear? Was his horse shot under him? Two writers mention this but two do not. Did he try to rally his men? Did he leave the field promptly or did he have to be persuaded — or even coerced?

Doubts such as these arise in connection with all sorts of incidents during the '45. Because the point is so important, a few further examples may be given. Stirling castle was unsuccessfully besieged by the rebels from 8 January 1746 until the end of the month. The siege was conducted by a French engineer, M. Mirabelle de Gordon, whose knowledge of engineering, according to Lord Elcho (who was present at the siege) was 'extremely limited' and who was 'totally destitute of judgment, discernment and common sense'. But according to Lord George Murray, who was also present, Mirabelle knew what he was doing, but was excitable and unreliable. And according to Lord MacLeod (also present) Mirabelle was always drunk. We must acknowledge that human beings are hard to understand and therefore to agree about — but surely events are easier? Not so — certainly not in the case of the siege of Stirling castle. The Chevalier de Johnstone (present at the siege, like all the others) says that 'we lost a great many men, sometimes twenty five in one day' and that Mirabelle's cannon 'produced very little effect on the batteries of the Castle'. But by Lord Elcho's account, the besiegers lost only thirty men killed during the entire operation, and their cannon (although soon silenced) 'did the walls much damage'. It is agreed that M. Mirabelle was not a success; but was he an utter incompetent or did he know his business? Was he or was he not able to inflict serious damage on Stirling castle?

Likewise, there are two very different versions of the way in which the Jacobite army reacted to the decision to retreat from Derby. According to Chevalier de Johnstone,

> The Highlanders, conceiving at first that they were on the march to attack the army of the Duke of Cumberland, displayed the utmost joy and cheerfulness, but as soon as the day allowed them to see the objects around them and they found that we were retracing our steps, nothing was to be heard throughout the whole army but expressions of rage and lamentation.[6]

But Lord Elcho gives a very different account:

> The inferior officers of the Princes army were much Surprised when they found the army moving back and imagined some bad news had been received, but when they were told everything, and found the army had marched so far into England without the least invitation from any English man of Distinction, they blamed their Superiors much for Carrying them so far, and Approved much of Going back to Scotland.[7]

It is tempting to conclude that each of these writers attributes to others (in the first case, 'the Highlanders' or 'the whole army', in the second, 'the inferior officers of the Princes army') the feelings that he experienced himself, or that he was prepared to approve in others. But once again the 'evidence' is confusing.

Let us take one last example. What happened immediately after the Jacobites were defeated at Culloden? It is clear that no rendezvous had been arranged in the event of defeat. Charles went with an escort down the Great Glen to Gortleck, twenty miles southwest of Culloden, and the remains of the army gathered at Ruthven, further south and on the other side of the mountains. What orders or messages did the army receive? Lord Elcho, who was with the Prince, states that the Scots who were with him were ordered to Ruthven but while on the road were told 'that they might disperse and every body Shift for himself the best way he Could'. The same brief advice, Elcho says, was repeated to the army at Ruthven. But according to Home, who gives Andrew Lumisden as his authority (and Lumisden was with the army), a message reached Ruthven a few days after the battle, in which Charles thanked his followers for their loyalty and bravery upon every occasion, but advised them 'to do what they thought was best for their own preservation, till a more favourable opportunity of acting presented itself'. Another version is that Charles sent a message to Ruthven notifying his commanders that there would be a review of the clans at Fort Augustus on the following day, but that news leaked out that the Prince was on his way to Glengarry, which is *west* of Fort Augustus. Not knowing what to do, Ker of Graden says that the army remained at Ruthven a few days longer awaiting clearer orders, but that none came; whereupon the army dispersed. The Chevalier de Johnstone, however, who was at Ruthven, says that Lord George Murray sent a clansman to seek orders from the Prince, and this man returned with the laconic reply, 'Let every one seek the means of escape as well as he can'. These variants are not trivial because they reflect very differently upon the Prince. None does him much credit as supreme commander, but according to Lumisden he at least thanked his followers for their past loyalty and bravery, whereas at the other extreme there is the suggestion that he was concerned only to escape at once to France, deserted his men, and even tried to deceive them as to his whereabouts and intentions.

So in the manufacture of history a second process of selection takes place, this time not in the eye of the witness, but in the mind of the historian. Out of all the information at his disposal (incomplete of course) he has to retain some items and discard others. His task is to provide a coherent explanation of events; to show what occurrences (in Oakeshott's words) 'mediate one circumstance to another', and what reasons may be supposed to have prompted men to act as they did. The satisfactoriness (or otherwise) of the explanation that he provides will, therefore, depend to a large extent on his ability to understand and explain the thinking behind the event. But because thoughts and actions are so complex, it is very difficult to make a brief explanation satisfactory. The more the historian has to abbreviate his history, the more serious become his problems of compression and omission, and the more the reader has to take the author's judgements on trust. But it does not follow that the more 'complete' the history the better it is. If our author has been invited (probably unwisely) to write the definitive study of whatever-it-is, and if he himself belongs to the exhaustive

school, whose members believe all 'facts' whatsoever to be as diamonds and rubies, abbreviation is no problem — it just does not
happen. The important and the trivial are set side by side, the
reader's attention is directed to nothing in particular, and, unless
the available evidence has been sifted in some way, conflicting
views and assessments abound. The historian has avoided one
problem and the reader is left with two: he has no light to guide
him through the chaos of information, and he is bored to tears;
l'art d'ennuyer c'est de tout dire. But if our author, like most
authors, feels obliged to limit what he writes to a certain length,
some information will have to go. He may decide, for example,
that there is no room for the Prince's horse, which may or may not
have been shot under its rider, or for the names of the units that
stood round the Prince at Culloden; his work, he believes, will still
be intelligible and useful without these details. Provided that our
author is clear in his own mind as to which question or questions he
is trying to answer, it should not be too difficult to decide, for
any given length of book, what is relevant, and what should be
excluded. It is true, admittedly, that in a sense everything is relevant; even the name of the Prince's horse, if we knew it, is relevant. But it is not important; and while it might add a touch of
verisimilitude to the narrative, its omission could make no difference to the logical structure of the writing.

It is when we come to the removal of inconsistencies and to the
question of what our author is willing to believe is true and important, and what he thinks is not true or not important, that the big
difficulties — the really monumental difficulties — arise. To a
large extent these two points merge into one. So let us take another
example where historical doubt arises, not so much because there is
conflicting testimony but rather because it is not clear what construction should be put on the testimony we have.

When the Prince's army approached Edinburgh it was a very
small force numbering between 1,800 and 2,000 men; it was ill-
armed — according to Elcho, 'the half Compleatly armed, the
others with pitch forks, Scythes, a sword or a pistol, or some only a
Staf or Stick'; and it had only one cannon. Edinburgh was the
capital of Scotland and the largest town north of Manchester. Its
capture by the Jacobites would be a remarkable triumph for them
and a serious blow for the government. The city was a walled city
and it had ample warning of Charles's approach. Yet not a shot
was fired in its defence.

The decision to fight or not rested principally with the Lord Provost. There is no doubt that he gave orders to repair the city walls, to mount cannon on them (these were brought up from Leith), and to raise and arm several companies of volunteers for the defence of the town. But the question is, were these orders intended to secure the town as far as possible or were they merely a cover-up for a surrender that was planned to take place from the start? Admittedly, the allegiance of the townspeople was divided — two-thirds of the gentlemen, it was said, favoured the government and two-thirds of the ladies favoured the Prince. But the fall of the city was no foregone conclusion. There is ample evidence that at least some of the volunteers wanted to fight; the eminent professor of mathematics who was put in charge of repairing the walls (for mathematics and fortification were closely connected in those days) thought the town defensible; the highlanders were 'averse to approach walls, and afraid of cannon'; so the idea that resistance, even if unsuccessful, might 'break the force of the rebel army' was not absurd. Doubts must therefore arise — as they arose at the time — about the Lord Provost's will to resist. He was, said one observer, 'slow in his deliberations, backward in executing things agreed'; according to another, all difficulties were 'a Handle for justifying the Provest to give up the Town to the Rebells'.[8] Home seems not to condemn the Provost for what happened but to lay most of the blame on one of the captains of the volunteers, whose leadership, he says, 'was merely a pretence of doing what he never had the most distant intention to do', and who sabotaged the city's defence. But against this, we have the word of another of the volunteers (Alexander Carlyle of Inveresk, a pillar of the eighteenth-century Kirk) that Home at this time was 'very fiery' and that the captain in question was actuated solely by 'Zeal and prowess — for personally he was a gallant Highlander'. The Lord Provost subsequently spent fourteen months in the Tower of London, was tried for neglect of duty — and acquitted. Doubts have none the less persisted. In his *Autobiography* Carlyle tells how he was in a coffeehouse in London when the news of the victory at Culloden arrived:

I was sitting at a table with Dr Smollett and Bob Smith . . . when John Stuart, the son of the Provost, who was then confined in the Tower, after turning pale and murmuring many curses, left the room in a rage, and slapped the door behind him with much violence. I said to my two companions, that lad Stuart is either a madman or a fool to discover himself in this manner, when his father is in the Tower on suspicion.[9]

Should this be treated as evidence, confirming the view that the Provost was a covert Jacobite, or is it just another good story that the conscientious scholar will set aside?

In this case, therefore, we are left to think pretty well as we please. Certainly the Provost was not determined to fight at all costs; but perhaps he was timid, or could not control his subordinates, or was irresolute in a crisis — or tried to save lives by keeping all his options open until at the last moment the Jacobites broke into the city by stealth and ruined his plans. Whoever reads the evidence has to make up his own mind, for it does not tell him what to think.

The task of the historian is therefore to select, and to prefer one interpretation of the evidence to another. On what basis does he select and prefer? The answer — although it is superficial — is obvious: he selects and prefers so as to produce a version of events which he himself finds believable and agreeable — agreeable in the sense that it accords with his view of human nature and of how things are apt to happen. The foundation of his work lies in his personality, in his attitude to life. If, for example, he believes that the world is dominated by greed and wrongdoing, or that society is arranged by the rich and the powerful so that they can retain their riches and their power, or that the British are always right, his account of — let us say — the Indian Mutiny or the General Strike in 1926 will inevitably chime in with these views. If, on the other hand, he thinks that most people are actuated at least by good intentions and is willing where necessary to give them the benefit of the doubt, and if he believes moreover that society changes in a variety of unpredictable ways, upon the desirability or undesirability of which it is not for him to pronounce, he will be more sympathetic to the aspirations of everyone, and may even have a kindly word for the rich and the successful. A couple of instances come readily to mind. In *Das Kapital* Marx gives an account of life in mid-nineteenth-century Britain. In writing this he depended on first-hand observation by his intimate friend Engels, and on government blue-books — careful compilations containing mountains of data and much invaluable personal verbatim evidence. Marx describes innumerable cases of men, women and children living in misery and filth, working long hours for a pittance in abominable conditions, tyrannised and cheated by employers engaged in a merciless and unending struggle for the last halfpenny of profit. It is an appalling picture, and it is almost certainly all true. But no one reading it would suppose that Victorian Britain destroyed the slave trade, founded the Society for Improving the Conditions of the Labouring Classes in 1844, built the railways, the Tate Gallery and innumerable other galleries, libraries and museums, increased its population and raised the general standard of living faster than any country had ever done before. Marx doubtless knew but he did not wish to say that far more families in Britain were wealthy or even affluent in 1867, when *Das Kapital* was published, than in 1827 or 1767 or any earlier date whatever. This fact he did not regard as significant — it did not accord with his view of life. Another obvious example is the treatment accorded by historians to Neville Chamberlain and his foreign policy. Many volumes have been written which dwell on Chamberlain's inexperience of foreign affairs, his remarkable confidence in his own judgement, the military potential of Czechoslovakia, the 'dishonourable' way in which the Czechs were left to their fate. But the emphasis can also be placed on Chamberlain's intense patriotism, his shrewdness and his remarkable administrative powers; on the widespread support that was given by the British public to his pacific policies; on the fact that the British armed forces were almost hopelessly unprepared for war in 1938; and on the unreliability of the French. There is lots of room for disagreement. We cannot tell, of course, chauvinism apart, why some take one side and some another; why some are sympathetic towards Chamberlain and some are against him, why some believe in 'the perpetual warfare between class and class' and some do not. One day, perhaps, biology will tell us. In the meantime it is clear only that many historians, whether they recognise the fact or not, base their work on some prior set of principles or beliefs, and that what they write is an elaboration or illustration or defence of these principles or beliefs; and that all the others, however impartial they may try to be, have their personal preferences and their natural sympathies and therefore inevitably, although perhaps quite unconsciously, design their version of events to be consonant with their ideas about life in general. This is not to say that the ideas of a good historian, even his unexamined postulates and his general view of life, may not be modified by his study of history; indeed, it would be disturbing if they were not modified in this way; but the influence of innate attitudes of mind or deeply-held beliefs is most unlikely to disappear.

The historian is therefore bound to like some characters and some patterns of behaviour better than others (we all do) and to present them in a favourable light, and is very likely to prefer some causes to others as well. This can result in very emotional writing — numerous histories of the '45 make a far greater appeal to the reader's emotions than to his intellect. But serious history springs from and acts upon reason. It is admittedly too much to ask that the historian should write like a machine, without love, without hatred, without approval, without disapproval, without even the faintest tinge of preference. This is why Oakeshott's 'specifically "historical" attitude' is really not possible. According to Oakeshott, the unique quality of the historian is to be interested in past events for their own sake, without reference in any way to present problems, and therefore without any intention of influencing future events. The 'historical' past, in his view, as distinct from the 'practical' past, is a purely logical construct obtained from documents, and it is not seen by the historian as having any relationship to or possible influence upon the present; that is to say, he chooses the data which he studies solely on the grounds of 'appropriateness and completeness' and not in the least on account of the events and circumstances of his own life; he is in no way influenced by the hopes and fears, the preferences and ambitions which surround him in his present on-going world and which limit or motivate his 'practical' activities.

> The place of an event is not determined by its relation to subsequent events. What is being sought here is neither a justification, nor a criticism nor an explanation of a subsequent or present condition of things. In 'history' no man dies too soon or by 'accident'; there are no successes and no failures and no illegitimate children. Nothing is approved, there being no desired condition of things in relation to which approval can operate; and nothing is denounced. This past is without the moral, the political or the social structure which the practical man transfers from *his* present to *his* past. The pope's intervention did not change the course of events, it *was* the course of events, and consequently his action was not an 'intervention'. X did not die 'too soon'; he died when he did. Y did not dissipate his

resources in a series of useless wars: the wars belong to the actual course of events, not some imaginary illegitimate course of events. It was not 'the Liberator' who addressed the meeting in Dublin; it was Daniel O'Connell.[10]

But this programme of complete non-approval and complete non-disapproval cannot be realised, because historians are human. They may not consciously wish to instruct their readers by recalling past events from the dead so that these events may deliver some message favoured by the historian. Certainly they would repudiate the idea that they construct a 'living past' solely or principally in order to have it repeat 'with spurious authority' the utterances which they themselves put into its mouth. But they cannot avoid interpreting the past, just as they are bound to interpret the present, in the light of their own nature and their own experiences. The juice of the historian's humanity cannot be altogether squeezed out of his writing — nor should it be. But sense should keep well ahead of sensibility.

The difficulty arises most acutely in respect of individual character. For example, there is not a lot of room for argument about what Neville Chamberlain — or Peel or Pitt or Charles II — did or said, but there is a great deal of room for argument about what influenced them and what they intended. The thoughts and motives of others can be surmised but never known, and so the historian has a fairly free hand in 'interpreting' character. If he sincerely believes that Chamberlain was weak and short-sighted in his dealings with Hitler, he can present sufficient 'evidence' to support that position; if, on the other hand, he is a Chamberlain supporter, he can emphasise actions and quote from speeches that show the Prime Minister as honest and resolute in a very difficult situation. The reader, not having access to or time to read everything there is about Munich and its antecedents, is presented, either way, with a convincing picture of the man, his colleagues and the march of events. He does not know what evidence is missing (and there is bound to be a lot); he does not know how just the emphases are; but above all, he does not know how far the *dramatis personae* whom he reads about in the book would correspond with his own understanding of these persons had he ever met them or had time to read all that is known about them. What Shakespeare (who was admittedly not a historian) did for Richard III (who may — it is just possible — have been a charming fellow), many historians have done in a small, unconscious, but significant way for many other historical persons; most of all, doubtless, for the heroes and the villains.

Thus, while the 'bare facts' cannot be denied (sometimes there are surprisingly few of them), the writer of history selects what suits him from a mass of accompanying information, creates such characters as he can understand and believe in, and sets them to act out their parts in a logical play. In short, he remakes the past, playing his tricks upon the dead.

It must be made clear at this point that we are discussing history, not propaganda. The genuine historian makes every effort to avoid bias. He must try not to be unjust. Those writers fail to be historians of whom it can be said:

> that they are seeking to secure our approval for one side, and, in order to achieve this, unfairly denigrate the other; that in dealing with one side they cite evidence and use methods of inference or presentation which, for no good reason, they deny to the other; and that their motive for doing this derives from their conviction of how men should be, and what they should do; and sometimes also that these convictions spring from views which (judged in terms of the ordinary standards and scales of value which prevail in the societies to which they and we belong) are too narrow; or irrational or inapplicable to the historical period in question; and that because of this they have suppressed or distorted the true facts, as true facts are conceived by the educated society of their, or our, time.[11]

Writing of this kind is not history, but propaganda. And the reader will scarcely fail to notice if passages of moral, philosophical, political or social argument are used to support or 'explain' some contentious movement or institution; or if some large group of people — say, the British in India, or the opium traders on the China coast — are steadily presented as better (or worse) than the rest of humanity. Only a very ingenuous reader would suppose that such writing is unbiased and designed to give a completely fair account of what happened.

History depends upon honest invention. Propaganda, on the other hand, is apt to require the suppression of undeniably important facts and sometimes the fabrication of quite new ones. For example, a small book entitled *The Opium War*, published in 1976, explains how, in 1839, the Chinese called a halt to the opium trade and put pressure on the foreign community by withdrawing all their Chinese employees. According to this volume, the British Chief Superintendant of Trade, 'seeing the futility of outright resistance . . . ordered the British traders to surrender their opium, promising that the British government would give them compensation'. There is no reference to the fact that the Superintendant, who had come to Canton to discuss the situation, had been made a prisoner as soon as he stepped ashore (and remained a prisoner for two months), along with some 270 foreign residents, and that a triple cordon of boats blocked the river approaches for six miles down to Whampoa. In the matter of fabrication, this well-devised little book contains several statements — such as, 'The Chinese people had long been deeply concerned about the spread of opium and firmly demanded its prohibition' — which, to say the very least, are thoroughly misleading, if only because the opium trade could not have survived without very extensive Chinese connivance. In general, omission is easier and safer than fabrication, and is the standby of propagandists; everyone has read, or heard of, accounts of Nazi Germany which fail to mention the concentration camps, or histories of Russia under Stalin whose authors seem not to know that ten million people or more simply disappeared during this period.

Crude propaganda is easily separated from history. But there is unfortunately no clear dividing line between them, because both are and have to be selective in their presentation of the 'facts'. It is a matter of degree and of honesty. For example, there are numerous histories of the '45 which make almost no mention of French support. Is this reasonable? The answer must depend, to some extent, on the length of the account; a very brief study might be fully taken up with more important aspects of the conflict. But who is to say what is more important? A chronicle of the battles that were fought might seem to be the essence of the matter, but this would scarcely be history at all for it would not explain how and why these battles came to be fought — it would not explain their meaning. To omit all reference to French aid is justifiable only if the historian believes that the '45 would have occurred and would have followed much the same course that it did even if Louis XV and his ministers had never known nor cared anything about it; and that it involved matters vastly more important than a mismanaged item in French foreign policy. The historian who concentrates all his attention on Charles Edward and the clans can indeed argue that French assistance was very little; and in any case he is entitled to believe that the '45 is worth studying because it concerns clan loyalties and the clan system in action, and so gives us a glimpse of the ancient celtic civilisation that was so different from our own. This obviously is another way of saying that the facts are selected to suit the sympathies and interests of the historian; but so it is also with the writer of propaganda. It cannot even be said that although the methods may be the same in the two cases the intentions are different; for some propagandists doubtless believe that their version of events contains all that is true and that matters; and historians, believing the same, hope to persuade their readers to adopt their point of view. The gap between honest history and honest propaganda may be very small indeed.

Let us confine ourselves, however, to the honest historian, anxious to persuade his readers of the truth as he sees it. He is going to present the actors in the play as they seem to him, and the facts as he finds them understandable — he cannot do anything else, he must choose what he believes in. But beyond this he still has a good deal of latitude, and there are four ways in which he can go a little further in his efforts to put across his own particular point of view.

First of all, there are sure to be minor incidents, or aspects of character, which may or may not have been significant but which take on a special significance when singled out from the mainstream of events and the general picture of what was going on. Take, for example, the impression that Charles made upon observers while he was in Edinburgh. All agreed that he was 'a goodly person'. He was of well above average height, dark-eyed and sunburnt, his features regular, a graceful and masterly horseman, physically extremely fit. To some he looked like a man of fashion, and to others like a hero. But everyone who was in a position to do so noticed a curious thing about him; as he had already demonstrated during several years in Rome, he had no taste for the company of women. 'At night their came a Great many Ladies of Fashion, to Kiss his hand, but his behaviour to them was very Cool: he had not been much used to Womens Company, and was always embarrassed while he was with them.'[12] Perhaps this is quite irrelevant to Charles's conduct in politics and war, or to his fitness for a throne. But somehow it is not reassuring. For most men and almost all women, a disinclination to female company is a defect in a man's character. It makes him seem peculiar, a less sympathetic person than otherwise he might be. So if the historian draws attention to it he makes the reader sympathise with Charles a little less than he might otherwise do, but if he says nothing about this peculiar trait — and why should he mention it? — the reader's sympathies remain unaffected.

Secondly, the historian, who is constantly using his imagination to enable him to understand people whom he has never met and events that he has never witnessed, can go a little further and indulge in a little downright invention. He can, for example, attribute to his characters thoughts of which, in the nature of things, he has no certain knowledge. In the old days, this was a favourite proceeding. At the christening of Prince Charles, we are told by one nineteenth-century historian, there 'must' [*sic*] have been several, who reflected and 'felt ready to cry out':

> Why all this pomp and ceremony? What has the line from which yon child has sprung ever done that there should be these rejoicings at its perpetuation? Were it not better for the God-cursed dynasty to die out and cease provoking the divine wrath? What are its annals but the history of bloodshed and oppression, failure and intrigue? Has there ever been a family whose history has been such a record of misery generation after generation? What awful details their pedigree discloses! The first of yon child's ancestors —[13]

and so on and so on for a further 250 words. The modern reader is not likely to be impressed; no one writes like that nowadays, at any rate no historian. But the modern reader is probably less on his guard against the same thing done in a different way. For example, Charles left a small garrison in Carlisle when he retreated from Derby to Scotland — three hundred unfortunate men who were made prisoner very soon afterwards and a number of whom were subsequently executed. Their fate was predictable. Why did Charles leave them in Carlisle? According to one eminent historian, he was 'actuated by a natural desire to keep his father's flag flying in England as long as possible'.[14] As far as I am aware, there is no evidence whatever of this 'natural desire', and it seems to have been invented two hundred years later in order to justify, as far as possible, what the same writer admits was 'a blunder'. (One of the Prince's own followers recorded his opinion that leaving a garrison in Carlisle was inconsistent with either humanity or self-interest, and resolved to 'draw a veil over this piece of cruelty'.[15]) Or consider the following: 'Most of [Charles's] advisers had not wanted to leave Scotland. They invaded England because Charles insisted that he would receive massive support there'.[16] The first of these statements may be correct, although accounts of what passed at Charles's councils differ. But how does anyone know that Charles's forecasts of 'massive support' (and what, in any case, is 'massive'?) were what made up the waverers' minds? We can be sure only that the miscellaneous collection of men who were his advisers were influenced by many motives — hope of booty, of preferment or of glory, love of war, loyalty to the House of Stuart, fear of more powerful neighbours — there are numberless possibilities in innumerable combinations. To say that the Prince persuaded his followers to invade England by raising hopes that were largely groundless and that were quite falsified in the event is at best a simplification of the truth, and — much more significant — in a few casual-seeming words it makes Charles appear in an unfavourable light.

Not content with imaginary thoughts, historians also sometimes make play with imaginary events. The '45 provides a classic opportunity. Suppose that Louis XV had provided more timely support — what then?

> If Earl Marischal Keith . . . had been able to land in Scotland early in September with 3,000 men from France, insurrection in Scotland *would have been* [my italics] near-universal and the Highland army might have reached London even before George II's troops had been recalled from Flanders. Alternatively, if Lord Elcho's suggestion had been implemented and the entire Irish Brigade had been landed in fishing vessels on the English coast before the British regiments returned from the Low Countries, the reluctant Skye chiefs MacLeod and MacDonald of Sleat *would have joined* [my italics] the Prince.[17]

But how can we be so sure? And it should be noticed that such speculations quietly prejudice the mind of the reader — they make it seem, in this case, that it was almost by chance that the rebellion did not succeed. But if we were to suppose something else that did not happen — let us say, that General Cope fell back from the Corriearrack to Stirling, or that Field-Marshal Wade was replaced by Sir John Ligonier just after Prestonpans — then the Jacobites might never even have entered England and the rebellion might very well have fizzled out after only a few weeks. Or let us take another field for speculation, a very popular one. Suppose that Prince Charles and his followers, having advanced as far as Derby, had pressed on to London. What would have happened? Many historians have answered this question with remarkable assurance — but not always in the same sense. 'Had the Prince been permitted to carry out his intention of advancing upon London, he would have taken his prosperity at the flood, and been led on to fortune.'[18] Perhaps. 'In the light of all the available evidence, then, it is difficult to resist the conclusion that if Charles had marched forward from Derby he would have won the crown for his father.'[19] It may be difficult, but it is not impossible. 'Charles proceeded throughout on the bland assumption that all troops sent against him would always run away without fighting. It was an idiotic assumption and only on it could a decision to advance from Derby to London be justified.'[20] To advance, therefore, as Charles proposed, was absurd; but surely an army of 5,000 could have overcome feeble or disjointed resistance, and the question therefore becomes, how much resistance are we to imagine? Clearly, what did not happen is being used by these three writers to support their opinion of the Prince — in two cases of his wisdom, and in the last of his folly. And in any case, the whole argument is nonsensical. Charles's followers were against an advance from Derby. How could they, *in that state of mind*, have gone on to take London? To imagine that they advanced requires us to imagine also a preceding change in their state of mind; and such a change would have had to depend upon circumstances or personalities being other than they were — that is to say, upon the existence of a fictional situation.

Nevertheless, the game of interlacing history with fiction is so popular that another example may be given. Let us return to the Lord Provost of Edinburgh. His actions (or inactions) are implicitly defended in a recent history by imagining what would have happened if the city had been defended: 'Resistance inflicting serious casualties on an army storming the utterly inadequate city defences would certainly have been followed by pillage and just possibly by massacre, at least of armed defenders. The game was not worth the candle.'[21] So the Lord Provost was right. But this couple of sentences provides an excellent example of conjuring in history. First, the city defences are described as 'utterly inadequate'.

They were certainly poor, but they were never put to the test and 'utterly' is a strong word. Secondly, 'serious casualties' are assumed in spite of the hopelessly feeble defences. And in the end there is certain pillage and possible massacre (always a nasty word) although the Jacobite army seems to have shown notable restraint until it began its retreat from Derby. No one can say that this version of the defence of Edinburgh is wrong, because no defence ever took place. But the Lord Provost comes out of it very well.

And incidentally it is worth noting that even reputable historians are sometimes a little less than candid when two views of a character or incident are possible. For example, when the '45 was over, the Lord Provost of Edinburgh was accused of treason and acquitted. Nevertheless, many of his contemporaries believed him to be a Jacobite at heart, and the truth cannot be known. It is therefore somewhat surprising to be told by a modern historian that 'whatever [the Lord Provost's] private convictions there is no doubt that he did his civic duty',[22] and equally so to be told by an older one that 'There can be no doubt but that [the Lord Provost] was a Jacobite . . . and was guilty of high treason inasmuch as he neglected precautions which a loyal subject in the face of an enemy should have . . . scrupulously observed'.[23] Perhaps readers should be especially on their guard when historians use the words 'no doubt'. Sometimes it seems that the more evidence one reads (and this has nothing to do with what historians, ballad-makers, scandalmongers and romancers have subsequently written on the subject), the less certain one becomes about what really happened.

This leads us on to the last and possibly the commonest device used by historians to support and strengthen the case they are trying to make. This might be described as the side-road assassination technique. Relatively minor characters with whom the historian does not sympathise are taken into a short paragraph where they are made to look wicked or ridiculous or very very small in a couple of sentences, almost in a couple of words; and done away with. There is no argument, no balancing of good with bad, no fuss. It is casual, almost offstage. The victims have been shot down before you notice. Falsehood is not required, for a partial truth will do. An excellent example was once provided by a very brief entry in a ship's log: 'March 30th. Captain sober today.' This was quite true, for he was always sober. But what a damning distorting impression these three words of truth must make, if left to themselves! No need to vilify by invention or exaggeration when the truth will serve the same purpose.

So historians, possibly helping themselves at the same time to some emotive language, covertly identify for us the sheep and the goats, those whom we are influenced to admire and those whom we are influenced to despise. Thus Murray of Broughton is led onto the stage by one distinguished scholar with the observation that 'one of the leading figures . . . was John Murray of Broughton, whom more than one historian has likened to Judas Iscariot'.[24] After an introduction like that, there is no recovering a man's character. Another scholar provides a portrait of George II in half a short paragraph, describing him as courageous, parsimonious and 'a middle-aged military martinet and bore of the first water. His naturally unengaging temper was not improved by the fact that he had become a martyr to piles'.[25] We must admire the King's courage and may be able to forgive his parsimony, but we certainly cannot forget his piles. We shall never be able to take George II seriously again, or suppose that the Hanoverian dynasty was anything more than a collection of the most ordinary mortals, whose claim to the British throne can have been no better than anyone else's. And we may even be inclined to conclude that the Old Pretender (about whose piles, if he had any, we have not heard), would have made a better king. A particularly popular subject of historic ridicule is Sir John Cope. Cope avoided a battle at Corriearrack, where he was in a hopeless position, and then marched to Inverness, which turned out to be (perhaps) the wrong direction. His army was subsequently routed by the Jacobites at Prestonpans. According to one writer, when Cope saw the situation at Corriearrack 'he was at a loss how to proceed . . . What should he do? In the multitude of counsellors there was wisdom: he would call a council of war . . . In his opinion they should proceed at once to Inverness . . . Nothing more clearly proves the incapacity of Cope for the position he held than his conduct on this occasion'.[26] Another historian says that at Corriearrack 'Cope's nerve broke',[27] and yet another describes his movements, which were designed to enable him to meet the Jacobites on equal terms (which he finally did), as 'a strategic blunder'.[28] Poor Sir John! He called a council of war; his nerve broke; his strategy was bizarre; he was 'a plain, stupid soldier'. No one would suppose that to call a council of war was standard procedure during an eighteenth-century campaign; or that a recent historian has called the diversion to Inverness 'the only prudent decision';[29] or that another writer found nothing worse to say about Cope than that he was 'a brave and honest though unsuccessful leader'.[30] And one cannot help suspecting that if Cope had won at Prestonpans, some historians would speak more kindly of his strategy while he was in the highlands.

This game of making the other side look ridiculous and small by means of one or two half truths and a peremptory judgement depends, for its success, on the reader not noticing that it is being played at all. Gone are the days of forthright statements of opinion such as were made by, for example, Sir Charles Oman: 'If Philip [II of Spain] had been merely an honest fanatic, ready to wade through any amount of blood, and to kindle any amount of fires for heretics, he would have been much less hateful than was actually the case. But he was also a systematic liar and hypocrite',[31] or, 'It was only as the years rolled on that [Henry VIII's] many detestable characteristics became gradually evident',[32] or, 'Protector Northumberland I take to have been quite as disgusting an example of the egotistic opportunist as Cromwell or Slaghoek'.[33] We are all given notice that the author does not like these persons and that the reader is expected not to like them either. But it is another matter when a character is briefly sketched in, intermittently, with the help of a few clever but one-sided remarks. What are we to make of a personality about whom we do not learn a great deal but are nevertheless told about 'the high sycophancy rate in his correspondence' and his 'neurotic fussing about the degrading effects of an excessive consumption of tea'?[34] This man surely must have been a crawler and an old woman, not in the least admirable. Surprising, then, to find him openly described by another historian as 'the celebrated Duncan Forbes, whose name will never die as long as Scotland values patriotism, uprightness, and humanity',[35] or that he was the fountain-head of resistance to Jacobitism in Scotland until Cumberland reached Edinburgh at the end of January 1746, by which time the rebellion had been going for over four months. Everything is in the selection; but sycophancy and neurotic fussing — even if granted — are surely less important than patriotism, uprightness and humanity.

Finally, it should be noticed how far the choice of words, even the use of a single word, will do the trick. The Earl of Nithsdale and Viscount Kenmure joined Charles at Edinburgh in October, but, after surveying the scene, returned to their homes on the following day and had nothing further to do with the '45. In the words of one historian, they went soberly back 'and skulked'.[36]

This does not sound like good behaviour. But he might have said that they went soberly back and kept themselves and their followers quietly at home; or out of harm's way; or — if this had been his attitude — free from entanglement in a rebellion of irresponsible folly. So much depends upon how things are put. It is easy, for example, to associate blood and agony only with the swords of one's adversaries. Thus a Jacobite sympathiser describes Cumberland's victory at Culloden as 'Twenty five minutes of butchery and all was over'; having a few pages before accorded Charles an apparently painless victory at Prestonpans — 'The Highlanders' impetuosity had carried the day'.[37] The presentation of history is a literary pursuit, and words and phrases may be so chosen and arranged as to convey a feeling of sympathy or antipathy, admiration or the reverse, even where there is very little argument, or in the extreme case — at least so it might seem — without any argument at all.

In the following pages I have tried to present two versions of the '45, one from the Hanoverian and one from the Jacobite point of view. Either of these could have been written in a romantic, exaggerated and misleading way — numberless exaggerated and misleading accounts exist already, every second or third sentence charged with emotion. To repeat that formula would have been too easy. So I have refrained from depicting Charles as a stainless hero and from suggesting that his followers were a band of brothers actuated only by the noblest and most selfless motives, and, *per contra*, I have not pretended that George II and his ministers constituted a popular democratic government nor that the Hanoverian armies lost battles simply as a result of bad luck. I have not even attempted, in either section, to win over the reader by lamenting hardship or extolling heroism on one side only — for example, by dwelling on the miseries of the Jacobite army before Culloden while saying nothing about the appalling conditions endured by the men who marched under Wade and, to a lesser extent, by those commanded by Cumberland. Instead, I have differentiated the two versions principally by adopting contrasting political points of view, and by giving the benefit of the doubt, where doubt is legitimate, in one version to one side and in the other to the other. At the same time, I have limited the differences between the two versions by sticking to a few important rules which would be observed, I think, by such a person as I have called 'the honest historian'. These rules are as follows.

First of all, everything in each of these accounts I believe to be true. This means that I have omitted all the apocryphal stories repeated so often by writers engaged in shoring up their prejudices and presenting their views as persuasively as possible, all too often regardless of the nature of the evidence and the probabilities of the case. Thus, to mention only a few instances, I have not repeated the tale that Charles breakfasted after Prestonpans on the field of battle amid the cries of the wounded; or that on the evening before the battle Cope was comfortably lodged at Cockenzie while his men slept in the open fields, or that he was the first to bring the news of his own defeat to Berwick — two inventions that we owe to the composer of a satirical ballad. Nor have I blackened Charles's character by inserting the story that when the Jacobite army broke at Culloden he refused to try to rally his men but rode immediately from the field, whereupon Lord Elcho, his follower and one-time friend, said, 'There you go for a damned cowardly Italian' — a dramatic invention springing from a conversation that took place in the High Street in Edinburgh some time during the first two or three decades of the nineteenth century. I have not even availed myself of the popular legend that Wolfe was ordered by Cumberland to shoot a wounded Jacobite on Culloden Moor when the battle was over, and refused, whereupon the man was shot by someone else. This may possibly be true, but the evidence is very poor. Furthermore, I have not credited the armies of either side with numerical advantages or disadvantages which I think they did not possess, nor have I turned the wind and rain around to blow in the faces of the Hanoverians or the Jacobites as it might have suited me, in one case or the other, to do.

Secondly, I have not omitted, in either version, any facts that I think a well-informed and fair-minded person would say were of major importance. For example, I have not pretended, in the Jacobite version, that there were no differences of opinion between Charles and his lieutenants, or that Scotland was overwhelmingly for the Stuarts. Nor have I pretended in the Hanoverian version that no outrages were committed by the King's troops at Culloden Moor and afterwards. And I have acknowledged that both armies suffered from desertions during the campaign and that both sides made foolish mistakes — Charles, for example, in leaving a garrison in Carlisle, and Hawley in assuming that he had nothing to worry about when the Jacobites sallied forth from Bannockburn.

Thirdly, all my quotations are from persons who were alive

during the '45 and all of whom, with only one or two exceptions, actually played a part in the events described. I have not, in other words, quoted the opinions of later historians. I have also refrained from repeating what anyone is supposed to have said before, during or after the campaign. Popular accounts are full of direct speech, at best an unreliable recollection by someone who was present, at worst an invention. A notable example is provided by the first meeting between Charles and Lochiel at Borrodale. According to Home, Charles and Lochiel 'retired by themselves'; and neither of them, to the best of my knowledge, subsequently provided a synopsis, frank or otherwise, of the very important conversation that took place. Nevertheless, Home produces a 450-word summary of what was said, and this has subsequently been turned into direct speech by innumerable writers, altered and expanded to suit their varying preferences and fancies.

So much for self-denial. But in order to write two different versions of the same 'facts', I have been obliged to adopt two different characters and two correspondingly different sets of preferences and prejudices. In each of these characters I exhibit, like every other historian, a particular way of seeing the world, and a particular way of presenting my case. And while remaining in both versions an honest historian, I have permitted myself some freedom of manoeuvre in five ways, all of them, as it seems to me, perfectly legitimate and commonly employed.

First, I have concentrated attention on those whom I befriend, especially when they are behaving well. The Jacobite version is mostly about the Jacobites, their ideals, their difficulties and their achievements; the Hanoverians remain more in the background, less human, less understandable and certainly less loved; they are 'the enemy'. But in the Hanoverian version it is of course the other way round. George II, Cumberland and Duncan Forbes move to the centre of the stage and turn out to be human after all; they too struggle against difficulties and disappointments. Secondly, while omitting nothing of undoubted importance in either version, I have selected for inclusion matters of lesser importance which are calculated to suit the case being made. Charles's drunken later years, for example, are referred to only in the Hanoverian version, as is the fact that when a column led by the Duke of Perth attempted to return to Scotland ahead of Charles, it was intercepted by a company of local volunteers from Penrith and harried southward through the hills for five hours; and only in the Jacobite version is there a reference to General 'Hangman' Hawley's dreadful reputation for brutality towards his own men, and to the orderly and civilised behaviour of the Jacobite army while it was advancing into England. Thirdly, and partly as a result of this process of selection, the emphases in the two versions are quite different. Thus the fact that the Stuarts had ruled in England for several decades and in Scotland for several hundred years was clearly a matter of the greatest moral and political significance for the Jacobites, and must, in the Jacobite version, be sympathetically stated. For the Hanoverians, however, this piece of history was hardly more than an old song, a memory overtaken and outdated by the Glorious Revolution of 1688, and it is therefore scarcely worth mentioning. Differing views are likewise possible about the amount of space that should be devoted to the atrocities committed at and after Culloden. For the historian with Jacobite sympathies these crimes are understandably important and are often recounted *in extenso*. But Hanoverian historians naturally see them as a less remarkable part of the conflict, however much they are to be regretted, and may remind the reader that the Jacobites seem themselves to have been responsible for needless slaughter at Prestonpans. Fourthly, I have put somewhat different — but I believe in each case, perfectly reasonable — constructions upon the same events. Did Lochiel (perhaps like many of the other chiefs) join Charles out of loyalty, or was he promised so much that he thought the gamble worth his while? Did Cope lose at Prestonpans because the highlanders were altogether too much for him or because his gunners lost their nerve just a minute too soon? Was the dash to Derby a mad escapade or a brilliant offensive that might have succeeded? No one knows, and different answers can reasonably be given to these and several other important questions. I have also, where history provides no answers, speculated as to what might have been — in favour of the Jacobites in one version, of course, and in favour of the Hanoverians in the other. Finally, and perhaps of most consequence, I have interpreted character to suit the cause. I have tried to avoid character assassination as earlier described, but the same person can legitimately be understood and presented in different ways. This can be done for most of the actors in the '45, but for no one more easily and with greater effect than Prince Charles himself. Thus he has appeared to some as a heroic adventurer, the youthful and dashing leader of a brilliant campaign conducted far from his own home and kindred, fighting in a strange

land where he inspired devotion among his friends and consternation among his enemies. Others have seen him as a mere opportunist, quite devoid of military experience or skill, basically egotistical
and heartless, his irresponsibility towards his friends and supporters thinly concealed by a veneer of good manners and a superficial
amiability. Who is to say which of these interpretations, if either, is
'correct'? And what can be done as regards the Prince can also be
done, although less remarkably, in respect of George II, Cumberland, Duncan Forbes, Lord George Murray, Cope, the Earl of
Perth, and possibly all the other characters about whom more than
a little is known.

What I have tried to show in the following pages is how the same
people and the same events can be described in two different ways,
legitimately, soberly and in all honesty, if one adopts two different
points of view, two different sets of sympathies. Neither version is
crude propaganda, because in neither is there resort to fabrication,
distortion, serious omission or blatant appeal to the emotions. But
even without these, what is past — and for that matter, what is
present — can be understood and represented in very different
ways. And this is important, because it means that there is no such
thing, in any significant sense, as historical certainty. It may be
possible to imagine an investigation into the past based upon
extremely full information, conducted without any reference whatsoever to the present, unbiased in any way and therefore, in a
sense, final and conclusive; but it is not easy to believe that such an
investigation could be carried out by a human being. Good history
can, of course, be written — history that is sympathetic to its subject and to ourselves, careful, accurate, fair and understanding.
But it is nevertheless fallible. And as soon as the writer's hopes and
preferences wrest control from his judgement, what is written
becomes, in Oakeshott's words, 'an essay in retrospective politics' — something that a good historian would hope — at any rate
as far as possible — to avoid. From that level there is a continuous
gradation to the depths of bad propaganda. Between the two
extremes there is bad history and good propaganda, and the difference between them may lie only in the intentions of the authors; it
is even possible that a good propagandist may believe what he
writes and a bad historian may not. In any event, no clear and
certain dividing line can be drawn between history and propaganda — or for that matter between any other kind of reporting
and propaganda — however much we might like to think so. And

therefore it is always for the reader — or the listener or the viewer — to beware.

Notes and References

1. Quoted in E.F. Loftus, *Eyewitness Testimony* (Harvard 1979), pp. 62–3.
2. A. Lumisden, 'A Short Account of the Battles of Preston, Falkirk and Culloden', in *Origins of the Forty-Five*, ed. W.B. Blaikie (Edinburgh, 1975), p. 418.
3. D. Elcho, *The Affairs of Scotland* (Edinburgh, 1973), p. 434.
4. 'Lochgarry's Narrative' in W.B. Blaikie, *Itinerary of Prince Charles Edward Stuart* (Edinburgh, 1975), p. 121.
5. John Home, *The History of the Rebellion in the Year 1745* (London, 1802), p. 240.
6. Chevalier de Johnstone, *A Memoir of the Forty-Five* (London, 1958), p. 61.
7. Elcho, op. cit., p. 342.
8. Account by Walter Grossett in Blaikie, *Origins*, p. 341.
9. A. Carlyle, *The Autobiography of Dr Alexander Carlyle* (London and Edinburgh, 1910), p. 123.
10. M. Oakeshott, *Rationalism in Politics* (London, 1981), p. 154.
11. I. Berlin, 'Historical Inevitability' in *The Philosophy of History*, ed. P. Gardiner (OUP, 1974), pp. 174–5.
12. Elcho, op. cit., p. 261. Many other writers who knew Charles might be cited to the same effect.
13. A.C. Ewald, *Life and Times of Prince Charles Stuart* (London, 1904), pp. 4–5.
14. C. Petrie, *The Jacobite Movement* (London, 1959), p. 379.
15. Chevalier de Johnstone, op. cit., p. 78.
16. B. Lenman, *The Jacobite Risings in Britain 1689–1746* (London, 1980), p. 258.
17. F.J. McLynn, *The Jacobite Army in England* (Edinburgh, 1983), p. 9.
18. Ewald, op. cit., p. 181.
19. Petrie, op. cit., p. 374.
20. Lenman, op. cit., p. 258.
21. Ibid., p. 252.
22. Ibid., p. 252.
23. Ewald, op. cit., pp. 115–16.
24. Petrie, op. cit., p. 342.
25. Lenman, op. cit., p. 214.
26. Ewald, op. cit., pp. 95–6.
27. Lenman, op. cit., p. 251.
28. Petrie, op. cit., p. 353.
29. W.A. Speck, *The Butcher* (Oxford, 1981), p. 36.
30. A. Lang, *Prince Charles Edward* (London, 1900), p. 104.
31. C. Oman, *The Sixteenth Century* (London, 1936), p. 92.
32. Ibid., p. 100.
33. Ibid., p. 132.
34. Lenman, op. cit., p. 249.
35. Ewald, op. cit., p. 85.
36. Lang, op. cit., p. 126.
37. G.R. Francis, *The Romance of the White Rose* (London, 1933), pp. 253, 259.

PART II

A HISTORY OF THE REBELLION

1 GLOBAL WAR

On 16 December 1740, Frederick the Great, twenty-eight years of age and at the head of an army of 40,000 men, invaded Silesia, having gone out of his way a few weeks earlier to assure the ruler of that country, Maria Theresa, Queen of Hungary and Empress of Austria, that he recognised her right to the throne and would give her military support if she were attacked. His preparations had been extensive but his advance was slow. Silesia, sloping eastward to the monotonous sand-flats of Poland, is mostly high country, with many pine forests and swift-flowing rivers. By early April Frederick was in the mountains about one hundred and fifty miles south-east of his starting point near Frankfurt on Oder, aware that the army opposing him was in the vicinity but not at all sure where it was. The Austrians, although better supplied with intelligence by mounted scouts or cavalry, were likewise unaware of Frederick's exact whereabouts. The nights were extremely cold, there was snow on the ground, and both armies were climbing and descending mountains, contending with steep, icy roads, laboriously creaking and jingling forward with heavy guns and ammunition wagons. On Saturday 8 April they came in contact, and two days later were drawn up for battle.

The battle-field was a plain of silent snow, the air crisp, a few scattered villages, a handful of low-growing bushes, here and there the skeleton of a poplar tree. At 2 p.m. the Prussian guns opened fire on the Austrians lying between the hamlet of Grüningen to the east and a sluggish, boggy brook called the Langwitz, stagnating towards the Oder, to the west. After enduring the cannonade for a short time, the Austrian cavalry successfully charged down the Prussian right wing and Frederick hastily left the field, riding thirty-five miles to cross the Oder at Oppeln and reach safe country on the other side. But the Prussian infantry in the centre stood firm, and at the end of the day the Austrians were defeated. Sixteen hours after quitting the field, Frederick learned that he had won the battle of Mollwitz.

This was the first battle of the War of the Austrian Succession, which continued until 1748. The war proved extraordinarily popular with the princes and potentates of Europe; at one time or another almost every European state took part in it, excepting Portugal and Russia. What began as a simple act of premeditated robbery directed against the possessions of Maria Theresa became a general war out of which everyone hoped to gain something. Bavaria and Saxony joined in the attack on Austria; the King of Sardinia came to Austria's support; an Austrian army attacked Naples, and two Spanish armies attacked Milan, Piedmont and Savoy; France for a time contented herself with sending 35,000 French 'auxiliaries' to help the enemies of Austria, and this — also for a time — helped to persuade George II, King of Great Britain and Elector of Hanover, to remain neutral; although his neutrality did not prevent a British fleet from interfering with French and Spanish operations in the Mediterranean. In 1743, however, the diplomatic fiction that France and Britain were at peace with one another faded rapidly. The British government had landed 16,000 troops in Belgium in the previous year, and these troops, along with a Hanoverian contingent, now manoeuvred to attack the French, who were so positioned as to prevent the British from giving assistance to Maria Theresa. The result was the victory at Dettingen, the celebrated last occasion when a King of England led his army into battle. Soon afterwards France declared war on Great Britain and Austria, and planned an invasion of the British Isles on behalf of the exiled Stuarts; as a result of which, a Franco-Spanish fleet fought an inconclusive action with the British navy off Toulon. In 1744 the French invaded the Netherlands. Such were some of the principal events of the first four years of the war; and the second four years, which included the battle of Culloden, were not very different.

Geopolitics is a new word but it is not a new idea; the rulers of the eighteenth century knew all about it. They competed with one another for wealth and security, just as their successors do today; and the means to wealth and security was national power. In an age when technology was relatively primitive and changed only slowly, national power depended principally on numbers of people and possessions, and therefore all rulers made and broke alliances, schemed, married and fought in order to extend the territories under their control. At the start of the eighteenth century, France, Spain and Austria were generally supposed to be the greatest powers in Europe. And from the time that George I ascended the throne of Great Britain in 1714 until the Treaty of Versailles in 1756, one of the principal bases of international relations was the enmity between France and Spain on the one hand and the Austrian Empire on the other. The remaining European powers, large and small and including Great Britain, tended to take their stance on one side or the other of this great division. From time to time the pattern changed in its details, and a whole series of wars proved, if nothing else, that many combinations of friend and foe were possible; but, with some exceptions, the numerous congresses which met to restore peace and distribute the spoils of war left national frontiers and the pattern of alliances pretty much as they had found them. Yet throughout the eighteenth century the facts of relative power were altering. Especially it was true that Spain was becoming less important than once she had been, and Prussia and Great Britain more important.

The rise of Prussia was sudden and spectacular, and was due in no small part to the efforts of Frederick I and his son Frederick the Great. The rise of Great Britain, which began sooner and was a great deal less spectacular, cannot be said to have been correspondingly due to the efforts of the first two Georges, for Britain was a European power with considerable influence at the very start of the eighteenth century. She had already fought and on the whole got the better of the Dutch; the political settlement of 1688 — the Glorious Revolution, or, as Chateaubriand called it, 'the useful revolution' — had brought twenty-six years of domestic stability before George I ever crossed the Channel; and the steady growth of British trade and the brilliance and effectiveness of the campaigns of Marlborough had further increased British strength and prestige. Britain was a power to be reckoned with long before George I came to the throne. But under the Hanoverians Britain's progress was much more remarkable than it had been before. This might seem surprising, because the succession itself was a subject of dispute, and George I seemed to many people to be a strange choice for King.

The Stuarts, after ruling in Scotland for many generations, had reached the throne of England in 1603 and had retained it over a period of eighty-five years, broken for fifteen years by the Cromwellian interregnum. They had proved to be a mixed lot. James I was dull and sententious (although his wife Anne was one of the best customers that the London jewellers had ever had); Charles I, although he showed much nobility of character, combined obstinacy with irresolution and ended on the losing side in a civil war; Charles II was a consummate politician whom no writer has ever been able to describe as a man of high principle; while James II, after three far from glorious years, found himself so unpopular that he deemed it advisable to slip out of his kingdom one dark December evening and leave his crown and his subjects to their fate. He was succeeded by William of Orange, who was both his nephew and his son-in-law. And when William, fourteen years later, was thrown from his horse and fatally injured during a ride from Kensington to Hampton Court, he in his turn was succeeded by his sister-in-law Anne, a grand-daughter of Charles I. Anne bore seventeen children, all of whom died, and it is difficult not to feel sorry for her; but she seems to have been a most unlikeable person. She was dominated by the Duchess of Marlborough who was a terrifying character; but she was also sly, malicious and unreliable. Her death in 1714 brought the reign of the house of Stuart to an end. Parliament, in 1701, had foreseen the situation that now arose, and had enacted that the Crown was to pass to the Electress Sophia of Hanover, the grand-daughter of James I, and her descendants, being Protestants; and that the King must be in communion with the Church of England. Sophia died eight weeks before Anne, and therefore Sophia's son, George, Elector of Hanover, succeeded to the British throne. He was proclaimed King in August 1714, without delay and without opposition of any kind.

It would not be true to say that George had the throne thrust upon him; but it would not be very far from the truth. As early as the 1690s it was plain enough that Sophia or her son might succeed to the British throne; and from 1700 there was no life between the Electress and the throne but that of Queen Anne herself. Nevertheless, Sophia entered into no schemes or intrigues with either Whigs or Tories in order to secure her interests; her policy was one of simple inactivity, of wait and see. As for George, the prospect of becoming King of England seems to have filled him with something very like revulsion. This is not at all hard to understand. For one thing, he was very much absorbed in the affairs of Hanover; and for another, the history of Great Britain from 1640 to 1688 made the position of the monarch of that country seem distinctly unenviable, for the monarchy was itself increasingly unimportant and frequently insecure. One king had been beheaded, one had gone into exile, and there had been fifteen years with no king at all; and all the while parliaments and parties had gathered more and more power into their hands. It is therefore easy to believe that George's interest in the throne was slight, and that the chief attraction of becoming King of Great Britain was that it might enable him to take a larger part in military operations in Europe, an activity for which he always had great relish.

The Hanoverian Succession thus cannot be described as the work of the House of Hanover. The succession was made in Great Britain, and it was approved because it was, in fact, the Protestant Succession. Anti-Catholicism, established in Great Britain chiefly by the activities of Henry VIII, Mary Tudor and John Knox, had been completely absorbed into British life and British political thinking and can fairly be said to have been a dominant force in the life of the country for at least one hundred and fifty years before a successor had to be found for Queen Anne; and the House of Hanover was notably and consistently anti-Catholic. It was unfortunate, certainly, that George was a German; he could not even speak English. But the alternative, as far as most people were concerned, was a good deal worse. James Francis Edward, the son of James II, was born only six months before his father fled from London, and the child preceded the father to the court at St Germain-en-Laye, where he was brought up. He had an obvious claim to the British throne. And when his father died in 1701 Louis XIV of France immediately had him proclaimed as King James III and VIII of England, Scotland and Ireland. This ill-considered gesture did neither James nor Louis any good. Recognition by the King of France of 'the pretended Prince of Wales' as his father's successor on the British throne was an insult to King William (who had occupied the throne for thirteen years) and was regarded by the British government and people as a gross interference in their affairs — which it undoubtedly was. At the same time it announced to the world that James was a protégé of France. With friends like Louis, James did not need any enemies; the unlucky youth — he was only thirteen at the time — was already on the way to deserving his nickname of later years, Old Mr Misfortune. He had supporters, of course. Hereditary kingship was the norm in the seventeenth and eighteenth centuries, and the chopping and changing that had taken place in Britain made many people uneasy. In many ways it would have been much simpler, more conventional and reassuring, if James Edward could have succeeded Queen Anne. But he was a Roman Catholic, which alienated most of the population; he was a tool of the King of France; and these disadvantages were not overcome by any force or attraction of personality, for James was inclined to be reserved and melancholy, displaying none of those attractive qualities of charm, magnetism or leadership which had been shown by some of his ancestors such as James IV or Charles II.

George I thus became King and a new era in British politics was started. It had been feared that with little knowledge of British practices and little sympathy with constitutional government, the new King would cause difficulties for his ministers; but none appeared. Both George I and George II interfered very little in domestic affairs, and when they did so it was often to perform a very useful function in striving to compose differences between rival religious sects and rival political factions. Their standards of personal conduct may have been in some respects low and their view of human nature uninspiring; but they did not rock the boat. Above all, there was no renewed conflict between Crown and Parliament, partly because in constitutional matters the first two Georges maintained, as would be said today, a low profile, and partly because they were much less interested in British politics than they were in European affairs. This too was initially a cause of anxiety. George I brought Hanoverian ministers to London, with whom he worked very closely, and he himself took the keenest personal interest in European ambitions, alliances and conflicts. Inevitably, he and his German ministers showed a strong concern for the advantages of the Electorate of Hanover. But the way in which the complicated chess game of eighteenth-century international politics was played out did not bring these and British interests into conflict; and in fact Britain almost certainly gained rather than lost by the Hanoverian connection.

When George I ascended the throne, war with France seemed almost certain, one cause of hostility being the protection afforded to 'the pretended Prince of Wales' by Louis XIV. But war was avoided, and within a few years Britain and France had become allies, in opposition, principally, to the ambitions of Spain. The Jacobite rebellion of 1715 received almost no help from France, while that of 1719 was supported solely by Spanish troops and money, and was a complete failure. The French authorities had already informed James Edward that as an enemy of the King of Great Britain he was no longer welcome in France and must leave the country. He therefore went to Lorraine and then to Avignon, which was Papal territory, and soon that city became the home and haunt of the Jacobites, several hundred of whom either resided in or around Avignon, or were frequent visitors.

The alliance between Britain and France lasted from 1717 until 1731, and the two countries remained on reasonably good terms until about 1740. During this period of approximately twenty years disputes between them were avoided, and it seemed that their own policies of territorial expansion and commercial development need not conflict. But as things turned out, these years of co-operation were only an interlude — an interlude in the long struggle between the two nations for maritime and colonial supremacy. The great events of this struggle were still to come. But while peace lasted it gave both countries a chance to consolidate their respective positions. In Britain it was rather like the start of modern times, for it was the age of facts, figures and material things. These two decades were dominated by Sir Robert Walpole, the greatest financier of the age, a man of all-round business ability, massive common sense and political moderation. His was a policy of cautious temporising, of letting sleeping dogs lie; of not provoking the country gentry, many of whom had Jacobite sympathies; of legislating only for those changes that promoted trade without creating trouble; of peace and consolidation. Twenty years of such government left many old abuses unchanged but gave time for the Hanoverian succession to become settled and established. What hope of real revival Jacobitism ever had after 1720 was probably killed by Sir Robert Walpole.

In 1739, however, another war began, a war of England against Spain — the so-called war of Jenkins' ear — and in 1742 Walpole fell from power. French and British interests were beginning to diverge, and the old rivalries and animosities to reappear. Expansion, not in Europe but overseas, was becoming a prime objective for both countries. Colonies were not new. But the idea of an empire that might stretch from the East Indies to the New World was a conception almost as novel as it was grand, and the ambition to achieve it took root at much the same time in London and Paris. Riches and grandeur, it was believed, depended on numbers of people and extent of territory, but came especially easily to that country which could exploit a far-flung empire by exporting its own manufactures to its dependencies and getting back in return, if not gold and silver, at any rate an ample and assured supply of foreign raw materials. The bigger the empire, it was believed, the greater the commerce, the security, the gain and the grandeur. London and Paris, Antwerp and Madrid shared the same ideas; but it was the two former which had the power and the position to fight for empire on an epic scale.

At the start of the 1740s, when peace between Britain and France was beginning to be more nominal than real, the two countries were opposed to one another, if they were not actually at war, not only in Europe but also in North America, the West Indies and the East. This opposition was one of the great facts of European history in the eighteenth century, and into the conflicts that it produced were drawn numberless lesser men and lesser causes. Formal hostilities between France and Britain did not break out until 1744, but they then commenced in earnest. French and Irish troops defeated the Duke of Cumberland at Fontenoy in 1745; the Duke of Cumberland defeated the Jacobite rebels, who were assisted by Irish troops and French money, at Culloden in 1746; and a few months later the roar of French guns off Madras announced that the war had spread to India.

In the context of global war the rebellion of 1745 does not seem of major importance. But from very early in the eighteenth century Jacobitism was a force to be reckoned with in European politics because in time of war the enemies of Great Britain could hope to use the Jacobites as a fifth column, a convenient means of weakening British efforts abroad by causing trouble at home. For almost fifty years the Jacobite card was a useful one in the hands of France or Spain; and on four occasions it was played.

When James II died in exile at the French court in 1701, the Most Christian King of France, Louis XIV, at once undertook to support the claims of James's son to the British throne. Louis was not especially fond of the house of Stuart or of the Jacobites, but he fervently believed in the divine right of kings and he longed even more fervently for military glory. He made many wars — the war of devolution, the Dutch war, the war of the League of Augsburg, the war of the Spanish Succession. In this last, which began in 1701, he was opposed by Great Britain; and it naturally occurred to him that it would be very advantageous if at some time a rebellion on British soil could be arranged, ostensibly on behalf of the would-be James III, but in reality on behalf of his own armies and his own dreams of conquest. The argument was that if all went well with such a rebellion, British troops would have to be withdrawn from the continent, and it was even possible that the government might collapse and the complaisant Roman Catholic James (who had been brought up at Louis' court) replace Queen Anne (who was a firm Protestant and had never even set foot in France) on the throne of Great Britain. The attractiveness of this scheme depended largely on the progress of the French armies; as long as they were doing well, a Jacobite rebellion was of no great use to Louis; but after 1703 they were not doing well. Overwhelmed by Marlborough at Blenheim, they suffered another disastrous defeat two years later, in 1706, at Ramillies, and Louis was aghast to discover that the war was being carried on in his own territories. A Jacobite rebellion, to take place in Scotland, therefore seemed at this time a particularly desirable counter-move, and a rebellion was accordingly arranged for early in 1708. Thirty vessels carrying 6,000 French troops sailed from Dunkirk in March, accompanied by James Edward, who was trying to recover from measles. After a rough voyage, during which it is said that James and his entourage were all very sick, the French entered the Firth of Forth, cast anchor, and endeavoured to contact friends and supporters on shore. But none appeared. Instead, a naval squadron under Admiral Byng came over the horizon, and the French supreme commander hastily stood out to sea and retired northwards. One of his ships was captured, but the rest set off on a circuit of the British Isles, which not all of them completed. There was no fighting on land, and very little at sea, but French losses were far from negligible. James was never ashore. Even by Jacobite standards the '08 was a ridiculously ill-contrived affair.

Six years after this fiasco took place, Queen Anne died, and was succeeded by George I. This created a new situation for the Jacobites, some of whom had entertained hopes that the Queen would be succeeded by James, who (although he had recently attempted to rob her of her throne) was her half-brother. But these hopes were quite illusory. Consanguinity counted for little compared to religion, and James was a Roman Catholic who at no time showed any signs of abandoning his faith. No amount of political manoeuvring would have brought a Roman Catholic to the throne, unless supported by an armed insurrection; and the politicians at Westminster understood this very well. So George became King, and the Jacobites saw that their only hope was to draw the sword once more, and again to look to France for help. They were not long about it. George ascended the throne in August 1714, and six months later there were rumours both in London and Edinburgh of an intended French invasion, or Jacobite revolt. For a while nothing important seemed to happen. But in August 1715 the 11th Earl of Mar went on board a collier in the Thames bound for Newcastle, made his way to Fife and then to Aberdeenshire, where on the braes of Mar he raised the Jacobite standard on 6 September 1715.

The Earl of Mar has never had a good press, and it is not difficult to see why. His family was an ancient one, with estates in central

Scotland as well as in the north-east. By the time he was thirty he had risen to be Secretary of State and in 1706 he was one of the Commissioners for the Union between England and Scotland. After the Union was achieved he became one of the representative Scottish peers at Westminister, and in 1714 he was appointed a Third Secretary of State, with special responsibility for Scotland. He was, in fact, a government man, and a moderately successful politician. But he was a Tory. And when George I ascended the throne Mar was turned out of office, along with all his political friends. His response to this catastrophe was rapid and extreme. Unable to obtain employment under the ruling King, he sought other work, and corresponded with the exiled James. He had never shown signs of Jacobite sympathies while William or Anne were on the throne, but this previous lack of zeal seems to have made no difference to James. The would-be King encouraged him, and Mar became the leader of the rebellion. He is the outstanding example of a not inconsiderable body of men, those Jacobites who took up arms for what they hoped to get for themselves.

It may seem surprising that a political adventurer such as Mar (he changed back to assist the House of Hanover a few years later) proved acceptable as a leader of the first major Jacobite rebellion. But so it was. And after all, Mar had friends — or at least he was well-connected. The Earl of Kinnoull was the father of his first wife; the Earl of Panmure was his uncle; both these families gave assistance to the rebellion, and many other noblemen of conservative and Jacobite leanings proved willing to serve under him.

Once the standard was raised, a readiness to fight for the restoration of the Stuarts was hardly discoverable in England, and in Scotland was patchy. The Jacobites south of Stirling who stood up to be counted were few and far between. The men of the Western Isles showed almost no interest. From the mainland north and west of the Great Glen the support that Mar received was likewise comparatively little. It was from central Scotland, Fife and the north-east that most of the fighting men came. They were therefore led, most of them, not by picturesque highland chiefs but by lowland noblemen, men like Mar himself; Lord Forbes of Pitsligo, the Earl of Southesk, Lord Ogilvy (son of the Earl of Airlie), the Marquis of Tullibardine (who had to come all the way from London to take part), son of the Duke of Atholl; the Marquis of Huntly (who showed no enthusiasm for the cause), son of the Duke of Gordon. These were the rich and the powerful, almost all of them Tories.

And because they were powerful and had many tenants, they brought with them many followers. What the followers thought about it, no one knows. But it would be naive to suppose that all came gladly. In one case, at least, some record remains of the kind of pressure that was applied. Mar himself wrote to his baillie in 1715 in the following terms:

> Particularly let my own tenants in Kildrummie know, that if they come not forth with their best arms, I will send a party immediately to burn what they shall miss taking from them. And they may believe this only a threat but, by all that's sacred, I'll put it into execution — let my loss be what it will.[1]

However it was got together, Mar was soon at the head of a formidable force, and he began to move south, occupying Perth at the beginning of October. Having been joined by some further recruits, he was now in command of an army which numbered, according to differing reports, between 6,000 and 10,000 men. The government was, as British governments usually are, woefully unprepared to meet such a challenge. Little preparation had been made, and there were very few government troops in Scotland. But such as were available were rapidly concentrated at Stirling. This was a sound move, for Stirling was the best possible position for an army trying to prevent a Jacobite advance from the north into southern Scotland and thence into England. The commander, appointed a week after Mar raised the Jacobite standard, was the Duke of Argyll, chief of the Clan Campbell (although this seniority was disputed by the Earl of Breadalbane) and the greatest territorial magnate in Scotland. He was known, moreover, as 'Red John of the Battles', and with good reason, for he had served under Marlborough at Ramillies, Oudenard and Malplaquet and had commanded the allied forces in Spain in 1711. Argyll was an excellent general; but he had only 2,000 regular troops under him, assisted by six hundred volunteers from Glasgow, and he thus appeared to be hopelessly outnumbered. What he needed was time; and the Jacobites gave it to him. Perhaps they were waiting for help from France, perhaps for good news from England. Certainly they were safe where they were, for the country behind them was secure. On 20 September, 'James VIII' had been proclaimed at the market cross in Aberdeen, and a week before that the same had been done at Inverness — 'the laird of MacIntosh and Borlum came into this town with about 400 of the best of their men' and proclaimed the Pretender as King. Not that the Jacobites north of Perth had it all their own way. Some of those who seized Inverness next marched to Culloden House but were told by the laird's wife that 'if they would dare to approach within gunshot of her house, (tho' she was but a woman) she would soon let them know that she had both arms and ammunition to assert H.M. King George's right and title'.[2] The rebels laid siege to the house, and were still besieging it when it was relieved seven weeks later.

Incidents like this, however, were not going to tie down the Jacobite army. Mar could have moved south and forced a battle. Instead, he remained where he was and detached about 1,000 men under MacIntosh of Borlum with instructions to slip past the Duke of Argyll and combine with the small rebel forces that were known to be in the south of Scotland and in Northumberland. Slipping past was no easy matter, but MacIntosh was an exceptional commander — like many other Jacobites, he had learnt his trade in the French army. He made his way to the little fishing ports on the south coast of Fife, commandeered some boats, and crossed the Firth of Forth under cover of darkness. Then he decided not to press on southward but to attack and if possible take the city of Edinburgh. It would have been a great triumph if he had succeeded. But Argyll was too quick for him. From Stirling to the Scots capital is only thirty miles. So the Duke collected what cavalry he had in his little army, mounted a few score astonished foot soldiers on spare horses, rode the thirty miles as fast as possible and clattered into Edinburgh. Borlum prudently turned round and made for Kelso. There he met up with the other rebels, English and Scots, a few hundred of them, ill-armed and worse led. After much discussion it was agreed that they should march into England, where they expected to be joined by fresh supporters. These hopes were quite illusory. Nevertheless, they crossed the border and marched towards Lancashire, helping themselves *en route* to a supply of public money; but their numbers, instead of increasing, decreased, because many highlanders, dispirited and far from home, deserted. Those who remained advanced as far as Preston where, after a little fighting, they negotiated an unconditional and abject surrender. The whole adventure had lasted less than four weeks, and had achieved precisely nothing.

While all this was going on, the armies in the north continued to keep watch on one another. Both had received reinforcements, so that the discrepancy in their size was now a little reduced; the rebels probably numbered about 10,000, Argyll's army a little over 3,000.

Perhaps realising that if he did nothing for much longer his supporters would begin to melt away, Mar at last, after wasting four weeks in Perth, advanced southward. Argyll, always well informed about the enemy's movements, at once concentrated all his available troops and moved north to Dunblane. On 13 November — the day before the rebels surrendered at Preston — there was fought the battle of Sheriffmuir. In spite of their great numerical superiority, the rebels failed to win this battle. Their tactics were traditional. The highlanders, flinging off their plaids, fired one volley and then threw away their muskets and charged, shouting battle-cries and brandishing claymores. To face a highland charge required steady nerves and good commanders, and Argyll's left wing gave way. On the right wing, however, the rebels had to deal with Argyll himself. He waited until the charge had begun, and then, before the attackers could reach the red lines of infantry, brought the Scots Greys, who were part of his small force of cavalry, down on the rebels' flank. The charge was broken, and now it was Mar's left wing that gave way. So while one wing of the Jacobite army was pursuing the King's troops towards Stirling, the other was retreating in confusion in the opposite direction. Argyll rallied what troops he could, and awaited a further attack. But none came. Mar, still with superior forces, retreated to Perth, and the Duke remained in front of Stirling. The road to the south was still closed to the forces of 'James VIII'.

The rebellion was now effectively at an end. And the more intelligent of the rebels seem to have realised it. Large numbers of highlanders, disillusioned in their commander and disappointed of plunder, made off for the mountains; some gentlemen and noblemen likewise hastened to dissociate themselves from Mar and all his doings — the Earl of Huntly, for example, trekked back to his estates in the north-east where he made his separate — and successful — peace with the government. The other Jacobites remained disconsolately near Perth, and the Duke built up his forces based on Stirling. At this point the Prince of Denmark — in the shape of James Edward — at last arrived on the scene, wafted over from Paris in a French man-of-war. He brought little help and no comfort. He did not inspire his supporters, for he was in no way an inspiring man. Neither he nor anyone else could retrieve the situation. So when it was discovered at the end of January, after some further shilly-shallying round Perth, that the Duke of Argyll with 10,000 men had begun to advance through heavy snow, the Jacobites hastily quit their quarters and made off to the north. They dispersed as they went. A substantial number kept together until they reached Badenoch, and there they separated. But long before then, as the remains of the army were passing through Montrose, James gave his loyal followers the slip, and along with Mar embarked on a ship for France. He had been in Scotland for just six weeks, and was destined never to return. Mar similarly never returned to Scotland but settled in France, and James made him a Duke in the mythical Jacobite peerage.

This rebellion, which did the Jacobites no good, fortunately did Franco-British relations no harm. Indeed, they continued to improve, and in 1717 a formal alliance between the two countries was signed. Co-operation between them should have stabilised the affairs of Europe, and to some extent did so. But war in and around the Baltic between Sweden and Russia was in those years almost continuous and one effect was that relations between Britain and Sweden became extremely strained. Trade was interrupted, and Swedish privateers attacked British shipping not only in the Baltic but even in the Thames estuary. Sweden looked for allies and so negotiations began between representatives of the Pretender and Swedish diplomats with a view to further harassing the British government, perhaps even to the extent of a landing on the British coast by combined Swedish and Jacobite forces. This scheme came to nothing — it is doubtful if the Swedes ever took it seriously. But at the time it caused some alarm in Great Britain. It was well known that the Jacobites were always intriguing with somebody. And indeed, even before the Swedes had had time to settle their differences with the British government (which they did in 1718), a new plan for the restoration of the Stuart dynasty had been concocted, this time between James Edward and Spain. Spain, of course, had no great interest in the Stuarts, except that they were Roman Catholics. But Spain's ambitions in the Mediterranean had brought her into conflict with Great Britain, upon whom she declared war in 1718, and so she was glad to do as the French had done ten years before and lend the Jacobites a diversionary hand. The Spanish effort to mount an invasion of both England and Scotland was real and substantial. Against England, twenty-nine ships carrying 5,000 Spanish soldiers sailed from Cadiz early in 1719. They were commanded by the Jacobite James Butler, Duke of Ormonde, who was one of the Old Pretender's confidants. Persuaded by Jacobite agents (against all the evidence) that on their arrival in the West

Country they would soon be joined by hordes of eager Stuart supporters, the Spaniards carried with them an additional 30,000 stands of arms. The British government was well informed about these arrangements, and disposed its forces accordingly, both on land and at sea. But the expected invasion never took place. A violent storm struck the Spanish fleet before it had sailed as far north as the Bay of Biscay, and the damage sustained was so great that the operation had to be cancelled. The parallel effort against Scotland was on a much smaller scale, and in this case the invasion force had the ill-luck to get ashore. There were only three ships, two from Spain and one which, in spite of French professions of friendship for Great Britain, mysteriously originated in the French port of Le Havre and was full of Scots Jacobites. The expedition was jointly commanded by George Keith the Earl Marischal and the Marquis of Tullibardine. Both had been 'out' in that conspicuous failure, the '15, and Keith had been exiled for his pains. The three ships rendezvoused at Stornoway in the Isle of Lewis, and quarrelling between the leaders began at once. Their prospects can hardly have seemed good. They had only three hundred or four hundred men and it was a long way to London. Some thought that it would be best to remain in Stornoway and to wait for news of the doings of the Duke of Ormonde. But it was finally decided not to delay but to land on the west coast of the mainland and to establish themselves in and around the ancient fortress of Eilean Donan. This was the land of the Mackenzies, whose chief was with the expedition, and it was a centre of Roman Catholicism in the highlands. It must have seemed safe enough, for Eilean Donan is remote in the intricate fastnesses of highland mountains and sea lochs. But the government's forces reacted with remarkable promptitude and effect. Scarcely had the Spanish frigates, their mission accomplished, cleared from Loch Alsh, than three ships of the Royal Navy reached and entered the loch and proceeded to bombard the castle, which was then stormed by the naval crews. The intruders escaped, but they lost men, stores and ammunition. They were now quite isolated on the west coast of Scotland, without hope of escape by sea. Their army was strengthened by some new recruits, however, most of them Mackenzies, local men; the whole force numbered about 1,000. There had been no rush to join the rebellion; but no doubt the leaders hoped that one military success would change all that, and they probably planned to march eastwards and seize Inverness. Unfortunately for them, they had to reckon with Major General Wightman, who had fought at

Sheriffmuir and was now field commander of the government forces in Scotland. Wightman got together what men he could, about 1,000 in all, and without waiting for reinforcements took the initiative, marching to meet the rebels before they could even leave the West Highlands. He found them in Glenshiel, a narrow inhospitable place almost within sight of the ruins of Eilean Donan castle. The enemy were in a good defensive position which they had strengthened, and they were about equal to Wightman's forces in number. Wightman had the advantage of four small mortars, but it seems unlikely that these can have done much real damage against the enemy in such country. The battle was fought on the steep, heather-covered hillsides and along the shallow, stony river. It did not last long; the rebels were out-generalled and out-fought. Before darkness fell, their army had broken up. And when morning came, only some groups of Spaniards were to be seen, anxious to surrender.

From the Jacobite point of view, this was a miserable ending to a poor affair. The '19 was first blown away, and then it fizzled out. But it could have been dangerous. Enough Jacobite and Spanish troops were assembled to cause a great deal of trouble in Britain, if ever they could all have been got there. A sympathetic rising by English and Scots Jacobites anxious to join the troops of Philip of Spain and to fight against those of George I was at all times extremely unlikely, to say the least; but even without that, serious fighting would have taken place. The '19 came to nothing, but this was because of good luck at sea and prompt action on land, not for want of trying by the enemy.

The Jacobites were disappointed; but they did not give up. Persistence was one of their most notable qualities. And after all, France, although officially on good terms with Great Britain, continued to give them assistance. James Edward and many of his associates were virtually pensioners for life of King Louis XIV, and when he died in 1715 they were granted the same position under Louis XV because one day they might again be useful to France. They lived at St Germain-en-Laye, Bar-le-Duc in Lorraine, Avignon, Urbino; and in 1719 they settled in Rome; for many of them, plotting became a way of life. It was a kind of avocation; and if all went according to plan it might bring big returns. Also, there were those in Britain who had grievances — because their religion was proscribed, because the Whigs kept them out of office, because their debts were great and their affairs went badly. And there were others — true conservatives, 'fellows whom the flood could not wash away' — who believed in precedent, tradition, status and the divine right of kings. So Jacobite sentiment and Jacobite plotting survived the discreditable disasters of 1708 and 1715 and 1719. But nothing came of it all and nothing could come of it as long as Britain remained at peace. If neither France nor Spain would move, the Jacobites could not move. They had been able to fish in the troubled waters of the first two decades of the century, but in the years of peace and mounting prosperity from 1719 to 1740 there was nothing very much that they could do. The cause languished. And this is why, although only four years separated the battle of Sheriffmuir from the battle of Glenshiel, twenty-six years passed before the battle of Glenshiel was succeeded by the final Jacobite attempt to overthrow the government of Great Britain.

Notes and References

1. Quoted in Petrie, op. cit., p. 238.
2. G. Menary, *The Life and Letters of Duncan Forbes of Culloden* (London, 1936), p. 23.

2 'A DESPERATE UNDERTAKING'

James Edward the Old Pretender was not yet very old when the Spanish fleet that was to take him to England was disabled by the gale and his diminutive forces on land were scattered across the hillsides of Glenshiel by a handful of government troops. To be exact, he was only 31. But although his cause did not prosper in 1719, his personal affairs did, for it was in this very year that he succeeded in marrying an heiress.

Clementina Maria Sobieski was the grand-daughter of John Sobieski, King of Poland. Equally important, she was one of the wealthiest heiresses in Europe. As a result, she was courted by many men of nobility and title, and was in a position to marry almost as she chose. She chose James Edward. She considered, no doubt, that by this match she had a prospect of becoming Queen of England in fact as well as in name (for among his adherents James was known as the Chevalier de St George, King James the Third), while her husband benefited to the extent of a 25 million franc dowry and the enormously valuable Sobieski jewels. It looked a very suitable match on both sides. The bride travelled from Vienna to Bologna and was there married by proxy, James being occupied at the time in intriguing at the court of Spain.

It was of course important that marriage should bring to James not only a handsome settlement but also an heir. Clementina did not disappoint him. The year 1720 had not yet drawn to its close when the hoped-for event took place, and after a prolonged labour Clementina was delivered of a son. In order to prevent any doubts about the genuineness of the succession (as were not infrequently raised in connection with royal or noble heirs) no fewer than eight members of the Sacred College of Cardinals were present, including the Protectors of England, Scotland, Ireland, France and Spain, while the chamber was thronged with ladies whose names and titles had for generations been noted in the Libro d'Oro. The city of Rome was filled with rejoicing and felicitations. An artillery salute was fired from the Castle of Saint Angelo. The Pope, who had offered up special prayers before the altar of Saint Thomas for a successful conclusion to Clementina's pregnancy, and who had provided consecrated baby-linen of high price, came to the palace in person in order to bestow his blessing. Cardinals and members of the Spanish court attended and brought gifts. By a special arrangement, the Palazzo Muti, close to the Church of the Apostles, was transferred to James Edward along with a handsome sum for its refurnishing. Medals of silver and bronze bearing on one side a likeness of James and Clementina and on the reverse a portrayal of a mother and child, along with the motto 'Spes Britanniae', were struck in large numbers. As for the infant himself, he was baptised Charles Edward Louis Philip Casimir. The King of France, the King of Spain and his great grandfather, the King of Poland, were all honoured by this arrangement.

Charles was brought up at the Jacobite 'court' in Rome. His education, including his religious education, was of course a matter of the greatest importance, and his parents quarrelled about this as they quarrelled about many other things. The trouble began when James appointed a gentleman of good family — James Murray, the so-called Earl of Dunbar — to be Charles's governor. Murray was a Protestant, and this made him extremely unwelcome to Clementina, who was a devout Roman Catholic. She was also well aware that Murray's sister, Mrs Hay, known in Rome as the Countess of Inverness, was on terms of the greatest intimacy with James Edward. Towards the end of 1725 (in the spring of which year Clementina had borne her faithless consort a second son) relations grew so bad that Clementina left Rome and retired into a convent, protesting at the indignities and affronts which she had suffered and which she attributed to the malign influence of Mr James Murray and Mr and Mrs Hay. The scandal was extreme, and was the gossip of every court and every coffeeshop in Europe. The separation was moreover most offensive to the Vatican, a fact which was pointed out to James by several papal envoys. But the crownless monarch remained unmoved by pleas, remonstrances or admonitions. He denied that he was intending to have his sons brought up as heretics, and said that the appointment of a Protestant governor was simply to gain the goodwill of Protestants in Britain. He refused to give up Mrs Hay, to dismiss governor Murray, to be reconciled with his wife; and Clementina remained in the convent. But after a while James began to find that his friends were deserting him. The atmosphere in Rome became increasingly hostile. The Pope, who had made his views very plain, refused to give him audience, and the erring exile, along with Mrs Hay, departed from Rome to enjoy the pleasures of Bologna. But he had been assured before leaving Rome that in Bologna he would not be beyond the ambit of papal resentment, and so it proved; for supplies began to dry up. James in these years depended heavily on the pontiff for frequent and large donations, and was moreover in receipt of a substantial pension from the court of Rome. The donations diminished, the pension was reduced, and James began to see reason. He returned to Rome, dismissed his three favourites and after an estrangement of some eighteen months, was reconciled with his wife. But the reconciliation was more a matter of convenience than of love. The couple lived together, but fought about money and, some said, mistresses. Clementina grew more and more difficult and exacting, James increasingly dull and sullen. And when his wife died in 1735 at the comparatively early age of 33, doubts were expressed as to whether the Old Pretender felt any genuine regret.

What effect these matrimonial disturbances had on the young Charles is not recorded. We know that after the dismissal of Murray he acquired a new tutor — in fact, he had a series of tutors, all reliable Roman Catholics. Through them, and by means of his privileged position in life, he became possessed of the accomplishments deemed suitable for a well-born and seemingly well-educated man of his time. At an early age he spoke French and Italian well; he was very fond of music, and played the cello at concerts given before Roman society; he was always ready to go riding or shooting, and was often to be seen with his younger brother boating on the Lake of Albano. His manners were those of one accustomed to command, of a young man who had always moved in the highest circles. After all, his father, in Rome, was King James III; the Pope was his friend and mentor; and a special papal writ enabled Charles to hold benefices of all kinds, a privilege calculated to bring him a good revenue in France or Spain. In order to widen his horizons, at the age of sixteen he was sent by his father on a tour of the chief Italian cities, accompanied by an entourage of fourteen members of the Jacobite 'court'. Everywhere he went he was welcomed by the rulers of whatever city he visited, and dinners, balls and receptions were held in his honour. At Parma the Dowager Duchess made him a gift of a gold snuff-box set with diamonds; at Venice he was presented to the Doge, and the magnificent gondola of the French ambassador was placed at his disposal; at Florence the coaches of the Grand Duke were sent to meet him. Charles's good looks, the charm of his manner, his air of high breeding, all of which he possessed at an early age and retained for fifteen or twenty years, made him a welcome guest in the aristocratic and courtly circles of Italy.

Favoured by the Pope, petted by the most important families in the land, flattered by everybody, it cannot have been easy for Charles to develop any inclination to self-criticism, or to obtain much of a grasp of the sterner realities of life. Those entrusted with his education did not find that their task was an easy one, for he was wilful and petulant, his manners in private being no match for his manners in public. His father found him at the age of fifteen to be 'wonderfully thoughtless for one of his age', and six years later Lady Mary Wortley Montague, significantly, used the same adjective; she saw him at a public ball 'very richly adorned with jewels' and added that he 'seemed thoughtless enough'. According to Aeneas MacDonald, who later accompanied him to Scotland, 'he seemed to have been badly educated and to care for little else than hunting and shooting'. He no doubt wanted, like most young bloods of his day, to lead troops in battle and gain renown as a great commander. But the elder son of a claimant to a throne had to be looked after carefully, and only once before 1745 did he have the opportunity to see any kind of military action.

This happened before the tour of Italy, when the young man was not yet fourteen years of age. France and Spain were at war with the Emperor of Austria, who was also King of Naples and Sicily, and southern Italy was full of French and Spanish troops. The Emperor's forces were on the defensive, and a number of them had taken refuge in the town of Gaeta, where they were besieged by the Spaniards. Gaeta is less than a hundred miles south of Rome. It was therefore natural that the Duke of Liria, son of an illegitimate brother of the Old Pretender and therefore a cousin of Charles, should pass through Rome on his way to join the besieging army. It was, no doubt, equally natural that he should propose taking his young cousin with him to see the action. It was proper, indeed it was desirable, that at some time Charles should experience at least a whiff of battle; and Gaeta looked like providing a good opportunity. It was nearby, and the siege promised to be an easy one and not likely to last very long. So James agreed, the Pope gave his blessing, and Charles set out with three companions, four servants, a confessor and a surgeon.

He remained at Gaeta for a little under six weeks, until the town capitulated. On his arrival the Spanish commander appointed him a General of Artillery, although it can safely be assumed that he was never allowed to give any orders. There is no doubt, however, that he witnessed such military operations as were taking place — the defenders of the town resisted but not desperately — and that he heard shots fired in anger. According to the Duke of Liria, he and Charles came under fire in the trenches that had been dug before the town, and at one point Charles insisted on entering and for a short time remaining in a house at which the enemy was directing cannon fire. Indeed, his inclination to expose himself rashly seems to have caused the Duke no small amount of uneasiness, and when the siege was over the poor man wrote a letter to his half-brother thanking God that there was an end to his anxieties. He can hardly have been surprised at what happened. A high-spirited young boy, brought up in a great city and accustomed to be made much of by important people, was taken on a grown-ups' outing; and he made the most of it. War, not horse-racing, used to be the sport of kings. Had not Frederick the Great campaigned in Germany? Had not George II led his infantry in person at the battle of Dettingen? And come to that, James II, Charles's own grandfather, had done the same thing (admittedly unsuccessfully) at the Battle of the Boyne. So the siege of Gaeta was an adventure-holiday for Charles, a lesson — a very small one — in the way that great and important men of action lived in the world beyond Rome. He must have enjoyed himself thoroughly. There was probably just enough danger to make the trip exciting; and Charles was just the kind of boy to delight in it. As usual, he made a good impression on almost everyone he met. Vivacious, adventurous, cheerful, self-assured — young Charles was all of these. To the French he spoke in French and to the Spaniards in Spanish. They were delighted with him. Whatever else he lacked, he did not lack the ability to charm.

While Charles was thus growing to manhood, his father and the Jacobite 'court' were occupied, as usual, in devising schemes for the restoration of the dynasty. The birth of a successor to the dreary James had raised his followers' hopes and their enthusiasm; but as luck would have it, the times were out of joint. Nothing with any real prospect of success could be devised. So in order to keep themselves in employment the Jacobite agents concocted the so-called Atterbury plot. They drew some encouragement from the financial distress and general political discontent in Britain caused by the bursting of the South Sea Bubble in 1721, and they timed their efforts to coincide with the departure of George I from London on a visit to Hanover in the summer of 1722. The idea was that the Duke of Ormonde, the same Irish peer who had been involved in the '19, would organise a tiny invasion force in Spain (it had to be small, because this time the Jacobites were paying for it), sail up the Thames and land near London. He was to be accompanied by the inspiring presence of James. The Tower was to be seized, the bullion in the Bank of England used to defray the expenses of the expedition, and a nation disgusted by Hanoverian oppression was to appear cheering in the streets for this dramatic restoration of the Stuart line. What was wrong with this scenario was that it might have succeeded on the stage but could not possibly do so in England in 1722. The failure of the '15 had proved conclusively that a substantial rebellion was not at all easy to organise, and that even professed Jacobite supporters were reluctant to take up arms against the government unless foreign military assistance, and plenty of it, was visibly and tangibly on the ground. Inevitably, the whole scheme came to nothing. Both the French and the Spanish were committed to prevent any invasion force sailing from their shores against Britain; and in any case, the Duke of Ormonde soon found that he had more debts than money, and he accordingly cancelled the invasion. In London, Sir Robert Walpole was following every move in the game. Much Jacobite correspondence across the Channel was opened and read by government officials before being passed on, and there were government agents in every centre of Jacobite activity. Several persons were arrested, and one of them spent fourteen years in the Tower before escaping to France. The principal plotter was the Earl of Mar, whose military incompetence had helped to bring the '15 to an early end. But when Francis Atterbury, Bishop of Rochester, who was to have managed the rebellion at home, went through Mar's papers in 1724, he concluded that Mar had been working at least as much for George I as for the Old Pretender. The quality of Jacobite conspiring was never high.

For the next seventeen years nothing very much happened. George I and then George II, along with Sir Robert Walpole, were secure in London, while the Old Pretender continued to occupy the Palazzo Muti in Rome. He did not have much choice. This was made clear to him in 1727, when the death of George I raised his dynastic hopes and he promptly removed to Nancy, in the independent Duchy of Lorraine, so as to be nearer to Britain and thus better able to take advantage of the situation. But Walpole promptly complained about his presence in Lorraine, the French government exerted pressure and James was expelled. He went to Avignon, which was papal territory. But the British complained again, the

Pope exerted his authority, and James was expelled a second time. So he returned to Rome. He was as well there as anywhere, as he gradually came to realise, because the accession of George II caused scarcely a ripple on the surface of British politics and gave the Jacobites no encouragement. There was no situation to take advantage of. And thus the years passed with little change. Throughout the 1730s every European capital had a Jacobite agent, or agents, on the look-out for arms or money. Atterbury went to Versailles, Ormonde to Madrid. There was a fairly extensive network of mostly unemployed exiles, a number of them titled, genuinely or otherwise, a lot of them living on hope, along with remittances from their families at home. They kept in touch with one another and with the dwindling ranks of Jacobite sympathisers in Britain, men who had been more careful or more fortunate than the exiles themselves. But so long as Europe remained at peace, the restoration of the Stuarts was a fading ideal. James himself seems almost to have lost hope — 'All that remains is for the world to see that I have done my part', he once said.

Until almost the end of the 1730s the Jacobite cause looked moribund; indeed, it was moribund. But a short-lived recovery was still possible. Revolutionaries thrive on the troubles of others, and troubles innumerable were soon to descend on Europe. Peace and prosperity could not last forever, and neither could Sir Robert Walpole nor Cardinal Fleury, chief minister of France. They were the chief architects and supporters of peace in Europe, and gradually their ability to control the situation weakened. In 1739 Walpole was driven into war with Spain, although he did everything he could to avoid it. There was no prospect that the war could be profitable to the people of Britain, but it was just what the Jacobites wanted. They knew that the conflicts of interest between Britain and France were again becoming acute, and that France might very well want to give support to Spain, directly or indirectly. A proposal was therefore put to Fleury for the landing of 5,000 French troops in Dorset, their arrival to coincide with Jacobite insurrections in several other parts of the country. Fleury seems not to have bothered to reply. But the Jacobites were not altogether discouraged; and eighteen months later the thunder of the guns at Mollwitz gave them new hope. War between Britain and Spain was good, but an extensive continental war was much better. It was bound, sooner or later, to involve both Britain and France, almost certainly in hostilities against one another, and the affairs of Europe would probably undergo great changes. In 1741, by which time Britain and France were clearly supporting opposite sides in the war although they were still formally at peace with one another, a Jacobite request was sent to Fleury for 7,000 or 8,000 troops to be landed in Scotland, where it was said that they would be joined by 20,000 revolting clansmen. This was the kind of talk that made sensible men reluctant to have anything to do with Jacobite plots. In 1715 Mar had been able to raise only about 10,000 men, and there was no chance that 20,000 would appear in support of a French invasion in 1741. The extent and strength of Jacobite feeling in Britain was something about which Fleury made it his business to know a good deal, and it must have been quite clear to him that those who now sought his help either did not know what they were talking about or were trying deliberately to deceive him. In any case, open French support for James would have meant war with Great Britain, and this Fleury was still trying to avoid. He told James's friends that he would give them some arms and money if they chose to start a rebellion in Scotland, but that he could not do more. These negotiations led to nothing and helped neither party: they simply increased mutual distrust. The French saw the Jacobites as irresponsible conspirators who would only lead them into trouble; while the Jacobites began to suspect that France was not interested in restoring the Stuarts to the throne but wanted only to use Jacobitism as a means to weaken Britain's ability to resist French ambitions on the continent and elsewhere.

There was much to support these suspicions, on both sides. From the French point of view, the Jacobites were very small beer. They might be able to cause trouble in Britain, even enough trouble, if the timing was right, to affect the outcome of some major military or political campaign on the continent or overseas; but the resources they could command in men and money were small and doubtful, and their influence on great events was therefore unlikely to be more than marginal. The Jacobites, for their part, had to recognise that France and Spain would always pursue their own interests, and that only when at war with Great Britain would they openly help 'James III', and even then they would do so just as far as they thought that it would be worth their while. However much friendship might be professed, these were the fundamentals of the situation, and they did not alter. Nevertheless, the course of events turned to some extent on how persuasively the Jacobites could talk and a great deal on the resolve of France to remain at peace. And when the *dramatis personae* in the diplomatic play began to change, both at Versailles and at Rome, the scene began to be set for the last Jacobite convulsion.

In 1738 James passed fifty and began to show even more signs of middle age than he had done at thirty-five; and the old generation of his followers had mostly died off — Lockhart of Carnwath in 1731, Atterbury in 1732, Mar at Aix-la-Chapelle in the same year. They were replaced by the new men who were to help engineer and then direct the final Jacobite rebellion.

The first of these to arrive in Rome was a young gentleman who came — or so it was said — with the intention merely of passing the winter. John Murray was the younger son of Sir David Murray, a Peebles-shire laird of orthodox Jacobite principles and no great importance. Young Murray had been educated at Edinburgh and Leyden and then, like most young men of his age and station, had gone on the grand tour. He went first to Paris and then to Rome, where he spent much of his time in the endless galleries admiring the paintings and the sculpture. He seems to have first met Charles some time between 1737 and 1740. Later, towards the end of 1741, he was admitted to the Palazzo Muti, and introduced to the Old Pretender. Murray was twenty-three years old at the time and Charles was almost twenty-one, and the two seem to have developed a strong liking for one another. Murray, who is said to have been of a handsome appearance and with very prepossessing manners, apparently saw — or thought he saw — the chance of a lifetime. He succeeded in recommending himself to James, and in a surprisingly short time he became a confidant and a favourite of the would-be monarch, and was taken into the secret of the many schemes and intrigues which were going forward in Rome amid the exciting atmosphere of a European war. He was soon officially recognised as a useful agent in Scotland. And in 1742, at the early age of twenty-four, he managed to get himself appointed as James's Secretary for Scottish Affairs.

The second arrival was Lord Elcho, the eldest son of the Earl of Wemyss. The old Earl was a Jacobite, but too shrewd to have become deeply involved in earlier risings; he contented himself with living in Paris — which in any case he preferred to Scotland — refusing to take the oath of allegiance to King George. Elcho was educated at Winchester in so far as education took place there in the 1730s, and when his time was up he returned to Paris and, in the winter of 1740, was sent by his father to Rome. Soon after his arrival there he was presented to James, who introduced him to Charles. He and Charles were respectively twenty and nineteen years of age when they first met; and Elcho was naturally welcome in Jacobite circles, for his father was a distinguished although not a prominent adherent of the cause. Elcho soon became a constant attendant at James's so-called court.

The appearance of these new recruits more or less coincided with another effort in Scotland to promote the Stuart interest. In 1739 a number of Scots Jacobites got together and formed what they called an Association. They were an odd lot, and the Association was a very odd sort of revolutionary cell. The most prominent members were the Duke of Perth, described by one contemporary as 'a foolish horse-racing boy'; his uncle, Lord John Drummond; the Earl of Traquhair and his brother; Simon Fraser, Lord Lovat; Sir John Campbell of Auchenbreck (very hard up); and Donald Cameron the younger of Lochiel, whose father had been attainted and forfeited for his part in the '15. Of these seemingly enthusiastic revolutionaries, only three — Perth, Lochiel and Lovat — actually joined Charles when the chips were down in 1745, and the support given by Lovat was, as we shall see, ambivalent at best.

The Associators made contact with Rome through one of Lochiel's uncles by marriage, a highland laird of modest pretensions called William MacGregor, or, the clan name being proscribed, William Drummond of Balhaldie. Balhaldie was sent first to Rome in order to acquaint James with the existence and objects of the Association, and then from Rome he went to Paris in order to talk to Cardinal Fleury. Balhaldie seems to have been a most irresponsible person, even by the standards set by other Jacobite agents. He it was who said that in Scotland alone there were 20,000 men ready to fight for the Stuarts, to which he added that the cause of the Old Pretender was strongly supported in England and that success was certain if only the French would send over a few thousand troops. The pacific Cardinal expressed interest but remained non-commital. This did not prevent Balhaldie from returning to Scotland early in 1742 and telling the Associators that the Cardinal was a true friend, and that French troops would be sent over in the autumn provided that sufficient encouragement was given by the English Jacobites.

For the next eighteen months Jacobite agents were constantly on their travels, and intriguing and planning went on at an exhilarating pace. The Associators met the English Jacobites in London, who declared their willingness to give all the help in their power once

French troops had landed, but prudently refused to put anything in writing. Murray was sent to Paris in order to discuss matters with the Cardinal. Yet another plan was put forward, this time for an invasion by 15,000 French troops led by James himself. Then Fleury died. This was a stroke of luck for the Jacobites, because the Cardinal's dislike of military adventures had been a serious obstacle in their way; no longer advised by Fleury, Louis XV was now likely to be more obliging. Early in 1743 Murray was back in Paris, talking with the new French ministers, and in the summer a select group of English Jacobites arrived at Versailles and had an audience with the King. Louis was sufficiently interested to send an agent to England, ostensibly to buy horses but in reality to gauge the strength of English support for the Old Pretender. After being handsomely wined and dined by his contacts, this man returned to France with the extraordinary story that at least half of the English aristocracy and gentry were Jacobites at heart; all that was needed for a successful rebellion was a little French encouragement. This was what he must have been told. One may seriously doubt whether Fleury would have been deceived for a moment by such a gross misrepresentation of the situation, but Louis XV was anxious to revenge himself on Great Britain for British activities in support of Maria Theresa; and even monarchs are doubtless apt to believe what they want to believe. However that may be, military plans for a French invasion now began to take definite shape.

The planned French invasion of Britain in 1744 is an essential part of the Jacobite story, because the intention to invade was genuine, and knowledge of this fact influenced many of the rebels in 1745. What had almost happened in 1744 would actually happen, they believed, in 1745, once the standard had been raised. And this, when the time came, Charles encouraged them to believe.

The invasion plan was very carefully worked out. The essence of it was to attack without warning. Britain and France were still formally at peace, but Britain's allies and sometimes British troops were making life very difficult for Louis, and toppling George II by one unexpected thrust would stop British activity on the continent and might even bring the whole War of the Austrian Succession to an end in a matter of weeks. It was a plan worthy of Hitler. There was to be no declaration of war, and the results of victory would be splendid. Moreover, the French appreciated that in order to ensure success there would have to be an internal rising timed to coincide with the invasion, and that the invading forces would have to be large enough to convince the Jacobites that it would pay them better to step forward and join the invaders than to stand on the sidelines and wait and see. Louis therefore decided to land 12,000 men at Maldon in Essex, close to London, and at the same time to send 3,000 troops to Scotland under Earl Marischal Keith, half of whom were to land at Inverness, where they could be joined by Lovat and his clan, while the other half were to land on the west coast; these latter were to 'persuade' the MacDonalds, the MacLeods and the MacLeans of Mull to march across Scotland and join the Frasers under Lovat. Finally, in order to sugar the pill and conceal the fact, as far as possible, that this was an unprovoked act of aggression by a foreign power against Great Britain, Charles Edward was to take his place with the invasion force and thus make it appear that the French came as liberators and not as foes. Charles did not hesitate, but agreed at once to act as a collaborator and to lend his name and presence as a cover for French designs.

Troops and ships for the invasion were duly assembled at Brest and at Dunkirk, but before they could depart it was necessary for Charles to travel from Rome and join them. This was not as easy as it sounds, because the disappearance of Charles from Rome, and still more his arrival in France, would have aroused the immediate suspicions of the British government. The French were anxious to achieve complete surprise. And both they and the Jacobites knew that British intelligence was usually good and that the Jacobite 'court' was under constant surveillance. A cloak and dagger operation that would do credit to a modern Hollywood movie was accordingly arranged, and early one morning Charles slipped out of the Palazzo Muti, and all the world (including James Edward) was given to understand that he had gone on a hunting expedition. In fact, he made his way in a variety of disguises to Paris, which he reached three weeks later, towards the end of January.

The British government seems not to have known about this journey until after it was over. But this made very little difference, because when Charles appeared in Paris and the cat was out of the bag, the French expeditionary force was not ready to sail; and in any case, British agents had begun to suspect that something big was afoot, and British ministers had begun to take steps for the defence of the country. Had the French forces been ready to sail before Charles left Rome (as originally planned), the danger to Britain would have been very great indeed. But sailing had to be postponed for several weeks, and France thus lost the invaluable advantage of surprise. Louis nevertheless, undeterred, resolved to press on with a full-scale invasion of Great Britain.

The prospects of success remained good. A French squadron was at Brest, ready to engage the British ships or to draw them away from the Channel. At Dunkirk (where Charles arrived late in February) there were sixteen battalions of foot soldiers and one of dragoons, a force of approximately 10,000 men. This was a very considerable army, to be landed within thirty miles of the centre of London, under the command of Marshal Saxe. Saxe had fought in several theatres of war on the continent, and was unquestionably the greatest general of the age (he was destined in 1745 to inflict two serious defeats on British armies). Also at Dunkirk there were three battalions of the Irish Brigade ready to sail for Scotland, where Murray had done some preparatory work among the highland chiefs. It was a well-worked-out plan and the forces looked sufficient. All that the French now needed was a fair share of luck, or so it seemed. But this they were denied.

Late in February, a British squadron intercepted the French battle-fleet off Dungeness. A severe gale was blowing and no engagement took place, the French ships escaping under cover of darkness; but their presence in the Channel converted rumours of an invasion attempt into certainty. A few days later, on 6 March, by which time French troops for the invasion were embarked and some transports were already at sea, including one with Charles and Marshal Saxe on board, a violent storm arose which damaged the French fleet and sank twelve transports manned and equipped for the crossing, seven of them going down with all hands; other vessels were driven onto the coast and the men in them saved with difficulty. A week later it blew again, with only less disastrous consequences. Surprise was gone and the armada was crippled. Saxe decided that enough was enough, and he informed Charles that he had given orders to cancel the expedition. An end to the War of the Austrian Succession was not yet in sight.

This series of events had important consequences. For one thing, it brought the conflict between Britain and France into the open. When the British government learned in February that Charles was in Paris, a note was sent demanding his expulsion from French territory in accordance with existing treaty arrangements. Louis temporised. But a few weeks later when the plans for a surprise attack had had to be abandoned and double-dealing was no longer worth while, His Most Christian Majesty replied with a declaration of war. And Charles was not forgotten. After his return from Dunkirk to Paris, he was granted by the French court a pension of 5,000 livres a month, on which he should have been able to live at least reasonably well. But this sum proved to fall far short of his needs, or rather of his profligacy. Within a few weeks it was discovered that the young gentleman's debts amounted to approximately 30,000 livres; and in order to avoid scandal the luckless French government had to take steps to relieve him of the burden. Charles may have been drowning his sorrows, for the cancellation of the expedition must have been a bitter blow to him. At one point he had expected, not unreasonably, to be in London with a victorious army within twenty-four hours; to recover the crown that his family had lost, so regrettably and perhaps even unnecessarily, half a century before; to reverse the failures of 1708, 1715, 1719; and to do all this while not yet twenty-four. No wonder he was disappointed. Nor was he alone in his disappointment. So confident was the father of the son's impending success that he ordered new liveries to be worn by his servants when the news should reach Rome that Charles had made his triumphant entry into London; and when the news did not come, he shut himself up for several days in absolute seclusion. All hope seemed suddenly to be lost. And in the bitterness of the downfall of their expectations, numerous supporters of the Old Pretender began to suspect that the French had not played them fair. The need for secrecy about the invasion plans had left many Jacobites quite unaware of what was going on, and when they learned about it afterwards some were inclined not to believe what they were told, others resented not having been let into the secret, and still others concluded that the French were half-hearted and had no wish to do more than create some temporary trouble at home for the British government. The French, too, had their doubts. How much support really existed in Britain for the Old Pretender? As one of Louis' subjects put it, writing to the King himself, 'There are always malcontents in England but what weight can one put on this? I would by now have had time to grow disillusioned with the Jacobites, had I ever been taken in by them; they are good for nothing but ruining themselves and those they draw into their schemes'.[1]

But the exiled Jacobites could not afford to be too disillusioned, and they continued their lobbying of French ministers. From the summer of 1744 until the spring of 1745 numerous projects for an invasion of some part or other of the British Isles turned up in the

French Foreign Ministry. Jacobite agents continued to assure the French that a large-scale rising would take place if only the French would supply the money, as well as sending men and arms. Murray came to Versailles and explained the deep disappointment felt in Scotland over the failure of Saxe's expedition, and stayed long enough to try to suborn officers of the Scots Brigade serving with the Dutch, and to conduct a brief fund-raising campaign. There was a proposal (by a Jacobite) for a French attack on the British fleet, and Charles formally asked for another expeditionary force to be organised. But the French supped with a long spoon; besides which, Charles's personal relations with Louis do not seem to have been good. What the French wanted was a rising first; then, they indicated, they would give it support. They were less than enthusiastic about the Jacobite scenario of a landing by French troops to be followed by a rush to arms on the part of a downtrodden and Hanover-hating population.

While all this went on, Charles remained in Paris remote from his father the Old Pretender and his 'court'. In some degree, the Jacobite cause was breaking up, divided into those who were trusted by James, in Rome, and the group of so-called 'Irish advisers' who were Charles's friends in Paris. It was to these latter that the '45 essentially owed its origins; in spite of appearances, the rebellion was really an Irish adventure. Among the group was Lord Clare, the commander of one of Louis XV's Irish regiments, and it was he, in the course of 1744, who introduced Charles to several shipowners *cum* traders *cum* privateers who operated out of French ports such as Nantes and St Malo. These men were Irish émigrés, some of them born in France, and they had strong Jacobite sympathies. They made their living by shipbuilding, by the slave trade, and through the organisation of predatory activities against British shipping in the Channel — an enterprise which in time of war was of course approved of and supported by the French government. Some of them were wealthy and important men, and they were in frequent touch with the French Ministry of Marine which was responsible for authorising privateering ventures. These privateers were, in effect, a special branch of the French naval forces. Privateering in the eighteenth century was not a field for amateurs, for it combined highly organised violence with profit. And just as the risks were considerable, the profits, if all went well, could be very large.

Within this circle of acquaintances, Charles was subject to new pressures and was made aware of new opportunities. He was staying with the Duke of Berwick, a few miles from Paris. His host, like most of his new friends, was a man of action — the kind of action that had so narrowly eluded Charles in the spring of 1744. The Irish officers who surrounded him, servants of Louis XV, were men of the same mould. So were the privateers. But the French, it seemed, were for inaction, at least as far as the Stuarts were concerned. In these circumstances it is hardly surprising that Charles began to talk of going it alone, of crossing to Scotland 'tho' with a single foot-man' (as he is reported to have said) and certainly without a body of French troops. When Murray visited him in the summer of 1744 Charles put this idea forward, and Murray reluctantly agreed to transmit it to Scotland and find out what the leading Jacobites thought of it. They thought very little. Cameron of Lochiel called it 'a rash and desperate undertaking' and others declared that there would be no rising if Charles came unaccompanied by French sol-diers. Only the Duke of Perth expressed support. But Charles per-sisted, and early in 1745 he began to make tentative plans. His sympathisers in Scotland grew alarmed, and letters to dissuade him were written. Cameron of Lochiel even offered to come to France in order to discuss the matter, but Charles put him off. His mind, evidently, was made up. What he now wanted was not advice from Scotland, but arms, money and transportation. These, along with plentiful encouragement from his new friends, were to be found more or less privately in France and Italy. Charles gave orders that his jewels at Rome were to be pawned. He borrowed 180,000 livres from two of his adherents, the Parisian bankers Waters and Son, who no doubt bore it in mind that even if Charles was a spendthrift his father was a wealthy man. (At the end of the day, the money was in fact repaid to the bank by James.) He obtained further help from a young Paris banker called Aeneas MacDonald and he sent an agent to Holland to buy arms but not to answer any questions about their ultimate destination. Most immediately important, he approached the wealthiest of the privateers, Antoine Walsh, who had made his fortune as a naval shipbuilder and slave trader, and asked him if he would make available one of his well-equipped vessels to provide Charles with a passage to Scotland. This was agreed in April 1745, and Charles wrote to Walsh 'what you have engaged to do is the most important service anyone could ever do me'. Back in Rome, James knew nothing about these arrangements. Neither did Louis XV nor the French court nor most of the leading Jacobites in Britain. It was all done by Charles, encouraged by Irish officers in the service of France, and by Irish bankers and merchants-*cum*-privateers. The former would join the rebellion, hoping for glory at least, while the latter were ready to venture substantial sums on the prospect of the positions, privileges and enormous gains that they would be able to secure in the event of a Stuart restoration. What Aeneas MacDonald said after it was all over contained only a small element of exaggeration: 'the expedition to Scotland was entirely an Irish project'.

The vessel that was to carry Charles across the seas was a small sixteen-gun frigate called *La Doutelle*. Previously fitted out for the prosecution of privateering ventures against British shipping, she was fast and well-armed for her size, like a modern destroyer. She was loaded at Nantes in June 1745, with 1,500 guns, 1,800 broadswords, a supply of ammunition and 4,000 louis d'or to get the rebellion started. Charles and his backers went aboard at Nantes, and early in July the *Doutelle* sailed for Belle-Ile where she was to rendezvous with a larger ship, the *Elizabeth*.

Before leaving France, Charles wrote a letter to his father which that bewildered man did not receive until his son was well out to sea, on course for Scotland. This letter still exists, and it is a revealing document. Charles begins by saying that 'I have, above six months ago, been invited by our friends to go to Scotland' — an absolute lie, as we have seen, the Scottish Jacobites being much alarmed at the mere idea. He goes on to explain that he could no longer, with honour, remain idle in France or return meekly to Rome, 'after such scandalous usage as I have received from the French court'. Louis XV had indeed refused to see him, and Charles apparently felt that he should show the world that he was not to be ignored, that, as he put it, 'I have life in me. Your Majesty cannot disapprove a son's following the example of his father. You yourself did the like in the year '15 . . .' It then occurred to Charles, apparently, that the comparison was not a very good one (his father having set sail, rather tardily, to join an on-going rebellion, he himself setting sail in the hopes of starting one), so he audaciously continued, 'but the circumstances now are indeed very different by being much more encouraging, there being a certainty of succeeding with the least help'. Poor James! He must have found this very surprising. He must have reflected that he had, to the best of his knowledge and belief, as good means of knowing the circumstances as Charles. And his doubts must have increased when he found no explanation in the letter of these improved circumstances of which he was not aware — 'the particulars of which are too long to explain' — but merely statements to the effect that 'how matters stood' and just why the prospects were so rosy could not be fairly stated in writing. He was informed only that the French court had not been told of Charles's departure because they would possibly have tried to stop it, and because they would not have believed the story about an invitation. James probably did not believe it either, or, if he did, he would have set little store by it. He must assuredly have considered Charles's actions to be, at the very least, 'rash', as is foreseen by Charles in the letter; but there was nothing that he could do. His offspring had gone, and had left him quite behind, high and dry in Rome. The venture, he was assured, would be decisive: 'Let what will happen, the stroke is struck, and I have taken a firm resolution to conquer or to die, and stand my ground as long as I shall have a man remaining with me'. It sounded very heroic; but perhaps not to James. And we know that he did not take the advice which the letter also contained, that he should travel at once to Avignon, in order to be in readiness to go to London.

While this letter was on its way to Rome, Charles had had his first adventure. The *Doutelle* had left Belle-Ile in company with the *Elizabeth*. The *Elizabeth* was a French warship of sixty-four guns, hired by the Irish privateers for use in the West Indies. It is not clear whether anyone in the French government knew that she was to be used to escort Charles to Scotland; or that when she sailed she had on board one hundred French volunteers, 2,000 muskets and six hundred broadswords. It seems unlikely that not a single French official knew or guessed what was happening — Jacobite secrets were seldom well kept. But whether France was officially involved or not, the *Elizabeth* proved to be of crucial importance to the expedition, because the day after leaving Belle-Ile the two French ships were spotted by HMS *Lion*. Britain and France were at war, and the *Lion*, although outgunned, immediately attacked. The *Doutelle* took no part in the ensuing battle, which is said to have lasted for six hours, and in which both warships were severely damaged. The *Elizabeth* could not remain at sea, and set course for Brest, which she was lucky to reach, and the *Lion* was too much reduced in speed to pursue the *Doutelle*, which escaped to the northwest.

Four weeks later the French frigate reached Eriskay, and Charles set foot on British soil for the first time in his life.

Note

1. Quoted in F.J. McLynn, *France and the Jacobite Rising of 1745* (Edinburgh, 1981), p. 25.

3 THE PROGRESS OF THE REBELS

In the year one thousand seven hundred and forty-five, Charles Edward Stuart, the Pretender's eldest son, calling himself the Prince of Wales, landed with seven persons in a remote part of the Highlands of Scotland. A few days after his arrival, some Highlanders (not a very considerable number) joined him, and descending from their mountains, undisciplined, and ill armed, without cavalry, without artillery, without one place of strength in their possession, attempted to dethrone the king, and subvert the government of Britain . . . The conclusion of this enterprise was such as most people both at home and abroad expected, but the progress of the rebels was what nobody expected; for they defeated more than once the king's troops; they over-ran one of the united kingdoms, and marched so far into the other, that the capital trembled at their approach, and during the tide of fortune, which had its ebbs and flows, there were moments when nothing seemed impossible; and, to say truth, it was not easy to forecast, or to imagine, any thing more unlikely, than what had already happened.

This is the opening paragraph of John Home's *History of the Rebellion*, the only careful and reasonably unbiased account of the whole affair written by one who had actually taken part in it. As a two-hundred-word summary of the '45, the paragraph quoted above could hardly be improved upon.

Charles and his companions landed on Eriskay, a small island in the chain that makes up the Outer Hebrides, on 23 July. A week or so later they crossed to the mainland, and went ashore to look for support. Their movements were not, at this stage, known to the government; but throughout the summer there had been rumours of a French invasion or a Jacobite rebellion. At the end of June, shortly before Charles left Nantes, a letter was written by MacLeod of MacLeod to Duncan Forbes in Edinburgh, in which there occurs the following passage:

I cannot help informing you of a (more) extraordinary rumour spread all hereabouts . . . which is that the Pretender's eldest son was to land somewhere in the Highlands in order to raise the Highlanders for a Rebellion . . . I shall spare no pains to be better informed, and if it's worth while, run you an express.[1]

For two reasons this was an important letter. It was, in the first place, the earliest report to the government that trouble might be brewing in the West Highlands; and secondly, the information came from a great highland chief, nineteenth chief of the Clan MacLeod, whose territories extended through large parts of the Hebrides and whose support for the rebellion many Jacobites hoped for, and some even expected. But MacLeod was too shrewd to be caught, and had already decided to keep his clan out of any dangerous adventures. Not only so; he also made good his promise in the letter, and sent men to enquire for news along the coast, as far south of Skye as Ardnamurchan, but no information about a landing was to be had. Rumours none the less persisted. Reports of a French invasion planned to take place during the summer were current in London at the end of July. And at much the same time genuine information was received that Charles had set sail from Nantes for an unknown destination.

In spite of these rumours and the 'undoubted intelligence' of Charles having left France, the British government remained unconvinced that any special precautions were required. Although it was widely believed that the Pretender's son had gone to Scotland, taking with him sufficient arms for a considerable number of men, there was for a time no evidence that he had actually landed, or, if he had landed, that he had been able to attract any support. Duncan Forbes, Lord President of the Court of Session in Scotland, to whom MacLeod directed his letters, wrote as follows on 8 August:

I consider the report as improbable, because I am confident that the young man cannot with reason expect to be joined by any considerable force in the Highlands. Some loose, lawless men of desperate fortunes may, indeed, resort to him. But I am persuaded that none of the Highland gentlemen who have aught to lose will, after the experience with which the year 1715 furnished them, think proper to risk their fortunes in an attempt which to them might appear desperate, especially as so many considerable families have lately altered their sentiments.[2]

But on the very day that Forbes wrote these words, definite news reached Edinburgh, through no less a person than the Duke of Argyll, that Charles was in Scotland; and on the following day this was confirmed by another letter from MacLeod of MacLeod to Forbes, reporting that the Young Pretender had landed from a solitary warship with a quantity of weapons and with approximately thirty officers on board, Irish or French. There were still some who refused to believe it. But by the middle of the month, when Charles had been in the country for over three weeks, everyone had to accept the almost incredible fact that he had actually arrived, and that he had secured a foothold, however temporary and however tenuous, on the far west coast of Scotland, and that he was possibly going to be able to cause some trouble.

Steps to meet this unexpected threat had to be taken, but the government was not yet greatly concerned. It was surprising, certainly, that Charles had landed. But it seemed very unlikely that his landing would bring a serious threat to life and property let alone to the government or to the Crown itself. The Pretender's son was young, inexperienced and impetuous; he wanted glory and he wanted it soon; he was just the man to begin a rash improbable adventure for he bore a famous name — and he had nothing to lose. But it seemed almost certain that he would not gain anything either. Duncan Forbes's assessment was a good one. If Charles was foolish enough to come to Scotland with scarcely any supporters, there were very good grounds for thinking that very few highland gentlemen of substance would be equally foolish, and risk their own lives and the lives of their followers by joining him. It therefore seemed very likely that even if a rebellion were started, the Jacobites would fare no better than they had done in 1715 and 1719, and that a skirmish somewhere in the hills, or a small-scale battle in the Great Glen, or in the neighbourhood of Perth or Inverness, would soon put paid to the whole affair.

That these reasonable expectations were falsified in the event was due to several causes. The first was that the rebellion, by accident or by design, was very well timed. Britain was heavily engaged in a major continental war. The King was in Hanover, and the Duke of Cumberland, with most of the British army, was also on the continent. Marshal Saxe, a month or two before Charles left France, had inflicted a serious defeat on the British forces at Fontenoy, and this had reduced the availability of British troops, lowered the credit of the government and damaged morale. The administration of public affairs was in the hands of politicians who were not particularly competent, Parliament was not sitting, and the members of the Privy Council, along with the other advisers of the Crown, were at their country seats. The King had stated his intention of returning at once to London if a French invasion should appear imminent, but there were no particular plans for countering a rebellion in the north. In those days it took the better part of a week for a letter written in Edinburgh to reach London, and therefore, as the Jacobites gathered their strength, the officers of the government in Scotland had often to act on their own initiative and to do what they could for the defence of the country.

During these critical months in Scotland, Duncan Forbes was the most formidable enemy that the House of Stuart possessed. Born in 1685, he was the younger son of the third laird of Culloden. He had studied law in Scotland and at the University of Leyden, and in 1709 was admitted a member of the Faculty of Advocates. His work in Edinburgh was interrupted by the '15, when the rebels, as we have seen, besieged Culloden House. Joining his sister-in-law (for his elder brother, who was detained in London, was at that time the laird) Duncan Forbes helped to organise the defence of the house and then, when the rebels gave up the siege, took part in the attack on Inverness which recovered that somewhat Jacobite town for the government. In the aftermath of the '15 he played a more prominent part, raising a fund for the legal defence of the prisoners held in Carlisle, and addressing a strong protest to Walpole against the inhumanity and impolicy of the government's intention to put Scots prisoners on trial in England, as well as to detain in prison in Scotland those who had not enough influence to secure a pardon. The wise course, as he told the minister, was to reconcile those who had rebelled by clemency, to respect the established rights of the Scottish people, and to punish 'only as many as was necessary for terror, and for weakening the strength of the rebels for the future'.

This letter, however unwelcome it may have been to the government in London, did not injure Forbes's legal/political career. In 1716 he was appointed Deputy Lord Advocate (he was to become Lord Advocate in 1725), and in 1721 it was suggested to him by the Duke of Argyll, who managed the affairs of Scotland for the government, that he should enter Parliament. This he did in 1722, remaining a member of the House of Commons until 1737, when he became Lord President of the Court of Session. Forbes thus entered politics at the age of thirty-six, abandoning a lucrative career at the bar, for he was already one of the leading men of his profession. He had excellent political connections and was supported by the Duke of Argyll, with whom he was on very good terms. He was also intimate with Lord Lovat, chief of the Frasers. This was a curious friendship, if such it can be called. Forbes was a man of great energy, who worked hard and consistently all his life. He also drank hard, and was one whom Doctor Johnson would have called an eminently clubbable man. Beyond all this, however, he was a man of firm principles, and more than once he took considerable personal and political risks in standing by them. Lovat, on the other hand, was a treacherous scoundrel even by the not very exacting standards of the eighteenth century. His chief aim in life seems to have been a dukedom, and he did not care by what means it was obtained. In his early 30s he kidnapped the widow of his cousin, the ninth Lord Lovat, forced her to go through a marriage ceremony with him, and then held her prisoner on a remote and desolate island off the west coast of Scotland. This did not bring him recognition as the tenth Lord Lovat — instead, he was outlawed for his pains in 1698. In 1702 he proclaimed James VIII at Inverness, and then made off to visit the Old Pretender at Saint Germain. He returned to Scotland in the following year on a mission for Louis XIV, but betrayed his employer, and spent the next ten years in a French gaol. On his release, he returned to Scotland, changed sides, and supported the government during the '15. This time his schemes were successful, for his 'loyalty' was rewarded by recognition of his right to the Lovat title and estates, and he at last (although not without some residual legal opposition) became the tenth Lord Lovat. He seems a curious person for Forbes (and his brother also) to have known well, for he was a Jacobite if he was anything; but possibly part of the explanation is that they were neighbours. At one time Lovat was Sheriff of Inverness.

In 1734 John Forbes died, and Duncan succeeded his brother as laird of Culloden. Two years later Edinburgh was in an uproar over the fate of two notorious smugglers and the captain of the city guard. That the smugglers were guilty was certain, and they were condemned to be executed. But the sympathy of the populace, as always in the eighteenth century, was with the smugglers, and when, during a service in the kirk of St Giles, one of them held down the guards in order that the other might escape (which he did, assisted by the congregation) sympathy turned into whole-hearted admiration. The remaining prisoner became a hero, and in due course an enormous crowd turned out to witness his execution. When it was over, some stones were thrown at the hangman, and Porteous, the captain of the guard, ordered his men to open fire. Eight or nine persons were killed and twice as many wounded. Porteous was flung into prison, but the rights and wrongs of the matter were not clear, and popular anger and excitement reached fever pitch. Would Porteous escape the gallows? Some person or persons unknown determined not, for a tumult arose one autumn evening in the Grass Market and a well-organised mob broke into the prison, overcame the guard, dragged out the prisoner, and hanged him in the street about a quarter of an hour before midnight.

The affair of the Porteous mob was extremely serious. A servant of the Crown, convicted of murder but almost certain to be reprieved, had been taken from custody in the heart of the Scottish capital and lynched. No government likes a riot, and a riot of this nature in the 1730s was sure to evoke a drastic response. Duncan Forbes, as the chief law officer of the Crown in Scotland, was intimately concerned in the whole affair. The ultimate responsibility for Porteous's conviction was his, and it was now his task to discover 'the ringleaders and abettors of these wicked and audacious proceedings' and to prosecute them with the utmost severity of the law. It could not be done. No one would talk. The government accordingly brought forward a Bill of Pains and Penalties which provided for the imprisonment of the Lord Provost and magistrates of Edinburgh and for the punishment of the city in general. This Bill, which was justifiably regarded as an unwarranted attack on the rights and reputation of all the citizens of Edinburgh whether guilty or innocent was strongly opposed by all the Scottish and many of the English members of Parliament. Duncan Forbes, in particular, spoke against the measure, and when commanded to appear before the House of Lords as a witness boldly declared, 'My Lords, we acted in that affair as our consciences directed us; and there is no power on earth that dare call our actions in question'. The Bill had to be watered down and the King's ministers were doubtless displeased. But the strong stand that Forbes had taken against the Bill in Parliament made him a popular figure in Scotland, and when he was appointed Lord President of the Court of Session in the summer of 1737 he was widely recognised not only as a champion of the law but also of the rights of the Scottish people.

Eight years later it was upon this man that there fell the main task of organising the defence of Scotland. The army was not his responsibility, but almost everything else was. The situation was extremely confused:

> everybody spake of nothing but the young Pretender, though very few people knew what to believe about him. One day it was confidently affirmed, that he had landed in one of the Western Islands with ten thousand French: the very next day it was asserted with equal confidence, that he had landed in the Highlands without any troops; but that wherever he came, the Highlanders to a man had taken arms.[3]

It was precisely such unreflecting readiness to rebel that Forbes made it his first task to prevent. His own estates, at Culloden, Mull and Tiree, were in or on the edge of the highlands; he had many personal connections among the chiefs; and he understood the highlanders and their ways. He saw that the first thing to do was to prevent the contagion of rebellion from spreading. He therefore wrote to the chiefs in order, as he put it, 'to preserve them in their duty and prevent their madness', urging them to resist the temptation to join the rebels and reminding them of the ruin that would overtake those foolish enough to be misled. Some who wavered but remained loyal, such as the Duke of Gordon and the Earl of Seaforth, may have been persuaded by Forbes's words; others, such as Lovat and Lochiel were, unluckily for them, not persuaded. Still others who hesitated had their fate decided for them. The danger was, as Forbes recognised and the government in London did not, that the rebels would compel to join them those who could neither escape nor resist. The usual procedure was to threaten lairds or chieftains that unless they produced a suitable quota of supporters for the Prince their properties would be laid waste; the famous 'fiery cross', which did its rounds in 1745, was in reality a warning that the huts would be burned and the cattle taken of all those who did not 'come out'. Cluny Macpherson provides the best example of the dilemma that many faced. His lands lay in the rebels' path; and as he put it in a letter to Forbes, the choice was to be 'burnt or join . . . What to do, so as to save this poor country from immediate ruin, is a very great question to me . . . force has often made people commit that which was no choice'.[4] He prevaricated, but in vain. On 28 August, while on his way to raise his clan for King George, he was seized by the rebels and carried off a prisoner. After some weeks with them he returned to Badenoch, gathered together about three hundred of his kindred and — reluctantly or not, we do not know — joined the Jacobite camp at Edinburgh.

Forbes did all he could to prevent this sort of thing from happening, and it was to a considerable extent because of his efforts that when the rebel army emerged from the highlands at the beginning of September it numbered not more than 2,000 men, a very inconsiderable force. It would have been easier to prevent an escalation of the rebellion if, after the '15, the government had not adopted the policy of disarming the highlanders. What this policy meant in practice was that the loyal clans surrendered their arms, while those with Jacobite sympathies concealed them, only handing in a few rusty old weapons of no importance. The result was that in 1745 those who were inclined to rebel had arms and those who sided with the government had not. To make matters worse, the second Duke of Argyll, mistakenly believing that highland wars were at last a thing of the past, had turned the energies of the Clan Campbell towards a progressive agriculture, emasculating its fighting power and virtually removing a major force for law and stability in Scotland. Thus the power to oppose the rebels at the very start of the rebellion was weak. Forbes was constantly being asked for arms. The chiefs in Skye, for example, Sir Alexander MacDonald and MacLeod of MacLeod, wrote to say that they could raise 1,800 men but with only two hundred guns and swords 'they would make but a foolish figure'. To be in the highlands at this juncture, unarmed and not on the side of the rebels, was distinctly unsafe. Guns, money and credit were all lacking. The government in London was caught unprepared, could offer little more than encouragement, and it did not always offer much of that.

It was from Culloden House that Forbes's letters to the chiefs were written. He had gone there within a day or two of learning that Charles had landed, so as to be better placed to counter the moves of the rebels; on the day after his arrival, General Cope, the Commander in Chief in Scotland, put him in command of the Earl of Loudon's Regiment, a sort of northern territorial force that had only recently been organised and was very poorly equipped. Cope himself had been appointed only eighteen months before. He was an energetic leader and when rumours of a Jacobite rising were still very vague and disbelieved by the politicians, he had begun his preparations to meet such an eventuality. His plan was to march his forces into the highlands and there 'to oppose whatever enemies I shall meet with'. Once the rebellion began, the government approved Cope's strategy, partly on the ground that he would be able to rely on the assistance of friendly clans, and he was ordered to carry additional arms to distribute to these — as it turned out, mythical — highlanders. His army, such as it was, gathered at Stirling. Unfortunately for Cope, almost every unit of real fighting quality was on the continent. All that Cope had at his disposal was a scratch collection of two regiments of dragoons, three and a half infantry regiments, a few men belonging to Lord Loudon's newly formed highland regiment, and a handful of garrison troops. The dragoons had never been on active service, and the horses, like their riders, were quite unused to the sound of gunfire; of the infantry, not one regiment had ever been in action. Thus almost all his men, as Cope himself expressed it, were 'raw and unused to taking the Field'.

That the country was so ill-defended was due to the situation in Europe — the summer of 1745 bore some resemblance to the summer of 1940. The Duke of Newcastle, Prime Minister of the day, wrote as follows to Argyll on 14 August:

I never was in so much apprehension as I am at present . . . the loss of all Flanders, and that of Ostend (which I am afraid must soon be expected), will, we apprehend, from the great superiority of the French in Flanders, be soon followed by some embarkation from Ostend or Dunkirk, or both. And there is reason to believe that the French and Spanish ships which are now in the Western ports of France, and in the Bay of Biscay (amounting to between twenty and thirty, twenty of which are of the line), may be intended to support the embarkation either by coming up the Channel, where at present we have not a squadron sufficient to oppose them, or (as I find is apprehended by some), by coming north, about Scotland to Ostend. Seven French men-o'-war sailed from Brest about five weeks ago. It is thought possible they may be somewhere lying to the westward to wait there till Ostend shall be in the hands of the French, and then proceed round Scotland thither. We are getting our ships ready, and I hope we shall soon have a tolerable squadron in the Channel. But if the French should come north about, they might surprise us. We are sending transports for 10,000 men to Campveer and Flushing, in order to bring part of our army from Flanders, if it should be necessary for the defence of this kingdom.[5]

In short, what Newcastle greatly feared at this stage was a French invasion. But only a few days later, instructions had to be sent to Cope to leave Edinburgh immediately in order to suppress a rebellion at home.

When Cope marched from Stirling it was with serious misgivings, for the rebellion looked every day more dangerous and to take all his forces north was to leave Edinburgh unprotected. But his orders were peremptory. He therefore left the cavalry behind, as being useless in the highlands, and thus set out with approximately 2,000 men, four field-pieces, carts, horses and baggage. His chances were not rated high by some good judges. Argyll thought that the rebels, if in sufficient numbers, would have the advantage, from their knowledge of the mountains and their experience of fighting in them; and that if Cope were defeated, very few of his men would be able to escape to the lowlands, and the whole of Scotland would be lost. Lord Milton warned that Cope would have 'no small difficulty' in getting at the rebels in inaccessible country, or in preventing them from slipping past him into the south of Scotland. Duncan Forbes expressed anxiety about the lack of provision for 'the worst and most unexpected events'. A great deal turned, of course, on the strength of the rebels, and on the strategy adopted by the two sides. It was known, as a result of the vigilance of Norman MacLeod of Sconsar, that Charles had landed with only a few companions and a score of Irish officers. These companions, upon whom history has bestowed the romantic title of 'The Seven Men of Moidart', were an odd lot. The 'Seven' seem to have been at least eight or nine. One was Aeneas MacDonald, who worked as a banker in Paris and who had lent Charles money; another was Sir John MacDonald, an officer in the service of Spain; another was the aged Marquis of Tullibardine, who would have been the Duke of Atholl had he not played a too prominent part in the '15, and who was described by Charles's half cousin Liria as a man of 'very little understanding or commonsense'; Sir John Strickland was an Englishman, John William O'Sullivan was an Irishman who had spent most of his life in France, Sir Thomas Sheridan, also an Irishman, was Charles's tutor, and Duncan Buchanan had served as a minor Jacobite agent in Paris and Scotland; finally, there was George Kelly, a non-juring Irish cleric who had spent fourteen years in the Tower of London after being involved in the Atterbury plot. It must have occurred to even so young and inexperienced a man as Charles that this was hardly the ideal group to start an insurrection in the west highlands of Scotland; but no doubt he relied more on the Irish officers, on his name, and on his monumental self-assurance.

Whatever his advantages and whatever his difficulties, he had some success — just enough for the rebellion to go forward. Recruiting at first in the wilds of Arisaig and Morar (a region where Roman Catholicism reigned supreme), Charles could not fail to attract some of the lesser chiefs and their clans who lived in remote glens or at the head of distant sea-lochs, almost inaccessible to government, making their own laws and living largely by protection rackets and by stealing other people's cattle. MacDonald of Keppoch, for example, was an early recruit. His father was described by Liria as 'nothing more than a highway robber' and as a man who had 'no regard for his word or for the law', and the son was equally sure to join in any rebellion against the government, and in any fighting that promised booty for him and his followers. The MacDonalds of Knoydart and some of the MacGregors (an outlawed clan) were also in this category. But other and greater chiefs whom Charles approached, refused. MacDonald of Boisdale, whom Charles met on Eriskay and who controlled Uist, was not to be persuaded either by promises or threats; he moreover cautioned several other chiefs against rising, prevented Clanranald's islesmen from joining the rebellion, and advised Charles to return home. (Charles could at this juncture have accompanied Antoine Walsh back to France, for whose shipping services, incidentally, he recommended to his father that Walsh be made Duke of Ireland.) Sir Alexander MacDonald of Sleat and MacLeod of MacLeod likewise refused, powerful chiefs upon whom Charles and his associates exerted every possible pressure. The numbers of the faithful were indeed so small and they were men of so little consequence that the decision of Cameron of Lochiel became crucial to the whole enterprise. 'Young' Lochiel (so-called because his father was still alive, but exiled; he himself was fifty years of age in 1745) was a moderately important person in the highlands, and a very important one in the hopes of the Jacobites. His grandfather — who died in 1719 — was already a legend, a barbaric figure who had understood fighting and killing and stealing and not much else — Charles II once called him 'the king of thieves' — and about whose name fond highland myths accumulated — for example, that he had once killed an English officer by tearing his throat with his teeth. The grandson was less primitive. He too was a Jacobite

— he had had a hand in the Atterbury plot — and misdemeanours by his tenants were apt to lead to a hanging or something similar. But he belonged sufficiently to the modern world to have up-to-date and extensive commercial connections. He exploited the woods on his estates for a profit, had an interest in the expanding eighteenth-century iron industry, and engaged in trade across the Atlantic as well as with the lowlands. Moreover, he had corresponded with Charles, and had spent time in Paris as well as Edinburgh. What now mattered to Charles, however, was his commitment to the cause, and the fact that he could bring to the field seven hundred men. Lochiel had too much to lose not to have reflected upon the chances of success and the costs of failure. When he met Charles at Borrodale, he advised him to return at once to France, just as he had previously joined with others in advising him not to come to Scotland unless accompanied by French troops. He would not join a rash attempt. And yet this is precisely what he did. What was Charles able to say that made him change his mind? We know that a long conversation took place between the two men, in private, but what was said is of course not recorded; some bargain must nevertheless have been struck and we know one relevant and indeed sufficient fact; when the rebellion failed and Lochiel fled to France, he was given command of a French regiment that brought in more than all the rents from his estates. Charles was always free with his promises; and some of them he kept.

With Lochiel secured, and a few minor chiefs emboldened to follow his example, Charles raised his standard at Glenfinnan on 19 August. On the day he had only about 1,600 men. Almost half of them were followers of Lochiel. Among the rest, Glengarry had brought four hundred men, Keppoch between two hundred and three hundred, and Clanranald perhaps a couple of hundred. A Council of War was held, and it was resolved to march immediately towards Perth. The rebels hoped that they would be joined *en route* by some further recruits, and in this they were not disappointed, partly for a peculiar reason. This was, that the first shots in the rebellion had already been fired, and to the Jacobites' advantage.

Small numbers of the King's troops occupied three forts in the Great Glen, Fort William, Fort Augustus and Fort George (sometimes called the castle of Inverness). These — especially the first two — were forward positions. When the Governor of Fort

Augustus realised that trouble was brewing, he sent, on 16 August, a small detachment under Captain John Scott to reinforce the garrison of Fort William. The distance is just under thirty miles. Scott left very early in the morning for he had to pass through wild country where 'incidents' were all too likely to occur, and he did not intend to spend a night on the way amid armed and disaffected clansmen. His party had got as far as High Bridge[6] when they heard the sound of bagpipes and saw some armed highlanders on the far side of the bridge. Two men were sent forward to investigate, and were seized. Unsure of the number of his enemies, and remembering that his own men were 'newly raised', Scott decided to retrace his steps and not try to force the bridge. When the soldiers' backs were turned, the highlanders followed them at a distance, keeping themselves largely concealed, and then, once the troops had reached narrow ground between Loch Lochy and the surrounding hills, began to fire from the shelter of trees and rocks. The soldiers continued their march 'with great expedition', but the number of their enemies increased rapidly, for the sound of firing attracted others to the scene. (The houses of both Lochiel and Keppoch, it should be added, were only a few miles from High Bridge.) Ordering his men to form the hollow square, Scott still marched on, now making for Invergarry. But he was intercepted by other groups of highlanders coming down the hillsides, and the game was up. Himself wounded, and with one or two of his men killed, he surrendered to MacDonald of Tiendrish. No sooner had he done so than Lochiel, with a body of his men, appeared on the scene and took charge of the prisoners. Three days later these prisoners were paraded at the raising of the Jacobite standard. This scuffle, in which the rebels did not lose a single man and which was in itself of no importance, greatly raised the Jacobites' morale, and encouraged those who wavered to join them.

While this was going on, Cope completed his preparations and left Stirling on 20 August. His orders were to march into the highlands and attack the rebels wherever he might come up with them. This was the strategy that had succeeded so well in 1719. But it was dangerous, because if the rebels slipped past the government forces they would be able to descend into the lowlands and seize control of the whole of Scotland, and perhaps also of the north of England; almost all the English army was on the continent and there were virtually no available reserves. It would probably have been better to follow the policy of the Duke of Argyll in 1715, and await the rebels somewhere near Perth or Stirling, with two or three men-of-war stationed in the Forth to prevent a crossing. But Cope's orders were absolute. He reached Crieff on 21 August and there found, to his astonishment, that neither the Duke of Atholl nor Lord Glenorchy could provide him with even one clansman. Without auxiliaries and encumbered by useless arms he was against taking his men north of Crieff, but he was 'tyed down' by his positive political orders and he therefore continued towards Dalwhinnie and Fort Augustus. He reached Dalnacardoch on 25 August, five days out of Stirling. Here he received intelligence that the rebels had already marched up the Great Glen from Corpach to Fort Augustus, where he had hoped to give them battle, and were moving south into the mountains. It was obviously their intention to engage his army as it crossed the Corriearrack. Corriearrack is a high pass through the mass of mountains that separates Loch Laggan and the Spey Valley from the Great Glen. Wade had built a nine-mile military road over the pass, where Cope had intended to go. The south side of Corriearrack is extremely steep and seen from a distance appears to rise almost vertically. The road, at the present day unusable, was carried up by seventeen traverses to a height of 2,500 feet; the long descent on the north side, to the level ground near Fort Augustus, was a steady incline, passing through several glens and valleys divided by small burns and gullies, with deep heather, trees and little bridges 'to facilitate the way'.

Pausing on 26 August amid the great bleak hillsides that surround Dalwhinnie, Cope reviewed the situation. He was only twenty-two miles from the beginning of the ascent to Corriearrack, clearly visible from his camp. But it could not possibly be crossed. His information was that the rebels already had possession of the pass, and that considerable numbers of them were actually also on the south side, concealed, and ready to attack his troops from the rear. Even supposing all this to have been untrue (and it was untrue), the risks of ascending the pass were obviously excessive. The rebels were certainly in the vicinity, and even small numbers of them, firing from behind rocks onto the road, especially at the traverses which were buttressed on the outside by walls ten to fifteen feet high, could have reduced the army to a shambles. The question was not whether to go forward or not, but which way to turn. Cope seems to have believed that as long as the rebels were not threatened by government forces they would continue to assemble men and arms and become increasingly powerful;

whereas, if he were soon to march further into the highlands the rebels would disperse, or offer little resistance. In believing this he was perhaps deliberately misled by covert Jacobite sympathisers, for the truth was that Charles was short of money, and probably could not have kept his army together for very long if he had remained shut up in the highlands. Inaction was for him almost as bad as defeat, but Cope did not realise this. In deciding what to do, the Commander in Chief also had to bear in mind that food supplies were running low and that the Atholl country, which now lay between him and Stirling, had proved, to say the least, unfriendly. Unable to cross the Corriearrack, and deeming the return march to the south too risky, he decided to make for Inverness, which was, after all, the capital of the highlands, and which the rebels might very well attack and occupy. Even this move was not without danger. The rebels might have been able to ambush Cope's army at Slochd Mor, between Carrbridge and Tomatin — indeed, they discussed doing so. But government agents brought in the news, and Cope at once set off on two forced marches in order to reach Inverness without opposition.

This move by General Cope was the second crucial factor in the initial success that Charles's campaign achieved. First, Lochiel had been persuaded to throw in his lot with Charles; and now Cope had had to extricate himself as best he could from a dangerous situation that was the result, to a large degree, of unwise orders from London. The highland army at the Corriearrack was not a formidable host. It was well suited for harassment and fighting in the hills, but it was small. Had Cope been able to advance from Stirling a few days sooner, or had he been able after reaching Dalwhinnie to fall back on Stirling, strengthen his forces and stand on suitable ground, he might well have achieved a victory like that of General Wightman in 1719. But by the time he reached Dalwhinnie there were no choices left. The rebels began their ascent of the pass before daybreak on 27 August, expecting that when they reached the summit they would see the zig-zag paths and the road on the south side thronged with redcoats. But when they got there, the hillsides below them were wrapped in solitude and silence. There was no one coming up the hill to be ambushed; no battle was going to take place. When the highlanders found out what had happened, they could hardly believe their good fortune. The only persons from Cope's army whom they encountered were some of their own kinsmen, either deserters or camp-followers or spies, who came with the news that only a few hours earlier the King's troops had struck camp and had set off towards Inverness. For the Jacobites, this was better than a victory. The government army, so it appeared, had not dared to meet them but had crept away, unwilling to risk a battle. They took it as an indication of their own strength. And accordingly, with new confidence, and much more sure of gaining further support as they went south, the Jacobites fell upon the low country, hoping that they might even be able to take Edinburgh before Cope and his men could return.

Meanwhile, the citizens of Edinburgh knew nothing whatever about the movements of the two armies; and many varying reports were in circulation. On the evening of Saturday 31 August, an express from Perthshire reached town with the astounding news that the King's army was still marching away from Edinburgh, and that the van of the highland army had reached as far south as Blair Atholl. Until that change of positions took place (which contemporaries likened to a figure in a country dance), the insurrection was looked upon less as a rebellion than a riot, which would be easily put down by regular troops. But when the army that had set out to fight the rebels was obliged to manoeuvre itself out of their way and leave them a free passage to the heart and capital of Scotland, the citizens of Edinburgh and other towns, like the inhabitants of Singapore two hundred years later, suddenly found that their trusted defences had disappeared and that they must shift for themselves.

Edinburgh at that time was a small, very crowded city of fewer than 50,000 people. It had never been fortified, but it was protected by the castle, and surrounded by a wall on three sides and by a shallow, boggy loch on the fourth. The town wall was from ten to twenty feet high in different places and was here and there strengthened with bastions, but there were no cannon; and great lengths of it were of no more use for defence than a garden wall of unusual height. In some places, even, houses had been incorporated into the wall, and some of these houses were overlooked by higher houses built outside the wall, but very close to it. As regards available manpower, the position was much the same. The Trained Bands — ludicrously misnamed — were a form of ancient militia, used occasionally for ceremonial purposes, and they had not appeared in arms since the revolution of 1688. There was also the Town Guard, whose members bore more than a passing resemblance, in age and general fitness for duty, to those members of the watch depicted in the plays of Shakespeare. And this was all that was immediately available to the Lord Provost and the magistrates for the defence of the capital of Scotland.

Nevertheless, when they learned of the rebels' approach, the city fathers resolved to defend themselves. They gave orders to repair the walls — a task scarcely worth attempting in less than a month — and to raise a regiment of 1,000 men. But time was not on their side. Eight days later, on 4 September, word was received that a detachment of Charles's army had occupied Perth, only forty miles away; and meanwhile nothing had been done about the proposed regiment because of the discovery that no regiment could be raised without a warrant from the King. An application was accordingly prepared and forwarded to London. But an answer would take days. And it was not much consolation to learn that Cope had asked for transports to be sent from Leith to Aberdeen, so that he might bring back his army and hasten to the relief of the city. He could not be expected to arrive within a week or ten days; and Charles was now within two days march of Edinburgh. In the meantime, a petition had been sent to the Town Council, signed by about one hundred citizens, asking that they be allowed to associate as volunteers for the defence of the city, and be provided with arms, which were available in the castle. This request was considered by Provost Stewart rather carefully, for associating in arms for any purpose whatever was doubtfully legal; but in the end the request was granted. On 10 September, a fleet of transports, escorted by one warship, sailed from Leith for Aberdeen, in order to fetch back General Cope and his army. On 11 September, cannon, to be mounted on the town wall (where possible), were brought up from armed vessels lying in the harbour of Leith. And on 12 September, two hundred volunteers, each issued with a musket, a bayonet and a cartridge-box (but no ammunition) began to take lessons in the art of war from some old soldiers living in the town.

Five days later, the city of Edinburgh was taken by the rebels without a shot being fired. Exactly what happened during these five days is far from clear, not because no accounts have survived, but because there are so many, and they conflict. But it is beyond doubt that considerable numbers of citizens were anxious to defend the town; that those in authority provided no leadership worth the name; and that even a slight resistance might have markedly changed the subsequent course of events. What took place seems to have been as follows.

On Friday 13 September, Charles, having spent a week in Perth extorting money in order to pay his troops, forded the Forth about eight miles west of Stirling (the bridge at Stirling could not be used by the rebels for the simple reason that it was commanded by the guns of the castle) and then turned eastward towards Edinburgh. His progress was well reported, because Colonel Gardiner, with his dragoons, was watching the river and he retired when the rebels crossed, keeping between them and Edinburgh. On Sunday, at daylight, 1,000 highlanders entered Linlithgow, hoping to surprise the dragoons who had spent the night there; but the dragoons were gone, already on the march to Corstorphine, which was then a small village about three miles west of Edinburgh. News that the highland army had reached Linlithgow, only sixteen miles from the capital, made the situation seem desperate, and it was proposed to General Guest, who commanded Edinburgh castle, that the two regiments of dragoons — Gardiner's and another then at Leith — should attack the rebels as they advanced on the city. The general demurred, very sensibly, but after a while it was agreed that if two hundred and fifty volunteers could be found, who would act as foot soldiers with the dragoons, then this little combined force might at least slow down the rebels' advance and weaken their army. This bold and possibly desperate plan to march out with the dragoons and engage the rebels met with only moderate enthusiasm within the city. The defenders of the town would clearly be heavily outnumbered — certainly by two to one, and many believed by ten to one — and the role of the foot soldiers sounded rather like that of a suicide squad. On the other hand, those who had looked round the walls knew that they provided a very poor defensive position; and many of the volunteers did not lack determination, and were as keen for military glory as Charles himself.

It was at this point that things started to go badly wrong. When the populace saw the volunteers ready to march, a 'universal consternation', in the words of Home,

> seized the minds of the people of every rank, age, sex, and party. The relations of the volunteers crowded about them, and mixed with their ranks. The men reasoned, and endeavoured to dissuade their friends: the women expostulated, complained, and, weeping, embraced their sons and brothers.[7]

The little army nevertheless moved off, but its morale was rapidly declining; and before it reached the west gate of the town, many of its number had quietly slipped away. In spite of this, it still amounted to about three hundred and sixty officers and men, apart from the dragoons, and was not a negligible force. Its next misfortune was that the Principal of the University intervened, and appealed most earnestly to the volunteers, pleading with them to remain within the city and reserve themselves for its defence. Their leader[8] responded by sending to enquire for the opinion of the Lord Provost. And the Lord Provost sent back word that he recommended the volunteers not to go. So the volunteers were marched back to the centre of the town and dismissed. Whether the Lord Provost and the captain of the volunteers ever seriously intended to fight in defence of the town has been much debated. The Lord Provost, upon whom most suspicion fell, spent fourteen months in the Tower of London after the rebellion was over, was tried and acquitted of neglect of duty. But if he was not a Jacobite at heart, he shuffled and dithered and stood on points of law and etiquette during these few days to such a degree that he could hardly have helped Charles more if he had indeed been a traitor. In any case, after this day of shilly-shallying, the volunteers had little faith in either their civil or their so-called military leader, and nothing more was heard of marching out to attack the enemy.

The walls and gates remained guarded, however, and Charles advanced only slowly. But on Monday 16 September, between ten and eleven o'clock in the morning, a message was received from the Young Pretender informing the citizens that if they admitted him freely into the city all would be well, but that if they did not they must look for military execution. This letter had the intended effect. The vagueness of its language conveyed a confused idea to unwarlike civilians of the horrors that might take place in a town taken by storm, and crowds began to gather in the market places and narrow streets, calling on the Lord Provost not to persist in defending the town, for if he did they would all be murdered. Rumours multiplied. The rebels, it was reported, were 16,000 strong, and the town was certainly to be given up. The spirit of resistance began to fail, and the volunteers who had again assembled, were marched up to the castle just as the sun was setting and, under the order of their leader, laid down their arms — some, it was said, with visible reluctance.

While this was going on, another letter addressed to the Lord

Provost was delivered at the gates, which read as follows:

> From our Camp, 16th Sept, 1745
>
> Being now in a condition to make our way into the capital of
> His Majesty's ancient kingdom of Scotland, we hereby summon
> you to receive us, as you are in duty bound to do; and in order
> to it, we hereby require you, upon receipt of this, to summon
> the Town Council, and take proper measures for securing the
> peace and quiet of the city, which we are very desirous to pro-
> tect. But if you suffer any of the usurper's troops to enter the
> town, or any of the cannon, arms, or ammunition now in it
> (whether belonging to the public, or private persons) to be
> carried off, we shall take it as a breach of your duty, and a
> heinous offence against the King and us, and shall resent it
> accordingly. We promise to preserve all the rights and liberties
> of the city, and the particular property of every one of His Maj-
> esty's subjects. But if any opposition be made to us, we cannot
> answer for the consequences, being firmly resolved at any rate
> to enter the city; and in that case if any of the inhabitants are
> found in arms against us, they must not expect to be treated as
> prisoners of war.
>
> Charles, P.R.

This letter from the self-styled Prince Regent was well calculated — Charles's propaganda was usually good. It said, in effect,
that if there were any resistance, no responsibility would be
accepted for (and presumably no orders would be issued to prevent) any murder, rape or pillage that might occur. Even this
threat, made by the leader of a virtually foreign army (for almost
all Charles's men were Gaelic-speaking clansmen who had
descended from their mountains and who knew not one word of
English) did not produce an immediate capitulation. Instead, it
was agreed to send a letter asking for more time to consider the
position, and at about eight o'clock that night four members of the
Town Council left the city in order to carry this request to the
Pretender.

No sooner had they gone than the situation changed again.
Information was received that the transports with General Cope's
army on board were off Dunbar, and the troops were expected to
land in the morning. From the time that the transports left Leith,
the people of Edinburgh had been looking up to the vanes and

weathercocks, to see from what point the wind blew, and calculating how soon they could expect the ships' return. Now, after only seven days, they were back. Messengers were at once sent after the four magistrates to prevent them from delivering the letter, but it was too late. At about ten o'clock at night the deputies came back to the city bringing a reply from Charles which stated that 'all His Majesty's subjects' should be able 'to accept with joy' the terms already sent to them, and that if there was no positive answer before two o'clock in the morning the most dreadful consequences were likely to ensue. But the magistrates thought that prevarication might still be worth while, and they sent their deputies forth once again, in a hackney coach, to beg a suspension of hostilities until nine o'clock in the morning. Charles, however, would have none of it. He, too, had heard about the return of the transports, and the deputies were peremptorily ordered to be gone. The coach brought them back to Edinburgh, and set them down in the High Street, in the darkness of the night. It then rattled off towards the Canongate, outside the city wall, where the coachman lived. When the gate in the wall was opened to let out the coach, eight hundred highlanders, led by Cameron of Lochiel, rushed in and took control of the gate. This was about five o'clock in the morning. Once inside the city, the rebels immediately sent parties to all the other gates, made those on duty their prisoners, and occupied their posts as quietly as one watch relieves another. When the inhabitants of the town awoke in the morning, they found, to their great amazement, that the rebels were in full possession.

This little triumph had important consequences, for it affected men's opinions about Charles and his supporters, and his supporters' opinions about themselves. Charles had raised his standard in the west highlands on 19 August; and twenty-eight days later he was master of the capital of Scotland. The speed of his success was astonishing. No previous Jacobite insurrection had done half as well. The King's troops had been outmanoeuvred and the defenders of Edinburgh first intimidated and then outwitted. It began to look very much, at any rate on the face of it, as if the old Jacobite notion of the magic effects of the presence of the 'rightful' king, even of his heir, had something in it after all. Waverers were persuaded. Lukewarm or apathetic supporters of the government became still more lukewarm, still more apathetic. Charles's army gained enormously in confidence and, to a limited extent, in numbers. As for Charles himself, he must have felt that most that had happened was due to him. That was what he always did believe, when things went his way.

Notes and References

1. Quoted in Menary, op. cit., p. 194.
2. Ewald, op. cit., pp. 86–7.
3. Home, op. cit., p. 54.
4. Quoted in Menary, op. cit., p. 205.
5. Quoted in Ewald, op. cit., p. 88.
6. This bridge, built by Wade in 1736 and now in ruins, crossed the River Spean over a gorge one hundred feet deep. Telford replaced it with Spean Bridge in 1819.
7. Home, op. cit., p. 82.
8. The captain of the volunteers was George Drummond, later Lord Provost of Edinburgh and a prominent figure in the making of the 'New Town'. There were some who thought that he had no intention of fighting against the Jacobites, and merely spoke and acted as he did in order to gain popularity, for he was a consummate politician, and an election to the Town Council was actually in progress. If this is true, the defence of Edinburgh was compromised and perhaps nullified by an election job.

4 INVASIONS ONE AND TWO

When the rebels seized Edinburgh, the governor of the castle was General Guest. The general was perhaps rather old for the job — he was eighty-five — and he was not very well; but he and the castle were a threat to the rebels which they were never able to remove, and when the main body of the Pretender's army advanced from Corstorphine to occupy the town they prudently did so *via* Duddingston, so as to avoid being fired upon by General Guest's men. They encamped in and near the King's Park, between Holyrood and Arthur's Seat, numbering between 2,000 and 2,500. To one observer they seemed to be 'strong, active, and hardy men . . . of a very ordinary size'; the kilts of the highlanders 'shewed their naked limbs, which were strong and muscular'; and their 'stern countenances, and bushy uncombed hair, gave them a fierce, barbarous, and imposing aspect'.[1] Their equipment, at this point, was poor. They had no cannon worth mentioning. Only about 1,400 or 1,500 men were armed with firelocks and broadswords; of the remainder, some had firelocks but no swords, and some had swords but no firelocks. The firelocks were of all sorts and sizes — muskets, fusees, even fowling pieces; the swords were mostly highland broadswords, but some were French. One or two companies — about one hundred men — were armed with a weapon which consisted of the shaft of a pitch-fork with a scythe attached to it.

The park was full of people anxious to see this extraordinary army and the young man who had called it into existence. When Charles appeared he made, as usual, a strong impression on those who saw him. He was tall, fair-haired and distinguished-looking; one observer thought his appearance 'not ill-suited to his lofty pretensions'. He wore the ordinary highland dress as it then was, a short tartan coat without a plaid, and a blue bonnet, thus identifying himself with his highland followers and not with the citizens of Edinburgh or other people of lowland Scotland. The Jacobites, especially the women, approved of what they saw; but the Whigs, although acknowledging that he was 'a goodly person', remarked upon his air of languor and melancholy; and said — or so it is reported — 'that he looked like a gentleman and a man of fashion, but not like a hero or a conqueror'.[2]

After showing himself to the people, Charles rode on to Holyrood, where he dismounted, and walked towards the door of the palace which stood open to receive him. Suddenly a gentleman stepped out from the crowd, drew his sword and, holding his arm aloft, preceded the Young Pretender up the steps. This melodramatic gesture was well-calculated to win friends for Charles among the spectators; he himself probably did not understand its significance, but the onlookers did. The person who thus ostentatiously declared his allegiance was Hepburn of Keith, a noted Jacobite — he had been 'out' in the '15, and was said to have kept himself in readiness for thirty years to take up arms again — but who was even better known as an opponent of the Union of 1707. It was a good move, from the Jacobite point of view, thus to make an appeal to anti-Union sentiment. The Union was not popular in Scotland — its material advantages were yet to be felt — and there were many Scotsmen who considered that the independence of their ancient kingdom had been taken away by English bribes and English politicians. It is true that Scottish independence and the House of Stuart had no very compelling connection, but there were many who confusedly associated the one with the other; and there were Scotsmen who did not find it too difficult to go on from that and imagine that a successful Jacobite rebellion would somehow restore to Scotland the glories of former times. So it was useful for the Jacobites to cast a fly over the Scottish nationalists in the political stream. One discontent, one unsatisfied ambition, might be used to support another. And this was true regardless of the fact that not all Scotsmen were opposed to the Union, still less that all Scotsmen were Jacobites.

Considerations such as these may have been uppermost in several minds when Charles entered Edinburgh. But the more pressing fact was the arrival of General Cope and his army at Dunbar, only thirty miles from the capital. Cope had hoped to arrive back in time to save Edinburgh; and had he been forty-eight hours sooner, or less, the course of history must have been different. As things turned out, his troops were disembarking at Dunbar at exactly the same time that the Heralds in Edinburgh — under duress — were proclaiming King James the Eighth, 'King of Scotland, England, France, and Ireland'. Charles's pretensions seemed very extensive; and many must have thought even his present position none too secure. But the danger that he faced was less than it appeared, for the army that had come to meet him had by now travelled a long way, and was in a poor state to fight a battle. It had marched from Stirling to the

Corriearrack, where it expected to fight; it had then been abruptly turned away and marched forty miles to Inverness, from whence it had departed almost at once and marched one hundred miles to Aberdeen; reaching Aberdeen, the troops next found themselves embarking on hurriedly arranged transports to sail down the east coast of Scotland, a rough voyage which occupied three days; and at Dunbar, the two regiments of dragoons joined the army — those regiments which had retreated from Stirling to Linlithgow, from Linlithgow to Corstorphine and finally from Corstorphine to Dunbar, without ever firing a shot. It is a reasonable deduction that morale in the King's army and the confidence of the men in their commanders must have been very low. And to make matters worse, there was not a single formation that had ever been in a battle before.

In this very unpromising situation Cope appears to have done as well as could be expected of any commander of good average ability. He marched from Dunbar on 19 September, and on 20 September took up a strong defensive position near Prestonpans. The place he chose, a flat area about a mile and a half long by three-quarters of a mile wide, was mostly stubble field, 'the last sheaves having been carried in the night before';[3] there was neither cottage, tree nor bush in its whole extent, with the consequence, in the general's own words, that it was an excellent spot 'for both Horse and Foot to act upon'. The Jacobites, when they first saw Cope's army drawn up for battle, did not know what to do. 'We spent the afternoon in reconnoitring his position; and the more we examined it, the more our uneasiness and chagrin increased, as we saw no possibility of attacking it, without exposing ourselves to be cut to pieces in a disgraceful manner.'[4] The rebel army, or parts of it, made several tentative movements, trying to improve the situation, 'hovering about the King's army, to find an opportunity, and rush in upon them',[5] and these movements obliged Cope to change front twice during the day. But his position seemed to remain secure. After nightfall, however, the rebels had the great good luck to be shown a way through the bog that protected the King's troops to the south, and in the early daylight of 21 September Cope had once again to reform his army, this time to face an enemy preparing to attack him from the east. The rebels had now certainly improved their position but they had gained no great advantage. Out-guards had given Cope early warning of their passage through the bog, and the manoeuvre of reforming was successfully completed before the rebels could launch their attack. Cope rode along the front of his line, 'Encouraging the Men, begging them to keep up their Fire, and keep their Ranks, and they would Easily beat the Rebells'.[6] It was just after sunrise when the left wing of Charles's army began the attack. Fifteen minutes later — some observers reckoned it nearer five minutes — the fighting was over, and the King's troops were utterly defeated.

How did Charles win such an easy (and important) victory? The two armies were equally matched in numbers, and Cope appeared even to have two significant advantages; he had cavalry, of which Charles possessed very little, and artillery, of which Charles possessed none at all. But it was in precisely these two departments of Cope's forces that the rot began. The highlanders under Lochiel led the attack in the customary way, advancing swiftly on Cope's right wing 'with a hideous shout'. The artillery — six field-pieces — was on this right wing, with an artillery guard of one hundred men. The first trouble was that the guns' crews resembled nothing so much as a detachment from some eighteenth-century version of Dad's Army. They were a caricature of fighting troops. The entire unit consisted of an 'old man' who had served in the Scots train of artillery before the Union; three old soldiers belonging to the collection of invalids in the garrison of Edinburgh castle; and finally, some sailors drafted from the naval escort that had accompanied Cope from Aberdeen to Dunbar and who had never, beyond a doubt, in their wildest imaginings, supposed that they would have to face a charge by several hundred ferocious highlanders. Lochiel's men fired as they came on, and the 'gunners' at once knew what to do; they ran. The two officers who remained at their post managed to fire five of the six field-pieces, which seemed to cause the attackers to waver for a moment, but they could do no more — the departed 'gunners' had taken the powder-flasks with them. One regiment of dragoons was now ordered forward to protect the cannon, but exposure to fire was a new experience for men and horses, and as soon as casualties were suffered the dragoons wheeled about, rode over the artillery guard and fled. The men of the artillery guard then followed their example. The highlanders continued to advance very swiftly on the main body of the King's army, which still awaited them. But panic is infectious. Having seen the cannon taken and the cavalry put to flight, the foot soldiers gave an undisciplined and unconcerted fire, which had almost no effect. And when the rebels, still running forward, threw away their muskets and drew their swords, Cope's army disintegrated.

Of the many examples that in war the moral is to the physical as three to one, the battle of Prestonpans is one of the clearest. Cope and his officers seem to have been confident of success, but this confidence evidently did not extend to the troops. These men had no battle experience. They had marched and sailed for four weeks and achieved nothing. According to one Jacobite report 'there was never such a parcel of poor mean fatigued creatures under heaven'[7] — and this was before they reached Aberdeen. It is small wonder that when at last the time came for them to stand and fight, and they saw some of their more gravely demoralised comrades collapse in a panic, their courage, and such determination as they had left, disappeared. Some officers and men behaved with great bravery. Colonel Gardiner, who commanded the reserve regiment of dragoons and who confessed before the battle that he had 'not above ten men in my regiment who I am certain will follow me', was ordered to attack the advancing rebels when the artillery-guard was overrun. He did so, but his squadron almost at once deserted him. Seeing some foot soldiers standing their ground without an officer, he moved forward to support them; a moment later he fell wounded from his horse, and was killed almost at once by sword-blows to the head. Captain Brymer, who had fought at Sheriffmuir and who considered the highlanders to be formidable adversaries, 'when the rebels broke in upon that part of the line where he stood, he disdained to turn his back, and was killed with his face to the enemy'.[8] Cope himself tried to rally the foot soldiers when they were little more than a rabble trying to escape ('For shame, Gentlemen, behave like Britons, give them another Fire, and you'll make them run') and when this proved impossible, he joined Lord Home and Lord Loudon in rounding up the dragoons. In this he had some success, but the troopers could not be prevailed upon to return to the battle.

Most of those in the defeated army who survived the battle were taken prisoner, almost a third of them wounded. Those who fled did not all live to tell the tale, for in the moment of victory the rebels gave little quarter, until compelled to do so by their senior officers. Many of Cope's men were killed as they ran, and many as they tried to climb the high walls of Preston House about half a mile to the west of the battle-field. Few were killed or injured by small-arms fire. The highlanders' favourite weapon was the broadsword, with the result that after the battle what had a few days before been a field of corn 'presented a spectacle of horror, being covered with heads, legs, arms, and mutilated bodies . . .'⁹ Scythe blades were also effective; they 'cut the legs of the horses in two'. According to the Jacobites, five hundred of the King's troops were killed, and an equal number wounded; as all this was done in ten minutes or less, it cannot have been against much resistance, and evidently was often against none at all. That afternoon Cope rode with the remains of the two regiments of dragoons south to Coldstream, which he reached that night.

On the following day Charles, who had seen little of the battle, having posted himself between the front line and the reserve, returned to Edinburgh. The streets were thronged with people and the prisoners were paraded. A council was set up, which was to meet every day in Holyrood House at ten o'clock. The magistrates of all the towns in Scotland were ordered to repair immediately to Edinburgh to pay sums of money which were demanded from every town. The officers of Customs and the Land-tax were obliged to hand over all the public money in their possession on pain of high treason. Regiments were ordered to be raised for Charles's service, and troops of horse-guards for the defence of his person. Nothing was spared which would give the appearance of royalty and magnanimous condescension. Most important of all, Charles issued two proclamations of a political character, like present-day party manifestoes, designed to weaken the allegiance of King George's subjects and to bring them over, if possible, to the Jacobite cause.

These two documents, besides containing many rhetorical questions ('Have you found reason to love and cherish your governors, as the fathers of the people of Great Britain and Ireland? Have you found more humanity and condescension in those who were not born to a crown than in my royal forefathers? Have their ears been open to the cries of the people?' etc., etc.), condemned 'the abuse of parliaments', 'the multitude of placemen', and the size of the national debt — all safe and familiar topics; insisted upon Charles's determination to respect the nation's religion, properties and laws; promised to establish a free parliament and to 'refuse nothing that a free parliament can ask'; and asserted that the 'expedition' now in progress, the current success of which was attributed to the good favour of God, was unsupported by either France or Spain. More specifically and of more immediate interest, Charles abolished the Union by a stroke of the pen. The 'pretended union', as he called it, was now 'at an end'. This peremptory abolition of an Act of Parliament was well calculated to please some Scottish nationalists, and may even have brought in a few recruits. But it sounded oddly in the programme of one who talked a good deal about respect for the law, the objectionable nature of 'tyranny and arbitrary power', and the need to act on the advice of Parliament. At least one very senior and valuable member of Charles's entourage was made most uneasy by this swift resort to unconstitutional procedures.

As to help from France, which Charles untruthfully said he had not received, one of his chief objects was now to receive a good deal more. He had won an unexpectedly swift success. But his army was very small, and a good many clansmen had returned to their remote habitations on the morrow of Prestonpans, taking their booty with them ('the army [after the battle] had a fine plunder', Charles had written to his father). He could not expect to be so lucky and to meet such feeble opposition in a campaign aiming for London, so messengers were forthwith dispatched to France with glowing accounts of the victory and instructions to his agents to persuade the French that they should use this unique opportunity and co-operate in the invasion of England. That Charles attached great importance to this is shown by his choice of messengers, among whom was the Irish priest George Kelly, one of the 'seven men of Moidart' and a fanatical Jacobite, and Sir James Stuart, who was Charles's most trusted negotiator.

News of the victory at Prestonpans was received in Paris with understandable enthusiasm. George II's troops had been defeated at Fontenoy in May and now they had been defeated at Prestonpans in September. To conquer Belgium first and then to neutralise Great Britain by establishing a Catholic dynasty on the British throne was an alluring prospect for France, and the most economical way to do it was quite possibly to give the Jacobites more support. They had already done a good deal with not very much — two ships, a score of officers, and some guns and swords. Early in October, a personal envoy of Louis XV was sent to Scotland with the French King's greetings and 4,000 guineas, and he was followed soon afterwards by two more French warships carrying a number of French officers, six cannon, 1,280 guns and small arms and ammunition for 1,200 men. In spite of a squadron under Admiral Byng covering the east coast, all the French ships got through. The question that Louis now had to decide was not whether more help should be given to the Jacobites, but how much and in what form. Before a decision could be taken, there were two underlying questions to be settled, questions of high policy affecting the interests of France, Britain and other countries in several parts of the globe. One of these questions was political, the other military. The political question was, what did France want to happen to the government of Great Britain? Britain and France were at war, and Britain was governed by the House of Hanover. On the face of it, if France could engineer a successful revolution in Great Britain, replacing the House of Hanover by the House of Stuart, great advantages would ensue; according to this way of thinking, the Royal Navy would cease to interfere with French plans, including those in Canada and India, subsidies to Maria Theresa would come to an end, the government of Holland would be overthrown, and the War of the Austrian Succession brought to a satisfactory conclusion. All this seemed to be correct, on one condition; that the Stuarts, once restored, would show suitable gratitude and do what was expected of them. But would they? They had never been very reliable allies of France; and even if they were restored to the British throne with French help, it was quite possible that the 'natural' rivalry and enmity between the two countries would soon obliterate all feelings of gratitude and lead to renewed war. And this war might well be more difficult to win than the one going on already, because as long as the House of Hanover ruled in Britain it was always possible to attack Hanoverian possessions on the continent and thus draw away British forces from other theatres of war; whereas if Britain were under the Stuarts she would no longer be vulnerable on the continent. Perhaps, some Frenchmen thought, there was a better way. Suppose that the Stuarts ruled in Scotland and perhaps Ireland, and the House of Hanover in England? Then the ability of the English to oppose French plans in various parts of the world would be very greatly reduced, partly from loss of resources and manpower, but chiefly because Scotland under a Catholic ruler (with or without Ireland) would be a continual threat and a source of endless trouble for politicians in London. Charles wanted (or said he wanted) to abolish the Union; but this plan would abolish it indeed! Great Britain would cease to exist and France would be free to pursue her plans of conquest across the world.

It is not clear that a final decision was ever taken on this important political question. In the French Council of State opinions differed. But all Louis' ministers agreed that as a diversion in the war against Britain, the Jacobite rebellion must not be allowed to fail. So as a first step towards strengthening the insurgents in the homeland, a Franco-Jacobite alliance was created by the Treaty of Fontainebleau. This treaty was signed only three weeks after the battle of Prestonpans, which is to say only one or two weeks after news of Charles's success reached Paris; or in other words, one or two weeks after his venture began to look credible. The main point of the treaty was a promise of French armed assistance for Charles against their common enemy, described as 'the Elector of Hanover'. There was explicit mention of the Irish Brigade, and provision for a future treaty covering French commercial relations with such territories as Charles might have secured by the end of his campaign. Precisely what these territories might be was left vague, so that the possibility remained open that Charles might become ruler of Great Britain, but equally possibly might become ruler only of Scotland. This careful ambiguity as regards French wishes and intentions for the House of Stuart was later to cause trouble. But in the meantime the treaty added to the political status of the Jacobites, and encouraged their hopes. When Charles heard about it, he immediately wrote to Louis to thank him for his assistance.

The military question remained; how much help to give, and how should it be given? What the Jacobites asked for varied, but they always made it clear that they wanted a good deal. When the English Jacobites learned that Charles was in Scotland, they called on Louis XV to land 10,000 men in Essex along with a regiment of cavalry, and arms and equipment for 30,000 Englishmen. Another version of what was wanted was an army of 6,000 men sent to Scotland, plus a separate force of 14,000 for England. After the surprise victory at Prestonpans, requests were toned down a little. Pleas for 10,000 men, or at any rate 6,000, became the order of the day, and the idea of French landings in both England and Scotland was dropped; possibly because James and Charles alike were known to favour a French attack on England. This clamour for foreign help was basically due to the smallness of Charles's army, and the lack of evidence that it was going to grow any bigger. Some 2,500 men or fewer had sufficed at Prestonpans, but no one in his senses thought that such an army would be able to conquer England — as matters stood, Charles did not control even the whole of Scotland. The unknown factor was the strength and earnestness of the English Jacobites. According to Charles's agents in Paris, as soon as a French force landed in England the English Jacobites would rise. The scale of this prognosticated rising varied according to which agent was telling the story, and what he thought it best to say. No one seems to have mentioned a figure of less than 5,000; and in the opposite direction, perhaps Sir James Stuart went as far as anyone when he told King Louis that he and his friends were 'morally certain that upwards of half the landed interest'[10] would join Charles as soon as the French landed. Louis and his Council of Ministers did not know what to believe. Nor did they know what to believe about the size of the forces that Charles had already got together. When Charles marched south from Edinburgh, Louis' representative there reported that he took with him more than 9,000 men. Emissaries sent by Charles from Edinburgh to Paris told stories of an army of 12,000 to 15,000 men, including at least 1,000 cavalry. Statements like this were risky (and were of course wildly untrue), because if the Jacobites were already so strong, what was the need of a French invasion force? Probably the French discounted the figures to some extent; and they soon realised — because the English Jacobites made this very plain — that there would be no rising in England against George II until a French army had landed. Yet their own preference was not to make a landing until the English Jacobites had convinced everyone of their sincerity by taking to arms. It was altogether a very difficult problem for Louis, and it is not surprising that he adopted a cautious approach. But whatever the truth about the strength of the Jacobites, they were obviously useful allies. They were already causing serious trouble for the British government and thus helping Louis' armies on the continent, and there was even a chance that they might draw off the whole British army into Scotland, which would leave the Low Countries at France's mercy and the south of England exposed to an easy French attack. The possibility of catching the British between two fires was especially tempting, and the stakes were high. To invade and destroy the United Kingdom would be the *coup* of the century. Charles offered Louis the chance, and cautiously Louis took it. Early in October, just when Charles was heading south from Edinburgh, Louis gave orders for an invasion force to be made ready.

In London, the news of Cope's defeat came like a thunderbolt. The three previous Jacobite attempts having failed miserably, no one expected that Charles would do any better, and it was generally assumed that Cope would dispose of the rebels as easily as Wightman had done in 1719. Until Edinburgh fell, the rebellion was treated very lightly. When his ministers proposed taking any steps with regard to the rebellion, the King said — according to Horace Walpole — 'Pho! don't talk to me of that stuff!' But within a few days of Prestonpans, almost everyone was demanding that battle-hardened troops be brought over from Flanders without delay. The King was reluctant and so were some ministers, but there was nothing for it: 'all other considerations must give way to that of the preservation of this country'. In fact, troops had been sent for already. Even before Cope's march from Dalwhinnie to Inverness, orders were given that all British troops at Ostend were to be 're-embarked forthwith and brought to Great Britain'. Two regiments and 1,000 men were moved from Dublin to Chester, and the Dutch were asked to make available the 6,000 men whom they had undertaken by treaty to provide if the Hanoverian dynasty were threatened. The King himself arrived in London on 31 August, prompt to return 'when there was any apprehension of danger affecting this country'. On 4 September, now aware that the rebels had given Cope's army the slip, the Cabinet ordered the Duke of Cumberland to send over ten of his best battalions immediately, under the command of Sir John Ligonier. It was a hard decision, for it gave the appearance of 'deserting our allies, and giving up the common cause'. But there were already fears of a French invasion across the Channel, and the country was so defenceless that Wade's well-known remark was made with a great deal of justice: 'England is for the first comer'.

Ligonier arrived with his men on the same day that news reached London of the disaster at Prestonpans. The Cabinet responded by sending to Flanders for six further battalions of foot and nine squadrons of dragoons, and followed this up a few days later by ordering all remaining British foot soldiers in Cumberland's army to return to Britain. This suited Louis XV admirably. After the victory at Fontenoy, Marshal Saxe had taken Tournai, Ghent, Oudenarde and Ostend and now threatened the Dutch Republic. To withdraw British troops from the continent looked like leaving the Dutch to their fate. And the Dutch might be tempted to conclude a separate peace with France if the allied army was seriously weakened. But the British government had no choice — Charles was playing Louis' game too well. As Cumberland's private secretary observed (not very grammatically), 'One must be deprived of his senses not to see that France is at the bottom of all this . . . If they can alarm us so far as to make a detachment they do everything; for if this allied army once comes to divide I am afraid all is irretrievably over'.[11] Later, in November, the British cavalry was also summoned home. No one supposed that all this build-up was wanted to suppress Charles and a few thousand highlanders. The real anxiety was a French invasion, made all the more difficult to deal with by rebels in the rear.

And with every week that passed it became more certain that the French threat was real. At the beginning of October the Duke of Newcastle began to receive reports of a large number of armed vessels assembling in the ports of Calais, Boulogne, Le Havre, Dunkirk and Ostend. Some ministers in London believed that this was a deception, designed only to keep British troops out of Flanders, but Newcastle thought not. Admiral Vernon was instructed to form several light squadrons so as to cover as long a line of the British coast as possible, and Admiral Byng's watch on the approaches to Scotland was intensified. These precautions were fully justified. At an early stage Newcastle learned that Louis had promised to send Lord John Drummond to Scotland with the Scots Royals and some Irish volunteers, a force of about 1,000 men; and while he could not be sure about a full-scale invasion, activity in French ports seemed to be increasing. In fact, not a great deal had yet been done, but ships were indeed assembling and the first important appointment had been made. Someone was needed to organise the large number of vessels of all kinds that would have to be assembled and equipped to transport at least 6,000 soldiers across the Channel, and who better than Antoine Walsh, the millionaire master-privateer, transporter of Charles to the west highlands and potential Duke of Ireland? There could be no doubt about his commitment to the cause, for he had put money into it. Walsh was appointed early in November, with complete authority over all maritime officialdom at Dunkirk.

While all this was going on, Charles remained in Edinburgh, having reached an agreement with General Guest that supplies would continue to reach the castle as long as the general did not bombard the town. He was there for just over six weeks, and some writers have argued that this was a mistake, that he was dilatory when he should have been sudden, that he gave the British government time to recover from the defeat at Prestonpans and time to organise their forces. But there were good reasons for Charles's delay. That he was eager to invade England is certain — he had no patience with those who thought that the Stuarts should be content to rule in Scotland alone. But there were very good grounds to doubt — as his council seems frequently to have been obliged to point out to him — that his army was strong enough. At Prestonpans he had beaten a force that it would be charitable to describe as the British third eleven. But some parts of the real British army were now back in England, notably ten picked battalions under Sir John Ligonier (including three battalions of guards) and two crack cavalry regiments under the Duke of Montagu and Brigadier St George. As for the Jacobite army, it had its problems. The highlanders had a primitive reluctance to march out of Scotland, and it was not certain that they would fight very well far from home; also, some men had deserted already and others had simply gone home, so that for a time the army was much smaller than it had been at Prestonpans. More men were essential, not only for the sake of numbers but because a larger force would look more like a winning force, would make a stronger impression on the English Jacobites, and would thus induce them to rise. Numbers would breed numbers; but a good figure on crossing the border was essential. For it was a melancholy fact, from Charles's point of view, that although he now controlled a large part of Scotland, not a single English Jacobite had yet declared for him.

So Charles remained in Edinburgh, looking for recruits and waiting for more help from France — help which he now realised was essential but which he had done nothing previously to organise. Some help did come. Four French warships reached Montrose in spite of the British navy, bringing guns, ammunition, money and several French 'advisers'. And Charles kept assuring everyone that there was more, much more, to come. Also, his army gradually increased in size. He had gained several fresh adherents on the march south from Corriearrack, most notable among them Lord George Murray and the Duke of Perth. Perth, who brought with him two hundred followers, was young and inexperienced — 'a foolish horse-racing boy', one contemporary said — and was well known to be an ardent Jacobite. But Lord George was a quite unexpected recruit. Exiled for his part in the '15 and the '19, he had been allowed to return to Scotland in 1725 and had lived quietly in Atholl for twenty years. But apparently he was not content. Feeling no obligation to the King who had pardoned him, he took up arms against the government for the third time, greatly to the surprise of both the Jacobites and the Hanoverians. His motives are obscure, but revived ambitions for military glory seem to have played the principal part. He went to see Cope during Cope's march to Dalwhinnie, and probably offered his services; and when they were refused, he went over to the other side. Many Jacobites never trusted him, and it is noteworthy that the Duke of Liria, who met him in Scotland during the '15, then described him as having 'plenty of intelligence and bravery; but he is false to the last degree, and has a very good opinion of himself'. He brought to the Jacobite army some much-needed military ability and a vast amount of conflict and trouble.

More recruits joined Charles in Edinburgh, although not many of them from within the city. As has often been remarked, few of those who were so eager to catch sight of the Young Pretender in the Scottish capital volunteered to help him to a throne. John Roy Stuart managed to raise a 'regiment' from among the dregs and outcasts of the population, but that was about all. Some of those who lived further north, however, and who had hesitated when the cause seemed more doubtful, now came forward, presumably persuaded by the rebels' victory that the days of King George were perhaps numbered. Gordon of Glenbucket came from the wilds of Aberdeenshire with a few hundred followers; the venerable Lord Pitsligo, 'of a wary and cautious temper', arrived from the northeast with several score of foot soldiers and enough country gentlemen to form a small body of cavalry; the Earl of Airlie remained peaceably at home, but insured against a Jacobite victory by sending his heir, Lord Ogilvy, to join Charles with six hundred tenants from the estates. (Several other families hedged their bets in the same way.) But still the wealthy and the truly powerful held aloof — not one Scottish landowner of major importance joined the Jacobites. In particular, the great chieftains in the west, Sir Alexander MacDonald and MacLeod of MacLeod, held aloof. Their action — or rather their inaction — was of critical importance, for each could bring out many hundreds of men. During October 'their were reports every day in town that Sir Alexander Macdonald, the Laird of Macleod at the head of their Clans, and the Frazers, Mackintoshes, and Mackenzies, were in arms and upon their march to join the Prince. Sometimes they were brought the length of Crief, but all these reports proved false'.[12] Charles sent a messenger to Sir Alexander MacDonald and MacLeod of MacLeod, with instructions to tell them that they were required to join the army 'with a strong body of men', and that he would 'allow no grudge to enter into our breast for their past procedure'. The messenger was further to acquaint them 'that we have most undoubted assurances of assistance from France and Spain' and that landings from France were about to take place both in England and in Scotland. But there was no response. Sir Alexander and his neighbour 'had resolved', as a contemporary put it, 'to stay at home, and not to trouble the

Government'. The Jacobites were very wrath, and thenceforth referred to MacLeod as 'the wicked Laird'.

In spite of these and other disappointments, the rebel army was a good deal larger by the end of October than it had been on the eve of Prestonpans. According to Louis' 'ambassador' in Edinburgh, Charles set off to invade England with 9,400 men; but this was a gross exaggeration. (He was accurate enough, however, in judging that the Jacobite army he saw might win one or two battles, but could not win the war.) Charles's numbers were usually exaggerated by friend and foe alike. As far as can be ascertained, he left Edinburgh with 5,000 foot soldiers and about five hundred cavalry. Of these, approximately 4,000 were Gaelic-speaking highlanders. These were the backbone of the army, but although they added to Charles's strength they were also something of a liability — for, as a leading English Jacobite said of his fellow-Jacobites south of the border, 'by no means would they trust themselves in the hands of the Scots highlanders'.[13] There was also a contingent of French infantry and a number of Irish and French officers. The army was weak in artillery. There were only sixteen guns, nine of which had been sent from France, and the officer in charge was an officer of the French army. It was a remarkably small and unbalanced force, almost international in its make-up, and the invasion of England looked like a reckless venture. But Charles 'was sure a great body of English would join him upon his Entring their Country, that the French would be Landed before he could join them, and that in Short every body in London was for him'.[14]

Members of his council had their doubts about these confident assertions, and many chiefs were decidedly opposed to the invasion of England. The matter was frequently discussed, but to little purpose, because Charles, although devoid of military or political experience, was opinionated and imperious, and never cared to listen to views which differed from his own. This trait in his character, which was to have fateful consequences, made meetings of the council disagreeable and divisive, as Lord Elcho discovered:

> The Prince in this Council used Always first to declare what he was for, and then he Ask'd Everybodys opinion in their turn. Their was one third of the Councill who's principals were that Kings and Princes Can never either act or think wrong, so in Consequence they always Confirmed whatever the Prince Said. The other two thirds, who thought that Kings and Princes

thought sometimes like other men and were not altogether infallable and that this Prince was no more so than others, beg'd leave to differ from him, when they Could give Sufficient reasons for their difference of Opinion. Which very often was no hard matter to do . . . The Prince Could not bear to hear any body differ in Sentiment from him, and took a dislike to Every body that did . . .[15]

So whatever his council might say, Charles was determined to march on London — determined, as he dramatically expressed it in a letter to one of his subordinates, 'to conquer or perish'. But in the event, as everyone knows, he did neither.

The Young Pretender left Edinburgh on 31 October. He had appointed Lord George Murray and the youthful Duke of Perth as his Lieutenant-Generals, and the army marched in two divisions, one, with the Duke of Perth, taking the road to Carlisle and the other, with Charles and Lord George Murray, going by a more easterly route to Kelso, which led on towards Newcastle. The intention of the insurgents was to march towards London, gathering strength as they went. They would be met — as they thought — by supporters and collaborators in and from the west country. The presence of Charles on English soil — so it was believed — would make hitherto coy and silent supporters declare themselves, and bring recruits flocking to his standard, so that the further the army marched the larger it would become. Also, a French landing would take place, as Charles constantly prophesied; local Jacobites would rise and seize control of numerous towns and strategic places; and the position of the government would thus rapidly become untenable. It was possible, even likely, that London would be taken without a battle.

By the time that Charles entered England on 8 November, the British government had been able to complete most of its arrangements for the defence of the realm. Vernon and Byng were at sea, prepared to intercept French supply ships or, if the worst came to the worst, a French invasion force. Field-Marshal Wade, seventy-two years of age and in poor health, had arrived in Newcastle with an army of over 9,000 men, and was positioned either to march north or to engage the rebels if they came down the east coast. In case of an invasion down the west side of the country, Sir John Ligonier with a smaller force had been ordered towards Chester, with instructions to prevent the rebels from crossing the Mersey if possible (for once across they would have the choice of proceeding towards London or on to North Wales), but 'in all events to stop them between the Trent and the Severn near Shrewsbury'. This plan suffered some delays, however, and Ligonier was only about one hundred miles out of London by the time that the rebels were entering Lancashire. A third army, or at least the nucleus of one, was collecting near London, to serve both as a reserve against the rebels and a first line of defence in the event of a French landing in the south-east. Nor was this all, for a variety of what might be called civilian armies appeared in many places. The country militias had long since fallen into desuetude, and there was little point in trying to revive them. Instead, voluntary associations were formed, organised by 'nobility, gentlemen, clergy and freeholders' and armed (sometimes only in theory) by the government; and subscriptions were raised to pay for local military preparations. Some private armies also appeared, and a few commissions were granted for noblemen to raise their own regiments. These efforts, which were widespread, were by no means unavailing. Yorkshire, for example, raised forty-one companies, most of them fully recruited by early October; Liverpool organised, clothed and maintained for two months between eight hundred and 1,000 men; Sir Gregory Page mustered five hundred men on Blackheath, 'rais'd and cloth'd at his own expence'. In most English counties — probably in all of them — there was some force or other organised to resist the rebels, or to deal with any local disturbance should one occur. The fighting value of these formations was, of course, doubtful. The Duke of Cumberland was not impressed — he feared 'that they will rather be a hindrance than a service to me' — but the best of them were clearly capable of harassing the rebels, slowing down their advance and providing intelligence. They made it evident that while Charles had supporters in Scotland — many of whom confined their support to drinking his health — in England he was in hostile country.

The Jacobite invasion of England began well. Wade was a little north of Newcastle, on his way to Berwick, when he learned that the rebels had left Edinburgh. Had he been certain that they were making for Carlisle, as they had decided to do, he might conceivably have been able to reach the town ahead of the division under Lord George Murray which had gone to Kelso. The march to Kelso was a feint, designed to make Wade think that the rebels were taking the east coast route and so persuade him to keep his army east of the Pennines, out of the rebels' way. But it is doubtful if this ruse was necessary, given the timing, the distances and the state of the roads over which Wade would have had to bring his artillery. In any case, Wade remained near Newcastle and the two divisions of the rebel army joined forces just north of Carlisle and proceeded to besiege the town. Carlisle was not much better equipped to withstand a siege than Edinburgh. The walls were in disrepair and the 'garrison' consisted of some eighty invalids long past the prime of life. However, units of the local militia — the despised militia — had been mobilised, there were some volunteer companies of townspeople and the officer sent to take command — Lieutenant-Colonel Durand — resolved to hold out as long as possible. When the rebels first arrived, demanding quarters for 13,000 foot and 3,000 cavalry and threatening to burn the town down if they were not provided, Durand opened fire on them with cannon. The rebels hastily retreated, but returned the next day with a letter from Charles containing the usual unlimited threat — that is, all would be well if he were admitted but he could not be responsible for what might happen to the citizens if he had to use force. The defenders again replied with cannon fire. A false report that Wade was on his way to Carlisle drew the rebels off for a couple of days, but they returned in earnest. Now seeing no prospect of help arriving, and the defenders continually on the walls without even 'straw for the poor men to lay upon', the city fathers decided, by twenty-four votes to fifteen, to capitulate. Durand and a considerable number of men retired to the castle, but the morale of the militiamen was sinking fast; when the insurgents threatened to destroy the town if the castle was not immediately given up, Durand was obliged to surrender. It looked like another easy success for the rebels, and in a way it was. But the Jacobite army had been held up for the better part of a week.

The siege had another consequence that did the Jacobites no good. Operations were plannned by Lord George Murray but the negotiations leading to the surrender were conducted by Perth and Murray of Broughton. Lord George Murray, who was always a difficult colleague, resented this. He had no time for the Duke, probably because he resented having to share command of the army with a person of little experience and still less judgement, and perhaps also because Perth was a Roman Catholic which Murray was not. However that may be, when the siege was over Lord George promptly resigned his commission as Lieutenant-General and announced that he would henceforth serve simply as a volunteer. The senior members of the army were aghast. They knew that without the drive and leadership that Lord George provided the rebellion might collapse. They knew, also, that Charles disliked and distrusted Lord George. But there was nothing for it — Charles, not for the first time, would have to adjust his fancies to the facts. So they petitioned Charles that Lord George 'should be desired to take back his Commission', which he did. In response, Perth resigned his commission. Thus Lord George got what he wanted, and the army was saved. But the Pretender no doubt felt mortified, and jealousy and recrimination among his followers increased.

Leaving one hundred men to hold Carlisle, the rebels marched south. Wade was now behind them. He had set off for Carlisle, but appalling weather had made progress both slow and painful. There was heavy snow and severe frost, and the supply position was wretched. It was reported that 'many of the soldiers were obliged to lye on the ground tho covered with snow', and that others 'could get nothing to eat after marching 13 hours'. Mercifully, by the time that he reached Hexham, Wade knew that Carlisle had fallen, and the army limped back to Newcastle. On the west side of the country there was not much movement either — except by the rebels. As luck would have it, Sir John Ligonier had fallen seriously ill, and his army remained at Lichfield. A new commander had to be found at once, and the King made a very popular choice. He appointed his son, the Duke of Cumberland, to the command. The Duke was very young — to be exact, he was only twenty-four, a few months younger than Charles. He was tall and well-built (not overweight as he became later) and he had first seen action under his father at Dettingen, where he was wounded in the leg. He had commanded in only one campaign, in which he had been defeated. But this had been at Fontenoy, where the victor was Marshal Saxe; and defeat by Saxe was not disgrace. In fact, the Duke's military reputation stood very high. His personal bravery was beyond question, his 'generosity and compassion of prisoners' were favourably commented upon during the campaign in Flanders, and he was popular with his men. When the troops learned of his appointment they 'leaped and skipped about like wild things', and were said to be immediately confident of victory.

Cumberland had left the allied army in Flanders as soon as the French went into winter quarters, and had returned hopefully to England on 19 October. Just over a month later he received his appointment, and he arrived at Lichfield on 27 November. The situation that the new commander faced was not an easy one. The rebels had reached Preston, less than one hundred miles to the north. Wade was labouring down from Newcastle, but had not yet got as far as Ripon and there was little prospect that even his cavalry would be able to join Cumberland's army before it met the rebels. But what worried the Duke was not the size of his army but the risk that he might not manage to intercept the enemy before they did further damage. The obvious threat was to Chester. Like Carlisle, Chester was a town of considerable importance (it should be remembered that Manchester, Liverpool and Birmingham were relatively small in the eighteenth century) and, again like Carlisle, its defences were in a very poor state. A regiment had been raised for its defence, but arms were few and far between and the walls were commanded in many places by large houses in the suburbs. Cumberland detached two hundred and twenty regular troops, which he reckoned would be sufficient to enable the town to hold out until more help was sent, if needed. (Significantly, these troops were welcomed and well provided for in every place they passed through between Lichfield and Chester.) But the rebels still held the great strategic advantage that from Preston they could either continue south towards London or turn west into Wales where they expected to gain many new recruits. The bridges across the Mersey at Warrington and Crossford had been made unusable, with the help of a company of volunteers from Liverpool, but they could be repaired. Repairs to Crossford bridge were in fact begun by the rebels, but on 1 December, only three days after Cumberland had taken up his command, the enemy marched into Macclesfield.

This still left them the choice of London or Wales. The Duke was in a great difficulty, because if he advanced towards Macclesfield he would be on the wrong side of the hills — 'a ridge of impracticable hills called Bow hills' — for preventing an advance into Derbyshire; but if he moved east of these hills, the road into Wales would be left open. He appreciated the risks, and he acted with caution; but there was not much time. On 2 December the Duke of Kingston reported enemy troops in Congleton, and Cumberland became convinced that the rebels were making for Wales. He therefore moved the rest of his forces forward, preparing for a battle in the neighbourhood of Newcastle-under-Lyme. But it was a feint. Lord George Murray had advanced to Congleton in order to make it seem that the Jacobites were for Wales, but most of the army had gone straight into Derbyshire where Lord George joined them on 3 December. One day later, the rebels entered Derby.

The Jacobite advance to Derby is usually represented as an astonishing achievement. Astonishing it certainly was. A well-commanded army of irregular troops with a strong tradition of tribal or guerrilla warfare (in England they were often referred to as banditti) had been recruited in north and central Scotland and was now encamped within one hundred and thirty miles of London. But apart from walking, the Jacobites had done very little. They had fought a five- to ten-minute battle near Edinburgh (according to General Wightman, who was an onlooker and entitled to an opinion, it was a scuffle, not a battle, and lasted for only four minutes). They had taken nearly a week to reduce a city that could scarcely be defended. And now here they were in Derby. Their success, such as it was, has to be attributed to two facts: first, and principally, that Charles was astute enough or lucky enough to launch his attack on Britain when the King and almost the entire British army were out of the country; and secondly, that Lord George Murray had insisted on invading England by the undefended west coast route and had made a successful feint to Congleton. It is not much by which to conquer a kingdom.

But of course the Jacobites were not going to conquer a kingdom. Their 'success' was entirely illusory. The senior officers in Charles's army were good judges of their position, which they saw to be full of serious disadvantages, and even very grave danger. The army, never large, had become smaller. The rebels had left Edinburgh with about 5,500 men, but a good number deserted before they crossed the border and a few more after entering England. At Derby Charles may have had scarcely 5,000 men. This made nonsense of the entire Jacobite strategy, for the invasion of England was partly an invasion but partly also a demonstration — a large-scale demonstration designed to bring out the English Jacobites. When they came flocking to his standard Charles would have 10,000, 15,000, 20,000 men. But where were these loyal supporters? Proclamations were read in every town that the Jacobites passed through, but the citizens 'testify'd no joy'. In Manchester, which the Jacobites fondly supposed to be especially ripe for revolution, only a few gentlemen and a couple of hundred 'common fellows' joined the Pretender; and this was by far the largest addition to Charles's forces that any place provided. The truth was, that the English Jacobites sat tight. They were a minority and they knew it. Indeed, Charles's invasion seems to have been more effective in rallying support for King George than for the Jacobites. There were more subscriptions and volunteers and

loyal addresses to the King after Prestonpans than before it. When
Charles proclaimed that attendance at the 'Elector of Hanover's'
Parliament would be 'an overt Act of Treason and Rebellion', the
Tories — many of whom were suspected of Jacobite leanings —
seem to have spared themselves no pains to get to Westminster. And
it goes without saying that the Presbyterian Church, supreme in
Scotland and not without influence in England, remained unrelent-
ingly hostile to the Roman Catholic House of Stuart.

The claim is sometimes made that if the French had landed, the
English Jacobites would have risen. As the French never did land,
this is yet another untestable historical hypothesis. Charles was forever promising his supporters that the French would intervene, and
he had some grounds for thinking that they might. But when the
French did not appear, it looked to the Jacobites as if they had been
betrayed. They had rebelled, captured Edinburgh, drawn almost the
whole British army out of Flanders, invaded England and what did
France do? Nothing. Louis was content, it seemed, to use the
Jacobites merely as a diversion. Perhaps it was his plan to have the
Stuarts rule only in Scotland, and thus make the diversion perma-
nent. Whatever his intentions, he was a faithless ally. Such thoughts
bred confusion in the Jacobites' ranks, and lowered morale. And it
must also have occurred to some of the rebels that even if French
troops did appear, the situation might be no better. If Englishmen
would not rally to their 'rightful king' when his son came supported
by a small army of Scots and Irish (the Scots, admittedly, almost all
speaking Gaelic), what would they do if he had French troops along
with him? There was no love lost in those days between Englishmen
and Frenchmen, and to be seen as an ally of France meant nearly the
same thing as to be seen as an enemy of England. Charles needed all
the help from France that he could get, but he had to keep it in the
background. A French landing would have advertised to the world
that Charles was an ally of France, and that would no doubt have
decided many who lay low that they must throw in their lot with
George II. So the Jacobites began to realise that they had got themselves into a very precarious position, a dwindling army in a hostile
country. In purely military terms the outlook was bad. Nearby there
was the Duke of Cumberland with at least 9,000 men, possessing
cavalry and artillery far superior to the rebels'. Further south, at
or near Finchley, there were over 4,000 regular troops, including
cavalry, with the city-trained bands, several thousand strong, alongside them. And to the north, seventy miles away at Wetherby, Wade

commanded considerably more infantry and cavalry than Charles had with him at Derby.

But if the Jacobites had worries, so had the Duke of Newcastle. The news that an army of highlanders had reached Derby caused deep gloom and alarm in London, but what made matters much worse was the circulation of a rumour that a French invasion was imminent. Having to fight on two fronts at once was the nightmare of every British commander and politician. Fortunately, Louis was still far from ready to cross the Channel, and when it became clear a few days later that they had only the Jacobites to deal with, the fears of the London population greatly subsided. The army at Finchley, deployed to cover the northern approaches to the capital, was strengthened with regular foot soldiers, regular cavalry and artillery, and the trained bands, several thousand strong, were kept on the alert. The Jacobites wanted to believe — what one of them afterwards claimed — that the King was 'in readiness to sail at a moment's warning'; but in fact George II announced that he was going to Finchley in order to put himself at the head of his troops, and also stated (according to another and more reliable Jacobite source) that 'he intended to remain and die King of England'.[16] Before the King could set out for Finchley, however, Charles and his army were on the way back to Scotland.

The decision to retreat, although it has been much debated, was the merest common sense. Charles met with his advisers, and the arguments rehearsed above were all put forward. According to Lord Elcho, whose account there seems no reason to doubt, Lord George Murray spoke for his fellow-officers, and said to Charles,

> that the Scots had now done all that could be Expected of them. That they had marched into the heart of England ready to join any party that would declare for him, that none had, and that the Counties through which the Army had pass'd had Seemed much more Enemies than friends to his Cause, that their was no French Landed in England, and that if their was any party in England for him, it was very odd that they had never so much as Either sent him money or intelligence or the least advice what to do, but if he Could produce any letter from any person of distinction in which their was an invitation for the army to go to London, or to any other part of England, that they were ready to go. But if nobody had either invited them or meddled in the least in their affairs, it was to be Supposed that their was either no party at all, or if their

was they did not chuse to act with them, or else they would ere now have lett them know it.[17]

Lord George went on to stress the unlikelihood that the Jacobites would be able to defeat three British armies in rapid succession, and concluded by observing that, even if they reached the capital, 'if the Mob was against the Affair, 4,500 men would not make a great figure in London'. They should therefore return to Scotland and join their friends there. Two gentlemen who were present were for going to Wales, but everyone else agreed with Lord George. Everyone else, that is, except Charles. Charles, whose military experience was nil and who had no first-hand knowledge of the British situation, never having been in the country in his life before, 'fell into a passion' and accused his commanders of trying to betray him. He would not hear of retreating — 'He Continued all that day positive he would march to London'. If, as is sometimes said, he truly believed that British troops would never fight against him, or if he believed, as is sometimes also said, that the highlanders in battle were irresistible, then his attitude was bound to be what it was. He was a prisoner of his own delusions. His romantic inability to face unpleasant facts, reinforced by the flattery of the Irish officers, who were his closest friends in the army and who, as servants of Louis XV, would be treated as prisoners of war if captured, and not as rebels, placed him beyond the appeal of reason. But reason and necessity prevailed. After one whole day in Derby the army began its retreat, and Charles went with them.

This day spent in deciding where to go next had enabled Cumberland to retrieve his mistake of advancing up 'the Welsh road'. He had pulled his forces back to Stafford on the day that the Pretender entered Derby, and when the rebels began their retreat the Duke already had detachments in Coventry and the rest of the army strung out between Coventry and Wolverhampton. Thus it was once more impossible for the insurgents to approach London without having to fight a battle. Cumberland's move was one of remarkable speed and determination, for neither the terrain nor the weather was favourable. Nor did everyone understand the difficulties. As the Duke of Richmond put it, 'I dare swear thousands in London now sit upon their arses, and say, why does not the duke march up to them? And if it was all Hounslow heath between us, it would be a shame if he did not. But it [is] not to be conceived what a cursed country this is for marching'.[18] So the rebels started from Derby

and, as soon as possible (which was three days later), the Duke
started after them from Coventry. It was a race for the border. The
Duke took all his cavalry with him and 1,000 volunteer foot soldiers
who were willingly provided with horses by the local people — the
city of Birmingham alone provided six hundred horses free of
charge. On 9 December this force entered Lichfield, having covered
thirty miles that day, but the rebels retreated so fast that
Cumberland doubted if he would be able to catch up with them. On
11 December he reached Macclesfield, and Wigan on 13 December.
Twenty or thirty miles further north the main body of Wade's army
moved too slowly to have any chance of intercepting the rebels, but a
body of five hundred cavalry under General Oglethorpe, after a
heroic ride over the Pennines in terrible conditions of ice and
snow — it took them seventy-two hours — entered Preston just
behind the Pretender and fought a brief but very minor engagement
with the rebel rearguard south of Lancaster. The distance that separated the main body of the pursuers from the pursued was now very
small, and a battle seemed imminent. But on 14 December, just
when the chase seemed about to end in success — the rebels were
said to be throwing away their arms, and morale must have been
very low — orders were received both by Cumberland and Sir John
Ligonier to return at once with the army to London. The reason was
that the Duke of Newcastle had been informed at three o'clock in the
morning of 12 December that 12,000 French troops had landed near
Hastings, and that there were additional signs of 'an immediate
invasion from Dunkirk and perhaps some other ports'. Cumberland
was downcast; 'It was the greatest disappointment that ever befel
me'. Within a few hours the order to return was countermanded, for
the reports were false and the south coast was still safe, but some
confusion was caused and Oglethorpe's operations in particular,
which might have had a decisive effect, were made abortive. In spite
of this, the King's troops again established contact with the rebel
rearguard at Clifton, just south of Penrith, on 18 December. This
was partly because the flight of Charles's army through Westmor-
land and Cumberland had been a good deal impeded by the slow-
moving baggage waggons and the artillery (which Charles insisted
must not be left behind) and by the activities of the local people.
They had broken up roads, felled trees across them and damaged
bridges. Between Kendal and Penrith a volunteer company had
attacked a column under the Duke of Perth, sent ahead by Charles
to make contact with his friends in Scotland, and obliged the

insurgents to retrace their steps to Kendal.

The contact made by the King's troops with the rebels at Clifton led to very little. It was a rearguard action, undertaken by Lord George Murray to cover the Prince's retreat, and as the terrain was entirely unsuitable for cavalry, Cumberland was obliged to dismount the dragoons he had available. The rebels lined the hedges leading to the village, and the soldiers were in the open. What happened is not very clear, which is not surprising because it was five o'clock on a December afternoon and the darkness was punctuated by only occasional moonlight. Each side fired on the other, and some of the rebels charged across the fields. The dragoons who were thus attacked prudently withdrew, much hampered by their long boots in the soft wet ground. They suffered some losses, but the rebels did not press home their advantage and at once sounded a general retreat. As a result, Cumberland entered Clifton and spent the night there. This scuffle was described by both sides, with some justification, as a victory.

The insurgents' flight to Scotland continued as fast as before. On 19 December Charles entered Carlisle, where he foolishly left four hundred unfortunate men as a garrison, 'against the Opinion of almost Everybody'. The expert view was that the town could not be held. Among those who were left were over a hundred Frenchmen, most of them artillerymen, and some Irish. These troops were reasonably safe in the event of surrender because they were not the King's subjects. But there were also the Manchester volunteers, who, rather than cross the border, agreed to remain in Carlisle as the lesser of two evils. It was to prove a very bad decision, for they had been in the town for only one day when the royal army appeared before the walls. Charles meanwhile made all speed to the north, and re-entered Scotland on 20 December, after almost exactly six weeks occupied in marching to Derby and back again. Ten days later the garrison at Carlisle surrendered, and Charles's English adventures were at an end.

But the major conflict between the British government and Louis XV continued without interruption. When the orders to Cumberland to return with his army were countermanded, those sent at the same time to General Ligonier were not. Ligonier had been left in charge of the infantry near Coventry when Cumberland set off in pursuit of Charles. Marches and counter-marches in the dead of winter had exhausted the troops, but they remained cheerful, and when the orders came to return at once to London Ligonier reckoned that his men could probably manage the journey within ten days. This did not please the government, which had reason to think that the French transports in Dunkirk were about to set sail, and the general was urged to do better. Making all possible speed — 'the roads are so extremely bad that men march faster than wagons can go' — Ligonier reached the capital on 23 December.

It was no more than a month since Newcastle had learned that Louis had appointed the Duc de Richelieu as commander of the French invasion forces. From this he had drawn some entirely correct and very disturbing conclusions:

> The Duke of Richelieu is to have the command of this embarkation. If so, the sending of an officer of his rank and quality shows plainly that the design is not only very serious but that the numbers of troops to be employed in it will be very considerable . . . all our advices agree that the Court of France intend now to support the Pretender in earnest.[19]

During the first half of December, when Charles was in England and appeared at his most dangerous, the British government made some further unpleasant discoveries about French plans. They found out that the entire Irish Brigade was scheduled to land in England; Vernon reported that all French fishing vessels had been ordered to assemble at Dunkirk; and agents at Dover provided the news that all types of craft were being sent from Blankenberg, Nieuport and Ostend in order to embark 12,000 troops now in Dunkirk. No wonder that London was full of rumours about an invasion! During December, and most of all until Charles began his retreat, it was a life and death matter for the British government to know what French plans were. That French actions would be concerted with those of their allies already in the country seemed certain — Charles kept telling everyone that 'his cousin Louis' would soon be sending an invasion force to his assistance, and except when Charles was actually in Derby the ministers in London were a good deal more worried about this invasion force than they were about the Jacobite army. Instructions were issued to set up five beacons along the coast, garrisons in the coastal towns were ready to march, and as many warships and privateers were at sea as were fit for service.

French preparations were pushed forward with the most intense effort in the last three weeks of December. But there were snags. Walsh was beginning to find it impossible to collect together enough ships, and he was also beginning to realise that if and when he had enough ships in the right place it would be impossible to conceal them or even to keep them together safely in the roads. The sailing date for the expedition, once thought of as approximately the 10 or 15 December, had to be postponed. Troops nevertheless kept pouring in from Flanders, and on 17 December Richelieu himself arrived at Dunkirk. On the following day news reached France of the retreat from Derby. This certainly changed the odds, because the British would now be free to concentrate all their forces against an invasion attempt and not have to fight with one hand tied behind their back by Charles and his associates. But the invasion build-up went ahead as before. There was always the hope — encouraged by every Jacobite agent in France — that the Jacobites in England would rise. And as long as Charles and his army were at large in the United Kingdom they were a useful anti-government force and would be a help to the French. As if to symbolise the common purpose of the 'Court of James III' and the court at Versailles, Charles's younger brother Henry turned up at Calais and then went on to Boulogne, where he expected to embark. And Voltaire wrote a four-hundred-word manifesto, of which 3,000 copies were printed and handed over to Richelieu, explaining to the British people that Louis was following the demands of all true Englishmen [sic] in coming to the assistance of their rightful prince, and that far from being an act of aggression this was a laudable effort to bring peace not only to Great Britain but to the whole of Europe. It was a well-composed piece, and it proves once again that double-talk is not an invention of the twentieth century.

But the ships that Walsh assembled and the troops that Louis sent to the Channel ports were destined never to sail. Even while the leaders of the expedition made their final preparations, the foundations of the whole enterprise were being destroyed at sea. French transports had to make preliminary moves along the coast, and they began to suffer dreadful losses. On 18 December a convoy of eleven sailed from Calais; two were captured and another sunk, while British privateers seized a French ship anchored in the roads before her captain could cut the cables. On the following day an artillery convoy from Dunkirk, consisting of sixty ships loaded with arms, stores and ammunition was sighted at daybreak by British privateers cruising in the Channel; seventeen transports were destroyed or taken to Dover. Still worse was to come. Two leagues out of Calais on the morning of 20 December a couple of Vernon's ships attacked the escorts of another convoy making for Boulogne, and a few hours later two privateers intercepted yet another group of French ships, of which two were taken and most of the others driven ashore and wrecked. An attempt to deal with the privateers that evening resulted in the loss of yet another French ship. It looked very much as if the Royal Navy had a stranglehold on the Channel ports. And it was quite certain that Vernon and the British government now had a very good idea of the kind of ships the French were concentrating, and where, and therefore of what their invasion plan (they were actually aiming for Dungeness) was likely to be.

Richelieu did not give up at this point, but henceforth his difficulties mounted and his confidence waned. There was no shortage of troops — British intelligence sources estimated at one point that there were 23,000 French troops in the Channel ports. But shipping of the right kind was scarce, below expectations; the weather was unreliable; Richelieu and young Henry did not get on together — which is hardly surprising, for while Henry was genuflecting and counting his beads (as he so often did), the Duke may well have been counting his mistresses; and most serious of all, British warships seemed never to be out of sight. Very near the end of the year (just a few days after Charles re-entered Scotland, as it happened) Richelieu summoned a Council of War. Embarkation seemed (not for the first time) to be imminent. The proposal was to sail on the afternoon of 26 December so as to reach Dungeness at high water. Someone pointed out that departure from Boulogne required a high tide so that the ships, heavily laden with men, horses and artillery, could clear the harbour. Further discussion revealed that not all the ships assembled would be able to get out of the harbour on one tide; it might take five days, and the British would be able to pick them off at leisure. Heavy storms would help the expedition to get to sea, and it was calculated by Lord Clare (who was second-in-command) that three tempests at Boulogne and two at Calais would do the trick. But once at sea in these conditions the ships might not, of course, stay afloat. And there was always the Royal Navy to contend with. Richelieu finally lost heart.

Thus 'the great enterprise', as the Jacobites called it, was found to be impracticable. The peace of Europe would not be suddenly restored on French terms, and a puppet regime would not be established in Britain, or even in Scotland — not, at any rate, with the help of a French invasion. Had Louis acted with more promptitude and decision; had he arranged something less cumbersome than an armada; had he been able to trust the English Jacobites to rise when French troops landed; had Charles made his plans clear to Louis before sailing from France; had reasonable secrecy been maintained about the invasion, compelling Vernon to disperse his ships, instead of being able to concentrate them as he did; had all sorts of things been different, the outcome would of course have been different also — although how much different no one can say. But history is about what happened, not about what did not happen. The Jacobite invasion of England took place, and it was not a success. The French invasion of England was prepared but did not take place. By the end of 1745 Charles Edward was back in Scotland and the Duc de Richelieu was back in Paris and George II was still in London. The War of the Austrian Succession was still going on. The events of 1745 had settled nothing. But 1746 was going to be different.

Notes and References

1. Home, op. cit., p. 104.
2. Ibid., p. 100.
3. Carlyle, op. cit., p. 147.
4. Quoted in K. Tomasson and F. Buist, *Battles of the '45* (London, 1962), p. 48.
5. Home, op. cit., p. 112.
6. Quoted in Tomasson and Buist, op. cit., p. 60.
7. Quoted in Speck, op. cit., p. 49.
8. Home, op. cit., p. 122.
9. Chevalier de Johnstone, op. cit., p. 41.
10. McLynn, op. cit., p. 122.
11. Sir Everard Fawkner, private secretary to Cumberland, quoted in Speck, op. cit., p. 29.
12. Elcho, op. cit., p. 298.
13. Quoted in McLynn, op. cit., p. 84.
14. Elcho, op. cit., p. 304.
15. Ibid., pp. 288–9.
16. O'Sullivan, quoted in Speck, op. cit., p. 90.
17. Elcho, op. cit., p. 337.
18. Quoted in Speck, op. cit., p. 92.
19. Newcastle to Wade, 19/11/45, quoted in McLynn, op. cit., p. 113.

5 AN ECONOMICAL VICTORY

While Charles was away marching in England, the friends of George II north of the border had time to organise; to set up, it would nowadays be said, some kind of resistance movement. The first sudden descent from the highlands had caught the government almost entirely unprepared. Aside from the efforts of the regular army, the rebels met with little opposition because there was almost nothing to oppose them with; no arms, no money, no organisation. So the first task of those left in authority had been, as Duncan Forbes expressed it, 'to prevent the contagion of rebellion from spreading'; and the second task, when there was time and means, was to get supporters under arms. In both matters it was Forbes himself who took the lead. As we have seen, he wrote to many gentlemen in the highlands, urging them not to declare for the Pretender, but to stay at home and thus 'save themselves'. Especially after Prestonpans it was essential to prevent reinforcements from the north reaching the insurgents, if at all possible. Parties of the rebels had gone north under Lord Lewis Gordon, and were trying to uplift money and raise recruits in Moray, Banff and Aberdeenshire. In the latter activity they did not have much success, because the Duke of Gordon, Lord Lewis's brother, remained loyal to the government. But similar efforts were being made elsewhere, and important groups might still be persuaded to 'come out', by fair means or foul, in spite of an inclination, if left to themselves, to do nothing, or even to risk supporting an apparently poorly defended government. Lord Lovat, for example, was making promises of unfailing loyalty to both sides, and Forbes feared (correctly) that the Frasers were about to defect; the Rosses in Cromarty were under arms, no one knew with what intent; many of the Mackenzies were doubtful. From his house at Culloden, Forbes was in close touch with all these developments, and the rebels knew it. They therefore decided that the Lord President should be captured or eliminated, and during the night of 15 October Culloden House was unexpectedly attacked by a party of two hundred Frasers. This was not a casual raid, for the Frasers came with a warrant in the name of Charles Edward as Regent of Scotland, England, Ireland and the Dominions, and signed by his secretary, 'authorising' them to seize the Lord Presi-

123

dent in his house and to bring him to Charles wherever he might be. The attackers were beaten off, and departed after pillaging the estate. This incident confirms the importance of Forbes's activities, which for a time he had to carry on with very meagre support. In November he summarised the position as follows:

> All the fine ladies, if you will except one or two, became passion-ately fond of the young Adventurer and used all their arts and industry for him in the most intemperate manner. Under these circumstances, I found myself almost alone, without arms, and without money or credit, provided with no means to prevent extreme folly, except pen and ink, a tongue, and some reputa-tion; and if you will except MacLeod, whom I sent for from the Isle of Skye, supported by nobody of common sense or courage. Had arms and money come when they were first called for, before the unexpected successes blew up folly to madness, I could have answered it with my head that no man from the North should have joined the original flock of rebels that passed the Forth.[1]

So the Lord President did what he could without any material sup-port from the government, and the rebels gradually gained recruits. But they gained them more slowly than they had hoped; and while in Edinburgh only a few hundred joined the standard, when Charles and his advisers had hoped for thousands.

Equally important was the task of organising military resistance. The Earl of Loudon, with his partially recruited regiment, joined Forbes at Inverness; but this was a force of only one hundred and fifty men. An extempore defence of the country had to rely on the raising of volunteer companies, more or less as was done in England, and early in September Forbes was authorised to raise in the highlands twenty such companies. Inevitably, this took time. In the end, Forbes issued commissions for eighteen companies of approximately one hundred men each. All but one of these indepen-dent companies were recruited from among the clansmen under their chiefs, and very delicate questions had to be decided concern-ing priority and seniority, especially in the choosing of officers, for possible jealousy among the highland chiefs would have ruined everything. Since the names of the clans that joined the rebellion are so frequently recited, it may be worth giving the names of those that provided independent companies to fight against the Pretender.

These were: the Grants, the MacDonalds of Sleat, the Mackays, the Mackenzies, the MacLeods of Assynt, the MacLeods of Skye, the Munros, the Rosses and the Sutherlands. Forbes gathered most of the companies into Inverness, which he made the headquarters of the government in Scotland, and where arms, sent by sea from London, gradually became available. The first companies reached Inverness early in November, and ten were in the town by the end of the year. They secured the safety of the city, and made it possible for Loudon, early in December, to get through with food and supplies to Fort Augustus, which was besieged by the Frasers. But some companies remained where they were raised, or 'at large', compelling neighbours with rebellious inclinations to stay at home, or engaged in protecting the lives and property of those who remained loyal to the government.

The insurgents likewise strengthened their position, some of those whom Charles had always hoped would support him at last coming forward, although rather late in the day. The Earl of Cromarty brought one hundred and fifty of the Mackenzies, whom he had 'debauched' in spite of the loyalty of their chief, Lord Fortrose. The Clan Mackintosh likewise divided, some two hundred of them rising under Lady Mackintosh ('Colonel Anne') regardless of the fact that her husband held a commission in the Black Watch. More important was the defection of the Frasers. Lovat, a double-dealer if ever there was one, sat on the fence as long as he could. While expressing in one letter (to Forbes in August) his 'zeal and attachment for His Majesty's person and Government' and referring to Charles as 'that mad and unaccountable gentleman', in another (to Lochiel in September) he conveyed 'My service to the Prince' and regretted only that some of his friends had perhaps been 'ower rash in going out ere affairs were ripe'.[2] He tried to cover himself by loudly professing his own undying attachment to the House of Hanover, while ordering his son (who seems not to have been a Jacobite) to take out the clan. The Master of Lovat did as he was told, and early in December marched with several hundred men to join the rebels. An attempt was made to place Lovat under house-arrest in Inverness, but he unfortunately escaped — an exploit which led him to the gallows. More important than any of these was fresh assistance from France. The Irish Brigade under Lord John Drummond (who had been educated in France and was an officer in the French service) was to have left Ostend for Scotland in mid-October, but it was delayed. A month later, however, five hundred men of the Scots Royals and at least four hundred men from various Irish regiments, including a regiment of horse, all of them in the service of Louis XV, were embarked at Ostend, elaborate measures being taken to conceal their destination. The British consul at Flushing was not deceived, however; express despatches were sent to London, and Byng disposed his forces to lie in wait for the enemy, who numbered eight vessels in all. Two troop carriers were intercepted and some two hundred and fifty of Louis' soldiers, including about four score officers, were taken prisoner. Drummond himself, however, and about seven hundred and fifty officers and men were landed at ports on the east coast of Scotland, making a very important addition of trained manpower to the Jacobite forces.

When Charles re-entered Scotland he therefore found his position to be a good deal better than his flight from Derby might have suggested. True, the castles of Edinburgh and Stirling, along with Fort Augustus and Fort William were held by the government; Inverness was under the control of Forbes and Loudon; and the city of Edinburgh was no longer in the hands of the rebels, for almost as soon as Charles had turned his back — to be precise, two weeks after his departure — the judges of Scotland, along with the Sheriffs of East Lothian and the Merse and numerous other gentlemen entered Edinburgh where 'they were saluted by a general discharge of the cannon of the castle'. They were joined one day later by several regiments of foot soldiers and dragoons from Berwick-on-Tweed. But at Perth, which had become the rebels' headquarters in Scotland, Charles now had a second army, for Drummond's Irish Brigade, and the Frasers under the Master of Lovat along with other smaller contingents of fresh recruits added up to a sizeable force.

After crossing the border on 24 December the so-called Prince Regent and his men did not return to Edinburgh, where a resolution had been taken to defend the city, but went to Dumfries, where, as was their usual practice, they seized what public money was available and 'fined' all those who had contributed to helping the government. They then proceeded to Glasgow, which was the rising commercial centre of Scotland. Glasgow had never made any secret of its hostility to the Jacobites, but it was quite defenceless. Charles therefore entered the city and remained there for seven or eight days, quartering his men upon the townspeople and requisitioning sufficient shoes and clothing to re-equip his entire army. No payment was made. The Jacobites then proceeded towards Stirling which commanded the passages over the River Forth.

It is just possible that even at this stage of his campaign Charles might have been able to accomplish something positive. The march into England had been a fiasco and had moreover soured relations between the Young Pretender and many of his senior commanders. Help from Louis, although not negligible, had not come up to expectations. As for the English Jacobites, far from rushing to his assistance they had kept out of his way. But the Jacobite army had not yet been defeated, and it was now far larger than at any time since the rebellion began, numbering between 8,000 and 9,000 men. All that opposed the rebels in Scotland, when Charles returned, was a scratch force of fewer than 2,000 men in Inverness, another and smaller collection of volunteers (of whom 'not above one half required to be paid') concentrating on Edinburgh, and a few regiments of foot and dragoons. Cleared out of England, Charles might have prevailed in Scotland if he had matched his capacity to make war with some political skill. He might, after all, have played the Scottish nationalist card. After Prestonpans he declared the union of the English and Scottish parliaments abolished; now, he might have declared the restoration of the independence of the ancient Kingdom of Scotland. Scottish nationalism, when not in the ascendant, lies always just below the surface of Scottish life. Rule from Westminster has never been popular, and sentimental ideas about 'the auld alliance' with France tended in the eighteenth century to crop up at least as readily as any sympathy for England. So the line that he was fighting for Scottish independence (like Robert the Bruce) might have gained Charles some additional supporters and have persuaded Louis at the same time to send more help. In addition, Charles could have declared himself a convert from Roman Catholicism. This, admittedly, would not have pleased Louis XV. But it would have undermined the implacable hostility of the Church of Scotland to a Roman Catholic pretender (significantly, many of those who paraded for the defence of Edinburgh in January 1746 'had their minister marching along with them'), and would have put Charles in the same religious camp as nine-tenths of the nation. Had he been able to pose as a national liberator who was also a protestant, it would have been much harder for many Scotsmen to withold their support for his campaign — whereas the way things stood, a great many were fighting against him. And if it is objected that Charles was above abandoning his religion for the sake of his political advantage, the answer is simple; this is precisely what he was to do in 1750.

Whether or not any of this passed through Charles's mind during the period when he was in or near Glasgow we do not know. But certainly he took no decision to modify the political objectives of his campaign. He seems never to have regarded Scotland as important or even to have cared much for the Scots, except as cannon fodder. He believed his rightful place to be in London. And presumably his overvaulting ambition to be master of England, Scotland and Ireland, which he thought no more than his due, prevented him from considering his position rationally, and made him unable to contemplate anything less than complete conquest. Moreover, his self-confidence was quite undiminished, for he regarded the retreat from Derby as purely the fault of the chiefs and the generals.

However this may be, he now decided to undertake the siege of Stirling castle. One of his armies marched from Glasgow and the other from Perth, the town of Falkirk was occupied, and the siege of Stirling began. As Stirling itself was not fortified, the magistrates had no choice but to capitulate, but the castle, which was defended by General Blakeney, was another matter. A call to surrender was treated with contempt, and the rebels realised that they would need artillery if they were to have any hope of achieving their purpose. Thanks to Louis XV, some modern battering cannon were available, landed at Montrose during the winter, but these were unfortunately at Perth. They were brought over the Forth, although their passage was seriously delayed by the activities of three hundred soldiers and two men of war operating out of Leith, and the siege began in earnest on 10 January.

Whether this siege was a wise move or not is a matter of doubt, but it seems to have been the occasion of the second outbreak of acrimonious argument in the rebel camp. Since Derby, Charles had begun the practice of taking no one into his confidence save Murray of Broughton, who was his secretary, and Sir Thomas Sheridan, who had been his tutor, and the Irish officers, who 'were of his own religion, and paid always more Court to him in their discourse'. Thus Charles decided what the army was to do next, and scant attention was paid to the opinions of more experienced men such as Lord George Murray and Lochiel; nor was their advice asked for. The chieftains evidently discussed the matter, and a document was drawn up asking that in future a Council of War would be summoned before any important military decisions were taken. Charles's answer, to men who had come to his support at the risk of their lives, was of breathtaking *hauteur*:

When I came into Scotland I knew well enough what I was to expect from my enemies, but I little foresaw what I met with from my friends . . . I am often hit in the teeth, that this is an army of volunteers, and consequently very different from one composed of mercenaries. What one would naturally expect from an army whose chief-officers consist of gentlemen of rank and fortune, and who came into it merely from motives of duty and honour, is more zeal, more resolution, and more good manners, than in those that fight merely for pay . . .

Thus corrected in their manners, the chiefs and the generals seem to have fallen silent, at least for the time being, and Charles retained his despotic control. But his behaviour was repeatedly a threat to his army.

Meanwhile, a steady build-up of government forces was taking place at Edinburgh. Cumberland had been recalled to London because there was yet another rumour of a French invasion, and many people besides the King wanted the Duke to command on the south coast. After some discussion it was decided that Lieutenant-General Hawley should command the government's forces in Scotland, and thus it fell to Hawley — so it was supposed — to give the *coup de grâce* to the rebellion. Hawley had fought with Marlborough, as well as under the Duke of Argyll at Sheriffmuir, and he was therefore an experienced officer. When he left Edinburgh on 16 January his army consisted of twelve regiments of foot — nine of them recalled from Flanders — two regiments of dragoons, a regiment of volunteers from Glasgow and another from Edinburgh, and some cannon. As is often the case, however, this force looked stronger on paper than it was in fact. There were no gunners worth mentioning, the regiments of dragoons were those that had been disgraced at Prestonpans, and even their best friends did not think that they could be relied upon. As for the infantry, most of them had spent half the winter marching up and down the north-east of England under Wade, and were, as Hawley put it, 'quite délabrée'. He considered, however, that he had sufficient men for his purpose, and he duly encamped in a field just to the west of Falkirk, only nine miles from Bannockburn, where Charles had set up his headquarters. On 17 January Hawley was reinforced by another regiment of dragoons — Cobham's — and by 1,000 Argyllshire highlanders, under the command of Lieutenant-Colonel Campbell, heir to the Duke of Argyll.

There is no denying that this force, suitably handled, should have been sufficient to defeat the rebels, although perhaps only just sufficient. Charles had left 1,000 men under the Duke of Perth to continue the siege of Stirling castle, so he had about 8,000 men in the field. Hawley's army numbered about 8,500, he had good officers, and some of the foot soldiers were among the best in Europe. What undermined the whole operation was a string of errors of judgement by Hawley himself — errors based on one fundamental mistake, that of underestimating the enemy. 'I do and alwayes shall despise these Rascalls', he said. It was a disastrous attitude.

Although the King's army had come from Edinburgh in order to dispose of the insurgents, it was the latter who took the initiative. A little before 1 p.m. on 17 January they were seen by some of Hawley's scouts marching towards Falkirk. This information was sent at once to Hawley, who was at Callandar House, one mile east of Falkirk, but his reply was that the men might prepare themselves but need not stand to arms. Within an hour, mounted scouts rode up to the King's troops 'on the spur' with the news that the rebels were only two or three miles away and were making for the high ground to the south-west of where the army was encamped. According to John Home, who was a member of the Edinburgh volunteers, 'this piece of intelligence alarmed the troops: one might hear the officers saying to one another, where is the General? What shall be done? We have no orders'.[3] Hawley's second-in-command ordered the drums to beat to arms, and the regiments formed at a professional speed that surprised observers. Hawley at last turned up, and ordered the dragoons to take possession of the high ground towards which the rebels had been seen marching; he ordered the infantry to follow. The day was overcast, and a storm of wind and rain blew directly in the faces of the King's troops, who were marching as fast as they could up the hill with their bayonets fixed, and unable to protect their precious cartridges from the heavy rain. The dragoons got a good way ahead, and reached the high ground at almost exactly the same time as the van of the rebel army.

The field of battle, upon which the respective commanders now hastily drew up their men, had two important features. To the south it was bordered by the boggy ground of Falkirk Moor, making encircling movements in that direction impossible. And on the north, where the ground shelved away towards Falkirk, the space between the rebel left wing and the royal right wing was taken up by 'a ravine or gully . . . which began on the declivity of the hill . . .

and went down due north, still deeper and wider to the plain'.[4] On account of the slope of the ground, those farthest north could not see all the troops south of them, standing higher up and over the skyline; and besides, the wind and rain continued, the darkness increased, and 'nobody could see very far'.

Just before four o'clock, and before all his men had taken up their positions, Hawley sent an order to the cavalry to attack the rebels. There is no understanding what prompted Hawley to send this order. It is credibly reported that when the officer in charge received it, 'he said it was the most extraordinary order that ever was given'.[5] The dragoons numbered about seven hundred, and they were drawn up facing approximately 4,000 rebels in the front line, with more than half that number behind them in the second line. There was no preparation by artillery (neither side had been able to shift its cannon in time). Because no flanking movement was possible, Hawley's order meant a frontal attack. Greatly to their credit, the dragoons advanced. Unfortunately for them, the rebel right wing was commanded by Lord George Murray, who, standing with his men, let the dragoons come within ten or twenty yards of him and then gave the order to fire. Men and horses were killed instantly all along the line ('I saw daylight through them in several places'[6]), and two of the regiments wheeled about and fled directly back, riding over some of their own infantry just as they had done at Prestonpans. The third went off between the two armies, receiving a good deal of fire as it passed in front of the rebels. With the dragoons out of the way, Lord George ordered his men to keep their ranks and stand firm. But discipline was never the Jacobites' strong point, either in plotting or fighting. There was a brief exchange of fire, and then the highlanders threw down their muskets, drew their swords, and fell upon the already disordered regiments of Hawley's left wing, both in front and flank. After a short contest, these regiments gave way, and a total rout seemed to be taking place, many of the King's troops fleeing for their lives, pursued by almost half the Jacobite army. Only a few hundred clansmen remained in their lines, as Lord George Murray had commanded them to do. Hawley was asked at this point in the battle — not very tactfully — if any of his regiments was still standing; he made no reply, but ordered the Edinburgh volunteers into a fold for cattle which stood close to hand. Then 'the disorder and confusion encreased, and General Hawley rode down the hill'.[7]

But on the other sector, matters had taken a very different turn.

Charles, although twice asked by Lord George to do so, had failed to appoint anyone to command the regiments on the rebel left wing. When at the start of the battle the King's army opened fire upon these regiments from across the ravine, they returned the fire, but the steady fire of the King's troops was so much more effective than that of the rebels that the latter lost a good many men, and fell back. Hearing all this noise of battle behind them, and perhaps already having secured enough plunder, many of the rebels who were in pursuit of the King's troops returned to where their lines had been, only to find that they were a company of stragglers on a darkening hillside, with heavy firing to the north of them. Unable to see what was going on, they concluded that the Jacobite army had been defeated, or was about to be defeated, and accordingly made off to the west.

The battle had now lasted for less than twenty minutes, and was almost over. A large part of the royal army had quit the field: an equally large part of the rebel army had done the same. In the rapidly falling darkness, commanders on each side were able to keep only a nucleus of men together. Lord George Murray still had some regiments with him, and he was joined by Charles, who had been in the rear of the second line with the Irish piquets and some horse. They went to the brow of the hill, where they found Cobham's dragoons, which had always kept together, riding up the hill. Neither side caring to restart the action, the rebels halted, and the dragoons turned back, going down to where the regiments who had fought so well on the right wing were standing. Horse and foot then withdrew together in good order, and joined the rest of the royal army who had rallied on the ground in front of their camp. That evening Hawley retreated to Linlithgow, and Lord George Murray, with a strong body of highlanders, took possession of the town of Falkirk.

This battle was undeniably a technical victory for the Jacobites. They moved forward to Falkirk, and the King's army moved back to Linlithgow. Also, the losses of the two sides were unequal. The Jacobite dead seem to have numbered no more than fifty or sixty, but on the government side at least three hundred men were killed including many officers, one of them Sir Robert Munro, chief of the Clan Munro. But the result of the battle, although a setback for the government, was not disastrous for them; the army was not gravely weakened, and more troops were still arriving in Edinburgh. It was otherwise for the rebels. They knew that they had had the advantage of the ground; of the storm blowing into the faces of their enemies; and of General Hawley's inexplicable order to the dragoons to attack a whole army; and yet with all these advantages, they had not won a decisive victory. What the insurgents needed to accomplish at Falkirk was the destruction of the King's army; and although presented with a very good opportunity, they had quite failed to achieve this. Falkirk was not another astonishing performance by the rebel army, such as the victory at Prestonpans or the march to Derby — performances which had made Louis XV and his ministers believe, fleetingly, that Charles and his men belonged to some more heroic age, that they were a force worth cultivating in European politics, and therefore deserving of French support. Already disillusioned by the retreat from Derby, Louis and his ministers were beginning to see the Jacobite rebellion as more of a liability than an asset.

The doubtful victory seems to have cast a gloom also on the Jacobite camp. Recriminations and animosities increased. Lord George Murray blamed Lord John Drummond for not taking control of the left wing, and Lord John Drummond and others blamed Lord George for restraining some regiments from taking part in the pursuit and holding them idle in the field; both probably thought that Charles had not done all that he should have done. But recriminations were not going to help. What the rebels had to do was to review their position, and decide what their next move should be. This seems to have taken a few days, for immediately after the battle Charles returned to Bannockburn, Lord George remained at Falkirk, and the siege of Stirling castle was resumed.

There is some evidence that the rebels contemplated fighting another battle in the immediate future. But if they did contemplate this they thought better of it, for an address to Charles, dated 29 January and signed by Lord George Murray and all the leading chiefs, was now presented in which the eight signatories stated 'that there is no way to extricate your Royal Highness and those who remain with you, out of the most imminent danger, but by retiring immediately to the Highlands . . .' Charles, as usual, huffed and puffed, declared himself 'extremely surprised' at the resolution, asked a string of rhetorical questions, and agreed 'with the greatest reluctance' to this unanimous resolution 'if you persist in it'. The arguments of his commanders, which he made no effort to meet, were simple and compelling. They pointed out, first, that a 'vast number' of highlanders had already returned home. Many of them had gone laden with plunder. But for everyone in the rebel army life had become very hard — food and clothing were often difficult to find, and the season was severe — and the natural response was to go home. Reduced in numbers by perhaps a quarter or a third — possibly by more — the rebels were no longer any match for the government forces. Secondly, the siege of Stirling castle was a waste of time. Persisted in by Charles and directed by a team of French artillery experts, the siege made no progress and the castle was as secure at the end of three weeks as at the beginning; a number of the rebels had been killed by fire from the ramparts. So the siege was raised, the rebels destroyed their cannon and blew up their magazines, and for the second time Charles and his army retreated — or perhaps one should say fled, for they crossed the Forth in great confusion — before the King's army, now commanded by the Duke of Cumberland.

Having been appointed to lead the troops whom Hawley had so dreadfully mismanaged, Cumberland left London on 25 January and arrived in Edinburgh on 30 January at four o'clock in the morning. The Duke was a popular commander and inspired great confidence in his men, who were 'in raptures at the Duke's coming'. Cumberland lost no time, but marched from Edinburgh on 31 January. The next day, while *en route* from Linlithgow to Falkirk, news came that the rebels had left Stirling, and were retreating into the highlands. This precipitate flight was a great disappointment to Cumberland, who had hoped, in his own words,

> that the rebels, flushed with their late success, would have given us an opportunity of finishing this affair at once; . . . but, to my great astonishment, the rebels . . . are retired over the Firth . . . leaving their cannon behind them and a number of sick and wounded . . . When the rebels crossed the Forth their leaders told them to shift for themselves, which is the first order they have yet obeyed.[8]

The Duke marched to Stirling, and to Dunblane, Crieff and Perth, where he halted. He was only a few days behind the rebels, who were fleeing north at great speed. Their army had divided at Crieff, after a Council of War — 'there never had been such heats and animosities as at this meeting'[9] — and one group, under Charles, was on its way to Aberfeldy (where it crossed the Tay using Wade's bridge, built in 1733 to facilitate the movement of government troops), while another, under Lord George Murray, was on the coast road to Aberdeen. Their objective was Inverness, which they reached on 20 February. Both groups had to struggle through heavy snow, and from both there were many desertions.

The rebellion was now in its final phase. Whatever they said to one another, many of Charles's followers must have realised that the game was up. From a not very promising start at Glenshiel the fuse had run crackling to Derby. But now, only eleven weeks after Derby, the government had established undisputed authority in the whole country south and east of a line drawn from Glasgow to Aberdeen. What remained to the rebels was almost entirely highland, and they did not control all of that. They had been beaten back, victories or no victories and, while they husbanded what strength they had left in the hills and glens, the government was still augmenting its forces and preparing to put an end to the rebellion for good.

In such a desperate and declining situation one may wonder why the insurgents persisted. To some extent it was probably because they too, like General Hawley, underestimated their enemy. George II was remarkably secure on his throne, for he enjoyed persistent if not enthusiastic support. Too many Jacobites mistook political discontent for a determination to rebel, and too many failed to realise the depth and extent of hostility to themselves. And, of course, they were committed. All the King's subjects who had rebelled were guilty of treason, for which the penalty was death. The ringleaders certainly, and their subordinates most probably, could not expect to return quietly to their homes if they laid down their arms. They had killed hundreds of government soldiers, terrified many civilians, assisted the King of France in his war with Great Britain and her allies, and put the whole country in an uproar. If the rebellion failed, as now seemed likely, death or exile would be the lot of the Jacobite leaders. As for those who were fanatical supporters of the House of Stuart — and there is no evidence that a great many were — there could be no turning back. So, as long as any chance of success remained, the rebellion continued.

And there were two other calculations that kept the rebels going. Back in the highlands where so many of them belonged, they felt secure. The great chiefs ruled in their respective territories with an absolute sway, frequently exercising the powers of life and death — when the gentle Lochiel, for example, hanged some of his clansmen for thieving, no one raised an eyebrow; it was perfectly legal — and they tended to believe that north and west of the 'Highland line' — from Glasgow to Ballater and from Ballater to Inverness — the government in London could not for long exercise its jurisdiction unless they allowed it to do so. Numerous Scottish kings had invaded the highlands; but they or their representatives had never been more than a passing influence. The forts built along the Great Glen were frontier posts; to all Englishmen and most Scotsmen the country beyond them was a strange country, mountainous and infertile, where there were almost no roads, where money seldom changed hands, and where everyone spoke Gaelic. Very few Englishmen or lowland Scots had ever been there; and the rebels no doubt believed that pursuit and retribution could not very well follow them into this remote and inaccessible land.

Secondly, there was that will o' the wisp, help from the French — or the Spanish or the Pope. The chiefs' address refers to their hopes of both 'a landing' and 'succour from abroad'. These hopes were not yet entirely fantastical. Lord John Drummond had brought valuable help from France late in 1745; perhaps the French would be even more obliging in 1746. Louis was, indeed, about to make a few final face-saving efforts, although after the retreat from Derby he began to look upon Charles as a born loser. When in 1744 France called off the full-scale invasion of England, the idea of a landing by 4,000 French and Irish troops in Scotland was substituted. These troops, or at any rate a good number of them, were actually embarked at Ostend and Dunkirk towards the end of January 1746. No sooner were they on board than eight British warships appeared outside Ostend, so the operation was cancelled, and a few days afterwards the French supreme commander left the Channel coast, never to return. A little later, however, three French transports did actually sail from Ostend for Scotland. Two were chased back into port by the Royal Navy, but one got through and landed a few hundred men in Aberdeen in late February. The final success was the landing of a handful of men, 2,000 louis d'or and some arms and ammunition at Peterhead at the end of the month. But the ship that got through had to be run aground and was destroyed, and out of seven other French ships that sailed for Scotland in February, none reached its destination and two were captured, along with 373 French soldiers and 23 officers. It cannot be said that Louis did not try, but he was not very successful. By the spring of 1746 there were more than 1,000 French prisoners in British gaols.

The fact is that the rebels were now waiting for something to turn

up — perhaps a British disaster in some other theatre of the War of
the Austrian Succession, a change of ministers in France, a Jacobite
rising in Wales, disturbance in Ireland, or even — *mirabile
mirabilis* — a French landing on the south coast of England. Their
plan while they waited was to be 'usefully employed the remainder
of the winter, by taking and mastering the forts of the North'. They
were destined not to succeed. They began with Inverness. Inverness
was held for the government by Duncan Forbes and Lord Loudon,
who had collected together a good number of men from the well-
affected clans, but their efforts were largely nullified by the failure
of the ministers in London to send one tenth as much help to their
supporters in Scotland as Louis sent to the rebels. In the early days
of the rebellion Lord Milton had complained that 'the well-affected
to the present happy establishment are not armed and properly
supported, and empowered to appear in a legal way for the defence
of His Majesty's person, and support of his Government', and now,
eight months later, Duncan Forbes stated the case very clearly to the
Duke of Newcastle:

> The too late arrival of the sloop [at Inverness] with arms and
> money which I had long solicited, was the cause why the rebellion
> gathered fresh strength in this country after the rebels' flight
> from Stirling. Had those arms come in time enough to have been
> put into the hands of men who were ready prepared to receive
> them, the rebels durst hardly have shown themselves on this side
> the mountains; but as those arms did not arrive in our road till the
> very day that the rebels made themselves masters of the barrack
> of Ruthven, within twenty-six miles of us, it was too late to
> assemble the men we had prepared, and in place of making use of
> arms we were obliged to keep them, as well as the money, on
> shipboard for security.[10]

Unable to defend the town or even themselves, Forbes and Loudon
retired with their men into Ross-shire, and the rebels took Inverness,
and two days later its castle, known as Fort George. They next
moved down the Great Glen to Fort Augustus, which they took a
few days later, after which a detachment set off to lay siege to Fort
William. While this siege was organising, Lord Cromarty and the
Duke of Perth moved into Ross-shire with very strong forces. Their
intention was to destroy the power of the government in the north of
Scotland and thus open the way for reinforcements to come out and

join the rebel army before the spring; and also to seize, if possible, MacLeod of MacLeod and the Lord President, for it was clear to everyone that because of their efforts a good many waverers had stayed at home who might otherwise have been foolish enough to march with the Pretender. 'Against these two their chief vengeance was levelled.'[11] Forbes and Loudon had only a small and poorly equipped army, and they had no choice but to retreat. They crossed the Dornoch Firth into Sutherland, but the rebels again followed them and a detachment of Loudon's forces was surprised and defeated near Dornoch. It was then decided to divide the army, such as it was. Forbes and Loudon marched via Loch Broom and the Gairloch to Kyle of Lochalsh, where they embarked with eight hundred men for Skye; while a smaller group went north, into Lord Reay's country. Forbes and his companions experienced 'bad weather, forced marches through mountains almost impassable, lying on roots or straw or heather, and a low diet from mere necessity',[12] and finally crossed to Skye 'in small boats, like canoes, in great hazard'.[13] The Lord President was over sixty years old, but he evidently had powers of endurance to match his determination.

This success by the rebels doubtless had some propaganda value in the highlands, but its military significance was small. The independent companies and Lord Loudon's regiment had kept the north quiet for six months while the Jacobites were campaigning in the lowlands and in England, and now their work was almost finished. They rendered one further important service, however. At the end of March a French ship with one hundred and forty officers and men (mostly Irish in the service of Spain) and a large sum of money on board was sighted by a British cruiser off Sutherland and after a five-hour chase driven ashore in the Kyle of Tongue. The officers and soldiers got ashore, taking the money with them (which was said to have amounted to over £13,000 in gold). But they were soon afterwards attacked by those of Lord Loudon's troops who had come north, assisted by some of the Mackays, and were obliged to surrender. This was an important success, for the money was seized by Loudon's troops, and money was a commodity of which the rebels were at that time in desperate need. Paying the men only in meal, to which the Pretender or his lieutenants were frequently reduced, was very apt to lead to desertions.

While these operations were taking place north of the Great Glen, commando-style raids were the order of the day farther south. This sort of activity was well understood by the highlanders, who had a wealth of experience in stealing cattle from lowland farms as well as from highland hillsides. These skills had already been put to good use by both government and rebels. Cluny MacPherson had been abducted from his own house by a party of rebels in August; two hundred Frasers had tried to seize Duncan Forbes in Culloden House in October; and Lord Loudon had succeeded in putting Lovat under house arrest in Beaufort castle in December, although he had escaped. In February, Loudon put another plan into execution which, if only it had succeeded, would have saved many hundreds of lives, possibly thousands, and would have ranked very high in the annals of military enterprise. At the end of his march north, and before attacking Inverness, Charles took up his quarters at the House of Moy, nine or ten miles from Inverness. Fearing nothing from Lord Loudon, he 'allowed his men to straggle about in their own country', and kept only a few hundred in the neighbourhood of Moy. Government agents got word of the situation back to Loudon, who that evening, as soon as it was dark, marched from Inverness to capture the Pretender. Unfortunately, government security on this occasion was no better than Jacobite security. Lady Mackintosh — who was Charles's hostess, while her husband served with Lord Loudon — learned of the plan and sent out a party of her own men with instructions to fire on the government troops whenever seen, to remain concealed themselves, and to give the impression that they were vastly more in number than was actually the case. In the darkness of a February night this old device worked well, and Loudon's men, attacked within three miles of Moy Hall by enemies whom they could not see, and thrown into great confusion, retired hastily back to Inverness. This attempted raid was a brilliant idea, carried out on the spur of the moment, and if the execution had been as good as the conception, the war would have been brought to an end by one bold stroke.

Similar tactics were employed a month later by Lord George Murray. His object was nothing grander than the capture of some government troops, but he was also no doubt anxious for family reasons to clear the Atholl country of government soldiers and servants of the Duke of Argyll, for he was himself a younger brother of the Duke of Atholl. Accordingly, he left Dalwhinnie when daylight began to fail on 16 March, accompanied by Cluny MacPherson and seven hundred men. Only he and Cluny knew what was planned. After marching south for ten miles, Lord George divided the men into numerous parties, and gave them their orders. A few hours later, before daybreak, and as far as possible at the same time, a number of isolated government posts were attacked and, except in one case, all their occupants made prisoner. The rebels lost no men. In the one case where the defenders broke out, they took refuge in Blair castle, which was Lord George's ancestral home and which he shortly afterwards invested. But his two small field-pieces 'made no impression upon walls that were seven feet thick', nor did the siege as a whole impress Sir Andrew Agnew, who commanded the castle and who, it has been said, inspired far more terror in his men than the whole highland army. The siege lasted a fortnight, and was abandoned just before a relieving force arrived under the Earl of Crawford. As for Fort William, Cumberland had taken prompt measures to strengthen its defences before the siege began, sending provisions, arms, ammunition and men from Liverpool and Glasgow. Had Fort William fallen, it would have given the rebels a supply port on the west coast and made it easier for them once again to invade the lowlands. The Duke was well aware of this — 'I look upon Fort William to be the only Fort in the Highlands that is of any consequence' — and so here, too, the rebels were denied. Their operations after Falkirk thus brought them very little advantage, and their position was very little improved.

The end of March had now almost come. And when 'the cold wind of the spring, that dries the ground more than the heat of summer, had blown for some time, and made the rivers fordable',[14] it was expected that the Duke would very soon march from Aberdeen towards Inverness, where Charles was gathering together his scattered detachments.

The Duke marched from Aberdeen on 8 April. He had systematically built up his forces, which were well trained and well supplied, morale was high, and a number of transports, escorted by warships, kept by him along the coast, loaded with provisions, artillery and ammunition. On 12 April, the army prepared to ford the River Spey. The Spey is a wide and fast-flowing river and a natural line of defence on the approach to Inverness from Aberdeen; the rebels should have been able to inflict casualties — perhaps severe casualties — on the King's troops while crossing the river. They must have thought of this, because a considerable force — the so-called 'Army of the Spey', between 1,000 and 2,000 men, commanded by the Duke of Perth — was on the west bank when the King's troops arrived, and some earthworks had been raised. But instead of exploiting their obvious advantage and opening fire, Perth and his men obligingly and at once retreated towards Inverness, and the crossing took place unopposed.

To understand why this unique opportunity was thrown away by the rebels, it is necessary to bear in mind two facts. First, although Charles knew very well that Cumberland was at Aberdeen and would march in the spring, and although he had had three months since the battle of Falkirk in which to lay his plans and collect his forces, he was caught largely unprepared. To some extent this was because the rebel army was plagued by the usual money and supply problems — little food and no pay — and many clansmen had therefore gone home to live for a while with their families, and had not yet returned. But it was also because elements of the army were still engaged in or were returning from operations elsewhere in the highlands. Lochiel was on his way back from the futile siege of Fort William; Lord Cromarty was in Sutherland, pursuing Loudon; Cluny MacPherson was still in Badenoch. With his forces thus dispersed, Charles may have wished to avoid yet another commitment, this time on the Spey; and it is said that the Duke of Perth was under orders not to engage the enemy. This may explain the rebels' inaction; but it does not justify it. Perth could have both damaged the enemy and delayed his advance without becoming heavily engaged, and this, especially any delay, would have been very valuable to the Jacobites. The second point is that there had been no Council of War since just after Falkirk. Charles took his own decisions, probably after consulting his Irish friends. The decision not to fight even a delaying action on the Spey was therefore probably his, and it was a decision that neither Lord George Murray nor Lochiel — nor probably any other of the chiefs — would have approved.

Two days after Cumberland crossed the Spey, Charles marched from Inverness to Culloden. He took all the troops that he could find and left orders for those that were not yet in the town to follow him as soon as possible. He had decided to seek a battle, and he had decided to fight it on Culloden Moor. It was his decision and his alone, and by all accounts it filled the chiefs and commanders with gloom — 'We were at variance within ourselves: Irish intriguers and French politics were too predominant in our councils'.[15] That evening Lochiel arrived with his men from Fort William, and the rebel army spent the night among the gorse bushes and pine-trees of Culloden Wood. Charles and his principal lieutenants put up in Culloden House, the home of Duncan Forbes.

Having made one serious mistake on the Spey, Charles had now made another. Even if it is assumed that a battle had to be fought sooner rather than later, Culloden Moor was a very bad place for the Jacobites to fight. On such open and gently shelving ground, two equally matched armies could have fought with an equal chance. But the rebels were fewer than 6,000 men to Cumberland's 9,000, and they were inferior in artillery and vastly inferior in cavalry. They were, in fact, outnumbered and outclassed, and their best chance — perhaps their only chance — was to fight on ground favourable to themselves. Lord George Murray and the chiefs understood this very well. They urged Charles 'to retire to a strong ground on the other side of the water of Nairn' which they had reconnoitred and where they were sure that the highland army, if the Duke were to attack, would be able to fight to much better advantage; and if not attacked, they 'proposed (if no opportunity offered to attack him to advantage) to retire farther, and draw him up to the mountains, where we thought, without doubt, we might attack him at some pass or strong ground'.[16] This excellent advice was rejected, with disastrous consequences. Charles could not appreciate the old adage, 'Il faut reculer pour mieux sauter'; his was not a subtle mind. He seems to have believed that he could always win a straightforward battle. The rebels had won at Prestonpans and Charles believed that they had won at Falkirk. So why should they not win again? The young man's simple-mindedness, along with his blind belief in his ability always to advance and to win, was a fatal liability, propped up on this occasion by ignoring the facts that at Prestonpans he had faced a third-class army and at Falkirk an army whose own commander contributed only negligence and folly. But the Duke of Cumberland was neither negligent nor foolish, and while at Aberdeen he had assembled a strong and well-balanced force, with all the men and equipment needed for success.

The rebel army was drawn up in order of battle on Culloden moor on the morning of 15 April; but the enemy did not appear. So in the afternoon Charles suddenly put forward a new proposal. Under the influence of O'Sullivan, a captain in the French army and throughout the campaign the Pretender's Adjutant-General and evil genius, Charles proposed to march that very evening with all his forces and attack the King's army before dawn. Had this plan fully succeeded, most of Cumberland's men would have been killed in their tents where they slept. But the new proposal met with a very cool reception — night attacks are liable to cause more losses to the attackers than the defenders — and only when it was supported by Lord George Murray (who may have thought that anything was better than fighting on 'a plain moor') was it agreed to. On mustering the men, however, it was found that a great many of them had gone to Inverness to look for provisions, which were very scarce. Officers were sent to bring them back, 'but they refused to come, bidding the officers shoot them if they pleased, for they would not come back till they had got some food'.[17] But Charles was determined — he had previously declared that he would attack even if 'he had but a thousand men' — and the army set out at eight o'clock at night.

Six miles were covered in complete darkness, over rough and often wet and boggy ground. But the going was very slow. At two o'clock in the morning, still four miles from the Duke's camp near Nairn, this 'desperate attempt' had to be given up. Fresh troops might have achieved it. But a large proportion of Charles's men were hungry and ill-clad (the supply arrangements were little better than disgraceful) and 'many of the men had left the ranks, and had laid down . . . this must have been occasioned by faintness for want of food'.[18] The army dragged itself back to Culloden, 'fatigued and famished'. Most of the men presumably then tried to get some sleep, but a good number soon afterwards went off to Inverness to search once more for provisions of all kinds.

The return to Culloden was completed by six o'clock in the morning. At five o'clock the Duke's army had begun to march, and at about eight o'clock this most unwelcome news reached Charles at Culloden House. Instructions were at once given to recall the men who had gone to Inverness, but barring some extraordinary accident or miscalculation, the position of the Jacobite army was now hopeless. They had manoeuvred and marched themselves into a situation where they had no choice but to fight, and to fight on the most disadvantageous terms imaginable.

The rebels formed their order of battle close to Culloden House, with park walls protecting each flank. The Duke's army came in sight of them towards noon, at a distance of two and a half miles. The regiments at once formed into two lines flanked by cavalry, and continued to advance to within five hundred or six hundred yards of the enemy. The battle began precisely as the Duke would have wished it, with an exchange of artillery fire. The Jacobite gunfire did little harm, but the King's artillery was modern and well-served, and for the first time in the campaign the rebel army was exposed to a heavy and accurate cannonade. This continued for at least twenty minutes: some reports say forty minutes. Charles seems to have expected Cumberland to attack with his infantry, but 'finding his cannon rapidly thinning the Jacobite ranks, without experiencing any loss in return',[19] there was every reason for his not doing so. The cannonade therefore continued, smoke from the Royal artillery drifted over the rebel lines, and the rebels 'fluctuated extremely'. Suffering heavy losses and unable to reply, the Pretender's troops became desperate and could endure inaction no longer. Before any order to attack was received — although Charles, on horse-back well to the rear, belatedly gave such an order — the rebel centre and then the right wing broke out. The charge began in some confusion, which grew worse when the King's gunners switched from cannon balls to grapeshot, which 'swept the field as with a hailstorm'; and then the advancing highlanders ran into heavy musketry fire, some of it enfilading fire from a party of Campbells and from Wolfe's regiment which Cumberland had positioned on the wing for just such an opportunity. In spite of terrible losses, the rebels still rushed forward and attacked the King's troops sword in hand. 'The High-landers fought like furies . . . . It was dreadful to see the enemies' swords circling in the air as they were raised from the strokes: and no less to see the officers of the army, some cutting with their swords, others pushing with their spontoons, the sergeants running their halberts into the throats of the opponents, the men ramming their fixed bayonets up to the sockets.'[20] This desperate and ill-directed attack by half the rebel army fell almost entirely on two of Cumberland's front-line regiments, which inevitably gave way; and the rebels who remained came directly on to the second line of infantry. These soldiers waited until the enemy was almost upon them, and then fired together. Great numbers of the attackers fell. And such was the effect that those who did not fall were forced to turn back, climbing over the dead bodies of their comrades.

Meanwhile the rebel left wing had begun its advance, but slowly and with reluctance, due, it is said, to Charles having deprived the clans there of the honour of being on the right wing. However that may be, the left wing never closed within a hundred yards of the King's troops; there was an exchange of fire, and then, seeing the clans on the right completely broken and put to flight, the left wing also began to leave the field. Those of the rebel army who charged towards the King's troops fought with the utmost bravery; but good troop dispositions, rapid, heavy and sustained cannon-fire and musket-fire, backed up by furious resistance in hand-to-hand fighting, were altogether too much for the rebels; broadswords and a great attacking spirit were no longer enough.

Cumberland, who had been 'riding from right to left all the time of the action with . . . calmness and courage',[21] retained complete control of the situation; when the enemy broke he ordered his own infantry to stand and reform. It was the dragoons and light horse, who had carried out a flanking movement and were already attacking the insurgents' second line, who pursued the rebels. Their flight is often depicted as an absolute rout, but this is incorrect. The Jacobite right wing — what was left of it — was collected together by Lord George Murray and retreated 'with the greatest regularity', fighting a few brief delaying actions and successfully covered by the meagre Jacobite cavalry. The left wing and the centre, however, disintegrated. Mostly in small parties of four or five, these men made for Inverness, pursued by the dragoons; 'our horse . . . pursued them with sword and pistol and cut a great many of them down so that I never saw a small field so thick with dead'.[22] The dragoons had old scores to settle, and in the heat of battle — for firing was still going on — they showed little mercy. When Cumberland and the infantry advanced, 'they could hardly march for dead bodies'.

There is no doubt that Culloden was Cumberland's battle. Charles decided the place and the Duke decided almost everything else. He is usually given scant credit for a well-planned and economical victory which was gained at the cost of fewer than a hundred government dead and between two hundred and three hundred wounded. Instead, he is held responsible for endless atrocities, many of them committed only in the imagination of Jacobite historians and raconteurs. That there were atrocities, no one can doubt; there almost always are. They were probably rather worse than usual, for it was widely believed in the King's army — and with some justice — that at Prestonpans the rebels had slaughtered many defenceless and wounded men. Moreover, Culloden was the end of a bitter winter campaign, and the highlanders were regarded by all Englishmen and most Scotsmen as alien and barbarous, little better than animals — 'they came running upon our front-line like troops of hungry wolves'.[23] They were not a regular army, men whom soldiers could understand. Contrary to what is often stated, few men were killed in cold blood, but almost all by pursuers 'warm in their resentment'. The number of the Jacobite dead is unknown. At least 1,000 were killed on the field of battle, and perhaps as many again, possibly even 1,500, between the moor and Inverness.

Charles got away without difficulty. Always well to the rear, he left the field when the retreat became general, accompanied by Sir Thomas Sheridan, O'Sullivan and some other preferred friends. He made no attempt to stay with his men but sought instead to secure his own safety, and travelled that night towards Fort Augustus, to begin his five months of wandering in the highlands. Had he remained with his senior commanders instead of hurrying off to the west, he would have been able to escape with them to France in May, instead of playing the fugitive — and thus endangering many lives besides his own — until September. Lord George Murray retired to Ruthven in Badenoch with what was left of the army — perhaps 1,500 men — and only then discovered that the Pretender was already on his way to the Long Island, and had resolved to leave Scotland. Charles had sent some money to Ruthven for distribution among his followers, but he now recalled this money for his own use — surely the most heartless of his many egotistical and ill-considered actions. His final order was, 'Let every man seek his own safety the best way he can.' There was not a word of thanks for those who had risked everything on his behalf, and many thought that he gave so little indication of his own intentions and abandoned most of his followers so promptly because he feared that the Scots would betray him. If so, it shows how little he understood the hearts and minds of those whom he professed to lead.

The rebellion was now over and there were rejoicings 'in every town and village, nay, even thro' the country, and in private houses as far as the news had reached'.[24] The government, however, was left with the disagreeable task of making sure that the power to rebel was finally extinguished. After the '15, a distinctly lenient policy had been followed, many rebels being pardoned and no drastic or punitive measures taken. This policy, it seemed, had resulted in yet another rebellion. Ministers in Whitehall were determined not to make the same mistake again, so troops were sent all over the highlands to restore order, disarm the rebels and arrest the ringleaders. Cumberland instructed his men 'to behave with discretion, and to plunder none but by order',[25] but several of his subordinate commanders seem to have done pretty well as they pleased. Those who resisted or who were 'found in arms' were shot; fugitives were pursued and killed if possible; and many who did not 'come in immediately' had their houses burned and their cattle driven off. The situation got so far out of control that even loyal highlanders suffered from the depredations of raiding parties. These excesses did harm to everyone. But the main point was unforgettably driven home: 'The people of these Wild Countries' — the writer is referring especially to the west coast from Glenelg to Ardnamurchan — 'could never believe that they were Accessible 'till the King's Forces Scoured them after the Battle of Culloden which was a prodigious Surprize to the Inhabitants'.[26]

These operations finally extinguished the spirit of rebellion, as well as the power of the clans to make war in or beyond the highlands. They were supported by a Disarming Act; by an Act which forbade the wearing of tartan (which had served as the uniform of the rebel army); by an Act which abolished the hereditary power of the chiefs to administer justice within their own territories; and by transferring to the Crown no fewer than eleven highland estates belonging to rebel chiefs and arranging for their management and modernisation by Commissioners who met in Edinburgh. The old order was thus undermined. Tenants were no longer at the absolute beck and call of their chiefs. And when roads at last began to be made in the highlands and the ancient systems of land tenure and agriculture to be modernised, the old subsistence economy began to give way to something more productive, and men and their families no longer had to live like their forefathers, on the margin of subsistence.

Steps had also to be taken to deal with the more prominent of the rebels who failed to make good their escape. Four peers were tried and found guilty of treason; three of them, including Lovat, were executed. Forty-one other individuals were attainted, that is to say, declared guilty of treason and thus made liable to execution, their titles being annulled and their property confiscated. In all, one hundred and twenty people were sentenced to death, a third of them deserters or spies, not a large number considering that 3,400 had been arrested, the very existence of the government threatened, the life of the country seriously disturbed, and hundreds of thousands of loyal citizens alarmed, many for their lives, for a period of over six months. The policy of severity where necessary, and lenience and mercy where these would not lead to further disaffection, owed not a little to the advice of Duncan Forbes.

Most of the well-known leaders of the rebellion got away. Perth escaped, only to die on board the ship that was taking him to France. Sir Thomas Sheridan made his way to Rome, where he died a few months later. Lord John Drummond, rescued by the same French frigate as Perth and Sheridan, died at Bergen am Zoom in 1747, and

Lochiel, having been rewarded for his services with well-paid command of the Albany regiment in the service of Louis XV, died in 1748. Lord George Murray, after eight months hiding in Glenartney, escaped to France and lived mostly in Germany until his death in 1760. O'Sullivan reached France, quarrelled with Charles, married a lady with money, and died about 1761. Lord Elcho, lonely and embittered, likewise escaped to France, settled nowhere for long, and died in Paris in 1787. He had spent much time (to no purpose) trying to persuade Charles to repay a debt of £1,500 which was certainly owed to him.

As for Charles himself, the author of a rebellion which cost the lives of at least 3,000 men and caused much bloodshed and misery besides, his life after Culloden was neither distinguished nor edifying. During the summer of 1746 the French navy made a number of unsuccessful and costly attempts to rescue him, and then in September he was finally taken off from Lochnanuagh by a privateer from St Malo and returned to France. One of his first acts was to write to his father, adding a postscript about Lord George Murray in which he stated that 'it wd be of ye most Dangerous Consequences iff such a Divill was not secured immediately in sum Castle'.[27] The Old Pretender, who could recognise venom and injustice when he saw them, wrote a soothing reply, in which, however, he observed that if Lord George 'has been on several occasions of a different opinion from you or other people, I don't see what crime there is in that'[28] — sure proof that he understood Charles's character only too well. Soon the young man resumed his intrigues in Paris and Madrid, showing his usual total inability to understand the political facts of the situation, including the facts of the Seven Years War, or the opinions of others. He thought, not that the world owed him a living, but that it owed him a kingdom. But his star had set. In 1748 he was ordered out of France, and a few months later out of Avignon. He went to Rome. In 1750 he appeared briefly in London, probably in connection with another ill-conceived plot, and it was then that he took the opportunity to be converted to the Anglican faith. He had also, in the meantime, taken to drink. (Back in 1745 his father had referred with significant disapproval to Charles's 'slight taste for wine'.) In 1752 he publicly established as his mistress a lady whom he had met in Scotland, Clementina Walkinshaw, and a year later she bore him a daughter. Not much is known about Clementina, except that she also drank. Their life together, which lasted for about ten years — it is not easy to say precisely when it began, or when it ended — was one of perpetual quarrelling and recourse to the bottle by both man and mistress. At the age of forty Charles was an irretrievable alcoholic, prematurely old, withdrawn, peevish and suspicious. At the age of fifty-one he married a girl of eighteen, who took refuge eight years later in a convent. What her life had been like can be gathered from a letter written to Charles by a correspondent in London in 1776: 'All my countrymen who return from Italy are surprised that your amiable consort stays with you: there is not a single person who would not go any length to deliver her'.[29] He died in Florence in 1788, and the Pope — although Charles had reverted to Roman Catholicism many years before — refused to allow the funeral service to be held in Rome.

As for the War of the Austrian Succession, which Charles had seen as his great opportunity, this was brought to an end by the Congress of Aix-la-Chapelle, two years after Culloden. Apart from King Frederick of Prussia and his acquisitions, all the nations involved had had their ups and downs. France had gained many victories, but she had also suffered reverses, especially at ·sea, and both her commerce and her finances were reduced to a sorry state. Great Britain had done moderately well, but the most noticeable result of her continental adventures seemed to most of King George's subjects to be that the prosperous and populated parts of their country had been attacked by an army of highlanders, and that the Netherlands were overrun by the French. When it came to negotiations, Louis was disposed to be generous. France regained Louisburg and Cape Breton — 'the people's darling acquisition' — but evacuated the Austrian Netherlands and Madras. The question of the boundaries between the British and the French settlements in North America was left entirely undecided, to cause further trouble in the very near future. But one matter was forever settled. France recognised George II as the King of Great Britain, agreed to respect the Hanoverian succession, and permanently excluded the Old Pretender and his son from France. The troops of the Duke of Cumberland and the sailors of Admiral Vernon had not fought in vain. Jacobitism, for just over half a century a minor source of trouble and of possible war in Europe, had ceased to be a factor of any importance.

Notes and References

1. Quoted in Menary, op. cit., pp. 243–4.
2. Quoted ibid., p. 202.
3. Home, op. cit., p. 167.
4. Ibid., p. 170.
5. Ibid., p. 176.
6. Quoted in Tomasson and Buist, op. cit., p. 105.
7. Home, op. cit., p. 172.
8. Quoted in Ewald, op. cit., p. 212.
9. Quoted in Tomasson and Buist, op. cit., p. 116.
10. Quoted in Ewald, op. cit., pp. 217–18.
11. Quoted in Menary, op. cit., p. 274.
12. Quoted ibid., p. 280.
13. Ibid., p. 276.
14. Home, op. cit., p. 211.
15. Sir Robert Strange, *Memoirs*, ed. J Dennistoun (Edinburgh, 1855), pp. 60–1.
16. Quoted in Home, op. cit., pp. 361–2.
17. Ibid., p. 220.
18. Lord George Murray, quoted in Home, op. cit., p. 365.
19. Quoted in Tomasson and Buist, op. cit., p. 152.
20. Ibid., p. 158.
21. Quoted in Speck, op. cit., p. 139.
22. Quoted in Tomasson and Buist, op. cit., p. 172.
23. Quoted in Speck, op. cit., p. 147.
24. Quoted ibid., p. 158.
25. Quoted ibid., p. 166.
26. *The Highlands of Scotland in 1750*, ed. Lang (Edinburgh, 1898), p. 68.
27. Quoted in K. Tomasson, *The Jacobite General* (Edinburgh, 1958), pp. 255, 256.
28. Ibid.
29. Quoted in Petrie, op. cit., p. 449.

PART III

THE LAST JACOBITE RISING

6 THE HOUSE OF STUART

'The blow I saw given; and can truly say, with a sad heart. At the instant whereof, I remember well, there was such a groan by the thousands there present as I never heard before, and desire I may never hear again.' These words were written by Philip Henry, a spectator at the execution of Charles I, which took place outside the Banqueting Hall in Whitehall on a bitter January afternoon in 1649. Those who were responsible for this act of judicial murder supposed that they had brought an end to the line of Stuart kings, who had ruled in Britain for almost three hundred years, and to the monarchy itself. They were, of course, mistaken. The execution of Charles was carried out 'in the name of the people of England' but beyond any doubt it did not have the people's consent; they had not been consulted, and their disapproval was widely evident although it could not be openly expressed; it is significant that as soon as the execution was over, two troops of mounted soldiers cleared the streets. Few who saw the terrible event were not filled with dismay, for Charles was a man of high principle, a king and a gentleman. Clarendon, who was a moderate in politics and a shrewd judge of men, left a fair and accurate portrait:

> He was the worthiest gentleman, the best friend, the best husband, the best father, and the best Christian, that the age in which he lived produced. And if he were not the best King, if he were without some parts and qualities which have made some Kings great and happy, no other prince was ever unhappy who was possessed of half his virtues and endearments, and so much without any kind of vice.[1]

When Charles was beheaded many may have divined, and certainly many must have hoped, that one day his cause would triumph again. But none could have foreseen that ninety-seven years after his death the last battle on behalf of the House of Stuart would be fought by his great grandson, and lost.

The problems which led to the Civil War and the execution of the King, and which neither the war nor the regicide solved, were of three different kinds, all complex, all equally important, and all

153

inter-related. Religion — almost inevitably in the seventeenth century — was one of these problems. The Reformation had carried most people in England and Scotland — but not in Ireland — into the Protestant camp, and because religion and toleration very seldom went together in those days of strong belief, a new reason appeared for persecution at home and war abroad. Fear and hatred of Roman Catholics and of the Roman Catholic Church — a great political as well as religious organisation — became a powerful emotion that affected everything. The Marian persecution, the Spanish Armada, the plots against the life of Queen Elizabeth, the desperate struggle of the Dutch against Spain — all these and other politico-religious events proved how strong and persistent was the threat to the religion and the order of life which Englishmen and Scotsmen cherished. Protestants felt that they had always to be on their guard. They understood very well that there were degrees of closeness to Rome, and subtle ways in which Romanisation might begin. And because of this, variations in religious ritual or doctrine which seem to us of little or no consequence assumed an importance so great that men were willing to die or emigrate rather than accept them.

Secondly, there was the question of the balance of power as between King and Parliament. Absolutism was not a popular idea in England. Parliaments expected to be heard, and rulers even as powerful as Henry VIII or Queen Elizabeth had depended to some extent on adroit parliamentary management in order to maintain their position and carry out their policies. By the early seventeenth century the Commons had a declared interest, which could be neither ignored nor set aside, in almost all questions of finance and religion, and of the conduct of foreign policy which religion fundamentally affected. In 1621 Parliament told James I that 'the liberties, franchises, privileges and jurisdiction of Parliament are the ancient and undoubted birthright and inheritance of the subjects of England'; and went on to remind the King that 'the defence of the realm and of the Church of England, and the making and maintenance of laws and redress of grievances . . . are proper subjects and matter of counsel and debate in Parliament'. None of which James I liked in the very least, for he firmly believed that kings were accountable to God alone; and he promptly dissolved Parliament. This struggle for authority continued throughout the reign of Charles I, when it was complicated and embittered by Charles's reliance — he was only twenty-five when he came to the throne — on a few favourite ministers.

It was Charles's misfortune to be the first monarch to take the idea of the non-accountability of princes and to oppose it, in practice, against the idea of the sovereignty of Parliament. In the political struggle in which he engaged, he was perhaps rather naive; and he had the further misfortune to be guided by ambitious, energetic and often remarkably narrow-minded advisers. Buckingham, extravagant and erratic, loved and trusted by the King and hated by Parliament, was assassinated in 1628. In that same year, Thomas Wentworth began to exercise jurisdiction in the name and in the interests of the Crown, first in the north of England and then in Ireland, and to use his absolute powers in so ruthless a manner that all men feared for their safety. The methods of Stalin were anticipated in England. In 1641 Parliament secured his condemnation and execution. In religious affairs Charles was no better served. The aim of Archbishop Laud was to restrict the intense and varied religious life of his day into a narrow cage of carefully specified rules and rituals; to secure religious conformity by means of political repression. His efforts inevitably produced more hatred than conformity. And when he attempted to impose his high church style and an Anglican prayerbook on the Scots, force was met with force. Presbyterian in religion, even less inclined to compromise than the English, and still possessing a military capability that was far from negligible, the Scots put an army into the field and occupied Durham and Northumberland. After this event, and the execution of Wentworth, civil war was inevitable.

The third difference between King and Parliament was of a more nebulous kind, but possibly, in the long run, was even more important. Charles put his finger on it when he said, shortly before his execution, 'A subject and a sovereign are clean different things'. This proposition, like many other propositions, is capable of two quite different interpretations. If Charles meant, as he sometimes did mean, that only a sovereign could command and all his people could only obey, then his position was untenable. But if he meant that a hereditary monarch was a special person, playing a vital role in the state and in the lives of all his subjects that no other person could possibly play, then he was on very strong ground. Monarchy was the normal and accepted state of affairs in the seventeenth century. Moreover, monarchs were accustomed to exercise a very great deal of personal authority, and to some extent they were expected to do so. This was because the anarchic and fissiparous forces within nations in the seventeenth century were quite powerful, and the prime necessity was strong government. The monarch was expected to give a lead, and if skilful and successful — like the Great Queen — there was little objection to that lead being continuous and all-powerful. The idea of a shared authority, on the other hand, gave rise to uneasiness because it implied discussion and delay, quite possibly indecision and even conflict. And if authority was to be shared, who was to share it? The wealthy landowners and great merchants who filled the House of Commons no more represented the nation than did the King; indeed, they represented it a good deal less, for they were all rich men and had sectional interests to defend. A king, so the argument ran, could be both just and generous; he could stand between the poor and their oppressors; and was more likely to do so than anyone else because, being king, he could not himself be oppressed. It was therefore better that he did not have to bargain, or bargain much, with the men of property in Parliament. And there is also the point that a king — especially one who claims to rule by divine right — is both a man and a mystery. He personifies the nation; and can be admired and perhaps even loved. Who ever loved a Parliament! And because life is not all strictly rational, hereditary kingship makes a profound appeal to deep-seated emotions of loyalty, drawing men to its support through their natural human sympathy for tradition and the continuity of human existence. And this is why the contemptuous treatment that was accorded by the Parliament men to Charles I's claim that 'a subject and a sovereign are clean different things' helped to make that claim seem acceptable to large numbers of people in Great Britain, both at the time and since.

As a political experiment, the Commonwealth that was established after Charles's execution was not a disaster, but neither, on the other hand, was it a success. Like most dictatorships, it began by achieving an enforced national unity and conformity which, because it was enforced, was more apparent than real and had within it the stresses and contradictions that were bound to make it fall apart in due time. The Royalists were treated with great severity. All those who had been in arms for the King had part of their income or their property confiscated, while large numbers were exiled or imprisoned. The Scots and the Irish fared equally badly. Having no sympathy for the Puritan extremists, the Scots welcomed Charles II in 1650 and crowned him King of Scotland at Scone; as a result of which Cromwell invaded Scotland, defeated a Scots army at Dunbar, abolished the Scots Parliament and the General Assembly of the Kirk, and installed an English army of occupation. Thus the existence of Scotland as an independent nation was at last, albeit temporarily, destroyed. In Ireland, a brief campaign to make the country safe for English Protestants led to the eviction of countless Irish families from their homes and their livelihood, the massacres of Drogheda and Wexford, the disappearance of the Irish Parliament and the proscription of the Catholic religion which was the religion of the great majority of the inhabitants of the country. A superficial order was thus imposed on a scene of profound confusion and misery.

In foreign affairs the Protectorate pursued policies which were almost equally unfortunate. Commercial and maritime rivalry with Holland developed into a war which lasted for three years and was at once succeeded by another, which lasted for rather longer, carried on in alliance with Sweden and France against Spain. The years of the Commonwealth, it has been truly said, were filled with aggression and bloodshed. Damage to trade was enormous and discontent became severe, so much so that several years before the death of the Lord Protector numerous influential people in Britain began to contact the exiled Charles and to make arrangements which would smooth the way for his return. When Cromwell died in 1658 the restoration of the monarchy was only a matter of time.

Charles II resumed his inheritance not by force of arms but by popular acclaim. Pepys saw him pass along the Strand on his way to Whitehall in May 1660: 'Infinite the crowd of people and the horsemen, citizens and noblemen of all sorts. The shouting and joy expressed by all is past imagination'. The Protectorate had made few friends; Charles was welcome because the restoration of the monarchy was welcome, and he was perhaps particularly welcome in London because he was felt to be a Londoner. His early career was what used to be called romantic; that is to say, full of stress, danger, women and sudden reversals of fortune. Born at St James's Palace, he lived in England until he was sixteen, when for safety he was sent abroad after the battle of Naseby. He returned five years later, in 1651, to fight Cromwell's forces at Worcester, where he was completely defeated, and after numerous hair-breadth escapes which demonstrated his courage and resource he reached the coast near Brighton and made his way to France. Here and in the Netherlands, at Paris, Cologne and Bruges, he spent almost ten years, living a peripatetic and sometimes hand-to-mouth existence, with no security and few friends, surrounded by unhappy exiles, some of whom were as poor as himself, and treated with scant courtesy by the courtiers and politicians of France.

The people of Britain knew very little about Charles when they welcomed him back in 1660. They were delighted to see him simply because he personified the monarchy and the dynasty. They had no idea that their new King was a man of the world, self-educated, urbane, of infinite charm and sympathetic to almost all the most advanced and modern tendencies of the age. They took him on trust; and he was a great success. Times more puritanical than our own have condemned Charles as licentious. Certainly his fondness for female company was unabashed. On his return to England he left behind him, it is said, his seventeenth mistress (if that is indeed the correct number) and she was at once succeeded by Barbara Palmer, to the exploration of whose charms the King is supposed to have devoted his first night back in London; Barbara Palmer was succeeded by — to name only a few — Nell Gwyn, Lucy Walters, Mary Davies and the Duchesses of Cleveland, Richmond and Portsmouth. The extended list could be described as impressive or deplorable, according to one's attitude; it is certainly very long. But his contemporaries were not much concerned — kings were expected to have mistresses. What was much more important was that Charles attended to the affairs of state to very good effect. He was, indeed, a man of high intelligence and good sense, and a master-politician. Unlike most of his critics, he was tolerant of the opinions and aspirations of others. He did not share the vindictive attitude of many of those exiles who returned with him in 1660; he did not seek to 'put down' either the Puritans or the Catholics; he did not try to challenge Parliament. Yet he always contrived to keep control of events. The struggle with Shaftesbury, which was the great crisis of his reign, left that nobleman and the other parliamentary leaders utterly discredited, and Charles ruled during the last years with despotic power — a power that was secured by consent and not by force. He was immensely popular. It is true that in some ways he stood for the old order. But he also moved with the times, for he introduced reforms into the administration of the Navy, the Treasury and territories overseas; he founded the Royal Society, the Mathematical School at Christ's Hospital and the Royal Observatory at Greenwich; and he was the patron of some of the foremost writers and artistic men of his day, such as Lely, Dryden and Wren. The country prospered. And all this was due in large part to the work of one who is often supposed to have been more interested in pleasure than in work, and who is sometimes remembered simply as a tall dark man who walked with his spaniels in St James's Park, and fed the ducks.

When Charles died suddenly at the age of fifty-five it was a great misfortune for the country. He was succeeded by his brother; and although the monarchy seemed marvellously secure, within four years James II and the House of Stuart were swept away by a revolution. James had several admirable qualities. He was a man of great personal courage, as he showed in several campaigns on land, and also at sea when he commanded the British fleet in a victory over the Dutch in 1665. He was moreover a man of principle, and he was honest and straightforward. Unfortunately, these qualities showed to better advantage on the quarter-deck than on the throne. James's fundamental trouble was that he was a staunch Roman Catholic and he did not try to disguise the fact. His chief aim was to secure religious toleration, which his enemies represented as the first stage in a relentless campaign to return the nation to Rome. To the great majority of James's subjects the ideal of religious toleration was not acceptable — in this James was far ahead of his time — and his attempts to achieve it were, to say the least, unfortunate. His task was made more difficult by his simultaneous campaign for a greatly increased standing army, which would have made him independent of the Whigs, who controlled the militia, and by the renewed persecution of the Protestants in France which began, as luck would have it, in 1685. But the chief obstacles were James's own haste and obstinacy. What might have been achieved in twenty years with some compromises and perhaps some dissimulation, the King sought to achieve fully, openly and in haste. Seldom have frankness and honesty served a good cause so ill. The birth of his son in 1688 gave every promise of a Catholic succession, and hostility to the King reached dangerous levels. A brave man but an incompetent politician, James seems to have been totally bewildered by events, and his accustomed resolution deserted him. He fled to France, although he still had distinguished supporters in Britain and he might well have retained his kingdom if he had stayed to rally his people against the Dutch troops of William of Orange.

The revolution of 1688, was, like most revolutions, the work of a minority. It took most of the country by surprise, because although the King had become unpopular, there was no national uprising and his sudden departure was quite unexpected; it is scarcely an exaggeration to say that the British woke up one morning and found that they were to be ruled by a Dutchman. As for William, his motives have always been perfectly clear. He was the inveterate Protestant enemy of Catholic France, and he accepted an invitation to 'bring over an army and secure the infringed liberties' of the people of Great Britain solely in order that he might mobilise British money and manpower in support of his tireless resistance against Louis XIV. He did not come for love. And although in the course of time he became respected, he was never loved, for he was cheerless, demanding and sullen. He used men as far as he was able; and his manoeuvres to extend his own authority resulted, on the whole, in a further diminution of the power and popularity of the Crown.

After fourteen years William was succeeded by Anne, who was a daughter of James II. Anne was a popular Queen, for two important reasons; first, she was a Stuart; and secondly, she was a devout and loyal member of the Church of England. Unfortunately, constant ill-health and domestic troubles conspired to prevent her from play-ing a dominant political role, and she was further hampered by the conflict between her religious principles and her genuine attachment to her family in exile. To add to her troubles, she was for some years unduly influenced by the domineering Duchess of Marlborough, who was a Whig; and in later years she had to work with a Tory administration managed by Harley and Bolingbroke, both addicted to the bottle and the latter with a passion for women which made the conduct of Charles II look like an essay in self-denial. A somewhat ineffective Queen gave politicians their chance; and historians are accustomed to rejoice that it was during Anne's reign that party government was inaugurated. But no one could claim that the spec-tacle was an elevating one. Bolingbroke explained the attitude of himself and his colleagues when he took office in 1710:

I am afraid that we came to Court in the same disposition as all parties have done; that the principal spring of our actions was to have the government of the state in our hands; that our principal views were the conservation of this power, great employment to ourselves, and great opportunities of rewarding those who had helped to raise us, and of hurting those in opposition to us. It is, however, true that with these considerations of private and party interest there were others intermingled which had for their object the public good of the nation — at least, what we took to be such.[2]

This statement of political motive seems to be valid for other centuries besides the eighteenth, and makes it easier to understand the value of there being some restraint upon the actions of elected politicians. The British people in the eighteenth century knew very well what rascals they had to deal with — Adam Smith's comment later in the century might well have been made much earlier: 'All for ourselves, and nothing for other people, seems, in every age of the world, to have been the vile maxim of the masters of mankind' — and they looked to the monarchy to keep the excesses of their so-called representatives in Parliament within bounds. But neither William nor Anne was very successful in this regard. And this was particularly unfortunate, because the succession — Anne having no heir — became a party struggle between Whigs and Tories, each faction desperate to ensure that Anne's successor would be someone — no matter what his or her qualifications — who would help to keep the other faction out of office and would otherwise interfere as little as possible in the government of the country.

The moment was a crucial one in British history, for the question came down to this: was there or was there not to be an effective monarchy? According to the Act of Settlement passed in 1701 the throne could not be occupied by a Roman Catholic. This meant, when Anne was dying in 1714, that she would be succeeded by George Louis, Elector of Hanover, who had never set foot in the British Isles and who could not even speak English. This possibility was so absurd that everyone was bound to consider the alternative; why not prefer James Edward, son of James II, grandson of Charles I, born in London and now living just across the Channel at St Germain? Alas! he was a Roman Catholic. And there was no other choice. The Whigs were committed to George, whom they were confident they could manage. The Tories were the Church of England party, the one-time Cavaliers, and those on the right wing of the party were Jacobites. The Tories were sympathetic to James, although they feared his Roman Catholicism; and this was very much the position of the great majority of the population. Had James been willing to renounce his faith and enter the Church of England the throne would have been his. But to his lasting credit he would not do so. Instead, he wrote to the Queen, Harley and Bolingbroke as follows: 'All the just securities that can reasonably be asked for your religion, liberties and properties I shall be most willing to grant, and as that can be expected from a man of principle and true honour I am ready to comply with it, and you know I have too much of both to require more of me'.[3] James was a Roman Catholic but he was not a bigot; he was always a most honourable man and he would have kept his word; the Church of England would have been safe with James as King. But this was not quite what men like Harley and Bolingbroke wanted. They were not accustomed to having to cope with honesty in politics, and a King who had a mind of his own did not much appeal to them. What they wanted was a complaisant King and themselves to stay in office, so they remained non-committal about James and at the eleventh hour Bolingbroke even tried to do a deal with the Whigs. But he had too little to offer. Queen Anne died, the Elector of Hanover became King of Great Britain, and the Whigs obtained control.

From 1714 until the last Jacobite rising in 1745-6 Great Britain was ruled by two kings and three principal ministers, all of the latter being Whigs. The Kings made only a very small contribution to the life of the country — it is significant that only students of history know anything about them. George I was born in Hanover and died there, which was reasonable enough because his interest in British problems was approximately nil. He is otherwise remembered chiefly for his meanness, his disgraceful treatment of his wife, his vulgar tastes, his vulgar German mistresses, and his reliance on indifferent Latin when he had to talk to his ministers. George II, who did not leave Hanover until he was over thirty, was not much of an improvement. On the battle-field he did well, fighting with determination at Oudenarde when he was twenty-five and leading the British infantry to victory at Dettingen when he was sixty. But his intellectual abilities were moderate, and his sympathies were entirely Hanoverian. His effectiveness as a King can be judged by his observation that 'ministers are the king in this country' and by his reputation for parsimony, carried to such lengths as made his father — whom he detested — seem generous. So far had the British monarchy fallen. Those who looked back to the nobility and splendid bearing of Charles I or to the wit and matchless political capabilities of his son must have wondered what the nation had done to deserve two such little kings as George I and George II.

With the Stuart dynasty out of the way the Whigs now reigned supreme, and for twenty years the country was governed by Sir Robert Walpole, the greatest Whig of all. Walpole was able, level-headed and a past master in the art of political corruption. Like many modern politicians, he had no serious political ideology and he believed only in the advantages of peace abroad and the continuance of his own power at home. Apart from fearing loss of office he was disturbed only by fear of the Jacobites, whom he persecuted when possible and against whom he maintained a network of spies spread through every capital in Europe. Under the Great Man, as he was facetiously called, the life of the nation became miserably utilitarian, and worse still, it became corrupt as it had never been corrupt before. The patronage of letters gave way to patronage of another sort. 'All these men have their price' is one of the few apothegms that Walpole has left to history; and it is a maxim on the basis of which he constantly and openly acted. Votes were bought and sold, and systematic patronage was used to such an extent that even men who wished to remain honest became corrupted. Only those who firmly believed in something higher than their own advantage could stand out, and this makes comprehensible Walpole's peculiar hatred of the supporters of the Old Pretender. Loyalty was not a thing that Walpole understood.

It is true that the people prospered; but nevertheless they were not content. The reason is not hard to find. Walpole's was a repressive regime, in which criticism of the Glorious Revolution was liable to be looked upon as treason and anything resembling active opposition to the government might easily lead to imprisonment or even to the gallows itself. The Whigs' sense of insecurity was enormous. In 1722, for example, an absurd Jacobite plot, which never had the smallest prospect of succeeding, caused the suspension of the Habeas Corpus Act for no less than twelve months. Fourteen years later, in 1736, Walpole and his colleagues responded to the Porteous Riot in Edinburgh, when the captain of the city guard was lynched by a midnight mob, with measures so tyrannical that even some of the government's own supporters opposed them. Civil and religious liberties, which were supposed to have been guaranteed by the Revolution Settlement, were never safe with Sir Robert Walpole.

Feeling against the government was particularly strong among four groups of people. First, there were the Roman Catholics. Numbering at least one tenth and possibly as much as one fifth of the population, they were relentlessly discriminated against on account of their religion. They could not conduct religious services openly, and they were debarred from holding any public office, civil or military, and from voting in Parliament. Inevitably they were dissatisfied with things as they were. Secondly, there were the Tories, kept out of office by the triumphant Whigs. The Tories were old-fashioned and traditional in their outlook, not 'modern' and commercial. They identified with the Church of England, and were strong supporters of the monarchy although they had serious misgivings about what had happened to it. Thirdly, a large but unknown proportion of the people of Scotland were opposed, many of them bitterly opposed, to the Union of Parliaments which had been engineered in 1707. The Act of Union was a political job, and the Union was in fact a euphemism for the abolition of the Scots Parliament and of the Scots Privy Council. The result, predictably, was rule from Westminster which few people in Scotland wanted. Advocates of the Union had predicted, possibly sincerely, that Scotland would secure numerous economic advantages from what was proposed, but for many years no advantages appeared. Instead, taxes became more oppressive than before and economic adjustment proved difficult. Finally, there were the Jacobites, who, by definition, were opposed to the House of Hanover and whose opposition inevitably merged into opposition to the Whigs. These four groups overlapped but were not identical — for example, not all Scotsmen were Jacobites and not all Jacobites were Roman Catholics. The government hated them all. But it was the Jacobites whom the Whigs and the Georges really feared.

Attempts to get rid of the House of Hanover began almost as soon as George I arrived. His coming caused no joy; during the summer of 1715 there were riots in so many different parts of the country that a general rising in favour of the House of Stuart seemed imminent. A rising was, in fact, planned for September; and had it been properly organised and led, it would almost certainly have succeeded. The Whigs were already very unpopular, and a well-informed estimate of the feeling of the population was that 'five out of six are for the King', i.e. James Edward. But the Jacobites were seldom good plotters. On this occasion the government either discovered or divined their intentions, and it acted energetically and ruthlessly to prevent the start of any serious challenge to its position, at any rate in England. The Jacobite plan was for several risings to take place simultaneously in the west, supported by subsidiary risings in the north and in Scotland. Arms were assembled. But before anything else could be done, the government began its arrests. Numerous prominent Jacobites were seized in their homes, others fled, one attempted to commit suicide, and the House of Commons supinely agreed to the 'preventive' arrest of six of its own members. With the Jacobite leaders out of the way, the government moved troops into the west of England, and James's plan to sail to Plymouth and put himself at the head of his forces became meaningless. In Scotland the Jacobites fared little better. The Earl of Mar, who raised the standard at Braemar on 6 September, was a complete disaster from the Jacobite point of view. He seems to have appointed himself to lead the rising; and it is something of a mystery why the other Scots Jacobites accepted him as their commander, for he had previously done his best (unsuccessfully) to ingratiate himself with George I and he had no military experience. In spite of these deficiencies, Mar soon found himself at the head of an army of 5,000 men, and his position was strengthened by the appearance of small Jacobite forces in the lowlands of Scotland and in Northumberland. There was now an opportunity to strike a decisive blow against the House of Hanover and the Whigs, but all that Mar did at this point was to detach 1,000 men from his army to join the Jacobites further south. Under MacIntosh of Borlum, this detachment carried out Mar's orders with great skill, crossing the Forth unseen and even manoeuvring to capture Edinburgh, but it could find no worthwhile strategic objective. Borlum joined the contingents from Northumberland and the Borders, and the little army marched south as far as Preston. They took the town and held it for a few days, but as the expected rising further south had come to nothing there were plenty of government troops to spare and the Jacobites in Preston were soon compelled to surrender.

On the day before the Whigs recovered Preston there was fought the battle of Sheriffmuir. Mar had at last decided to move south, now being in command of an army of over 9,000 men. He encountered the Duke of Argyll near Dunblane, and the battle was fought on ground of Argyll's choosing, suitable for cavalry. This put Mar at a disadvantage, for his cavalry was weak; on the other hand, his forces outnumbered those of Argyll by at least three to one, and he should have been able to win a convincing victory. The battle began with the usual exchange of musketry fire, followed by a highland charge against Argyll's right wing. This charge was somewhat broken up by a flank attack by the government dragoons, the highlanders began to fall back, and in a short time Argyll and half his army had the upper hand and were pursuing Mar's left wing towards the River Allan. But elsewhere the position was reversed. The Hanoverian troops gave way before the Jacobite right wing, and fled back towards Stirling, pursued by Mar's men. Both commanders realised, too late, what had happened, and tried to rein in their pursuing forces and regain control of the situation. Argyll could collect no more than 1,000 men. His position appeared to be hopeless, for the Jacobite army had not scattered to the same extent, and before nightfall Mar had gathered together enough men to resume the battle with a numerical superiority of approximately four to one. Had Mar made a second attack, that evening or the next day, Argyll could not have survived, for he was without reserves. But Mar seems to have had no grasp of the situation, and instead of attacking he quietly withdrew to the north, leaving the astonished Hanoverians in possession of the field; the '15 was over.

The story of this affair is in some ways even more surprising than that of the '45. In 1715 the Jacobites had a far better opportunity to get rid of the House of Hanover than they were ever to have again. That the Whigs were very unpopular there can be no doubt — the riots and demonstrations that took place all over England in those years are proof of that; and the men who were ready to rise in Plymouth, Bristol and Bath were stopped from doing so only by the promptitude of the government (well served by its spies) in throwing their leaders into jail. In Northumberland the Jacobites took to arms, and had they been able in good time to reach Lancashire or Wales, they would certainly have been joined by many others. Men were under arms for James in the south of Scotland; and Mar had had no great difficulty in recruiting an army of 9,000 or 10,000 men, one that was between two and three times as large as all the Hanoverian forces in Scotland. The Jacobites therefore had all the · means they needed for the overthrow of the House of Hanover, except one; leadership. There was no one in the west of England with the qualities required, and when anything was done it was done too slowly, and too late. In Scotland, Mar assumed the mantle of leader unasked, and conducted a campaign of quite absurd incompetence. A good Jacobite general, given Mar's forces, would almost certainly have reached London. The Duke of Berwick, a first-class commander who was James's half brother, and who was prevented solely by his service in the French army from accepting James's request that he would replace Mar as commander-in-chief, would surely have done so.

Moreover, it must be emphasised that Mar was not only an incompetent Jacobite commander; he was also a most incongruous one. Causes depend upon persons, and if persons are worth anything they depend upon ideals. Mar seems not to have had any. And yet the Jacobites were, above all, men of an ideal, the ideal of

hereditary monarchy. They believed that kingship was above politics, and that loyalty to the annointed King and to his heirs was the
only true foundation of social existence. Their support for the
House of Stuart was thus not a matter of expediency or commercial
advantage, but of honour and loyalty. No doubt there were
schemers among the Jacobites, men who thought only of their own
advantage, of getting the better of their neighbours, of rising in the
world, of political manoeuvring, commercial prosperity, economic
progress and all the other forms of vanity and futility which are now
so familiar to us and which are no doubt the proper objects of
admiration in a materialistic age. But the alternative style of civilisation still existed in the eighteenth century. There were traces and
vestiges of it all over Great Britain — there still are — and in the
highlands of Scotland before 1750 the old patterns of belief and
behaviour were predominant and continued almost uncorrupted by
'modern' ideas.

Celtic civilisation, which found its last refuge in Ireland as well as
in the highlands of Scotland, was already old when the Romans
invaded Britain. The Romans despised this civilisation, and so did
the 'enlightened' men of the eighteenth century; in both periods of
history the members of celtic society were often referred to by their
enemies as 'animals'. Yet this society had prevailed all over Western
Europe for many centuries. It maintained itself by a system of
graded obligations of relationship and service; counted its wealth in
terms of fighting power, of herds and flocks, and in treasure of
metal; and produced an art of aristocratic patronage, devoted to the
adornment of warriors and their equipment, sometimes of their
women — an art which is at once refined, elaborate, clever, ambig-
uous and uncanny. It was also a civilisation built upon personal
loyalties and devoted to war. Raiding for booty or revenge was the
supreme and perpetual occupation of the heroic celtic world. Great
deeds were celebrated in poems and sagas, for example in Cu
Chulainn's boast:

> Three things countless on the cattle-raid
> Which have fallen by my hand:
> Hosts of cattle, men and steeds,
> I have slaughtered on all sides.

Largely destroyed by the Romans, this civilisation nevertheless continued for centuries in more remote areas because it was immensely

tough and resilient, maintained great continuity of tradition, and satisfied deep-seated human cravings for comradeship and battle. For all of these as well as for more immediate reasons it was from the highlands that the Old and Young Pretenders drew their chief support. During the '45 Charles Edward often referred to 'his brave highlanders', and it was right that he should do so, for they were the backbone of his army.

In the eighteenth century most Englishmen and many Scotsmen thought of the highlander as 'a wild man dwelling in the woods and mountains, and a born thief', and they no doubt shared the opinion of James VI, who once said that Inverness, for long a frontier town where Gaelic and English were spoken side by side, was 'surrounded on all sides by most aggressive and rebellious tribes, the clans'. For two hundred years after the death of James VI the highlands changed only a little. By the 1740s the clans had begun to be affected by the spread of commerce, and of law as understood in Edinburgh and London; but almost everywhere the structure of society continued to consist of close-knit families and clans, ruled by a chief, below whom came the 'grades of nobility' — the chieftains and the tacksmen. The system continued in the highlands long after it had vanished elsewhere because the country was so mountainous and difficult to traverse that unified military control, and hence unified government, could not be established. Small, rural, largely isolated communities therefore remained, organised in separate districts each under the leadership of a chief, making their own laws and conducting their own affairs. The chief settled all disputes and regulated the life of the community at his discretion; from his judgement there was no appeal. His habitation was the centre of the clan's existence, and a number of his followers constantly attended him both at home and elsewhere.

The land was the chief's; but the glory of the chief was the glory of all his kinsmen and his followers. The clan looked upon the chief as the father of his people, and themselves as his children; they believed him bound to protect and maintain them, while they were bound to regard his will as law, and to lay down their lives at his command.

The most sacred oath to a Highlander, was to swear by the hand of his chief. The constant exclamation, upon any sudden accident, was, may God be with the chief, or, may the chief be uppermost. Ready at all times to die for the head of the kindred, Highlanders have been known to interpose their bodies between the pointed musket, and their chief, and to receive the shot which was aimed at him.[4]

Loyalty, both to the clan and to the chief who symbolised its unity, was the master principle of the clan system.

The great objective of this ancient form of society was to maintain its customary way of life. Progress was not one of its illusions; nor was perpetual peace. Every man wished to be a fighting man, and the value of a property was reckoned, not by the rent it produced, but by the number of men whom it could support and send into the field. In the first half of the eighteenth century the highlands were more peaceful than once they had been, but the highlanders were still imbued with what Boswell called 'thoughtless inclination for war'. Raids and counter-raids were still the delight and the principal by-employment of most of the clans, their members 'profuse of their own lives, and of those of others; vehement in their attachment to one society, and implacable in their antipathy to another'.[5] Bravery in battle was the supreme virtue. It was said to be a maxim of the MacLean's 'never to turn their Backs upon an Enemy, tho ever so unequal in Numbers; but either to Conquer or Fall upon the Spot'; and partly for this reason two-thirds of the clan were left dead upon the field at Culloden.

Inured to conflict, the highlanders were famous long before 1745 for their great fighting qualities. But these depended principally on their attitude of mind — upon their ardent attachment to their clan; upon their contempt of suffering, and even of death, on its behalf; upon their consciousness of their own merit and standing within their own society. And this sense of dignity and independence existed because of the close connections between the chief and his people, because they all shared the same dangers and depended every day upon one another for their immediate safety. The meanest clansman, however poor, knew his chief, and expected to be treated by him as a friend and in many ways as an equal. The subordination of ranks existed, but it did not mean what it means in a commercial society. This point is admirably made in a story which recounts how George II wished to meet a highland soldier. Two young men, privates in the Black Watch, were sent to London, were seen by the King, and on leaving received a guinea each. This pourboire they handed to the porter as they passed through the palace gates. No doubt the King (not noted for his generosity) thought that he had behaved very handsomely. He did not understand that gratuities were for servants who worked for hire (like his own soldiers), not for independent clansmen.

With this sort of organisation and with these social norms it was inevitable that the clans should sympathise with the cause of the House of Stuart and rally to the support of Prince Charles. Hereditary leadership was something they understood. It made no sense in the highlands to have a king who was both a foreigner and a figurehead. But a king who was a Scotsman and whose family was connected, both by blood and by history, with the families of many highland chiefs and therefore with the clans themselves, was altogether a different matter. The forbears of numberless people in the highlands had died fighting for Charles I, for Charles II, for James II and for his son, James Edward. Most clansmen saw Prince Charles as the heir of the hereditary chief of all the clans, and therefore to fight on his behalf against a usurper was the most natural thing in the world. Sir Walter Scott relates that in 1788 a gentleman of the name of Stuart was seen in mourning, who, when asked for what relative he wore it, replied, 'For my poor chief'. Charles Edward had died in January of that year. The problem for the highland chiefs in 1745 was not to get men 'out' but — for those who were eccentric enough to wish to do so — to compel them to stay at home.

Notes and References

1. Petrie, op. cit., p. 26.
2. Quoted in Petrie, p. 187.
3. G.M. Trevelyan, *England under Queen Anne* (London, 1930-4), vol. III, p. 267.
4. Home, op. cit., pp. 9-10.
5. A. Ferguson, *An Essay on the History of Civil Society*, ed. Duncan Forbes (Edinburgh, 1966), p. 194.

7 'THE HOUR IS STRUCK'

James Edward, son of James II and known throughout Europe as the Chevalier de St George, who would have been King James III if his unquestionable right to the throne had ever been recognised, was a man of many excellent qualities. Like his grandfather, Charles I, he was a great gentleman; his word could be relied on; he bore his many misfortunes throughout life with a splendid natural dignity; always pursued whatever course he thought was required by his duty to his country; and was sincere and unswerving in his Catholic faith, although he had no passionate wish, like his father, to proselytise his countrymen. He probably would have made a very good king. But other qualities are needed in a prince who seeks to regain a throne, and James unhappily did not possess them. He was cautious and sensible, where what was needed was dash and fire; he was melancholy, where men would have liked to see a cheerful heart and an optimistic spirit; he was reserved where it would have been better to be cordial; and he was tolerant where firmness and a few little unreasonable prejudices would have done no harm. Only his courage suited the occasion — he charged twelve times with the Maison du Roi at Malplaquet — but this heroic virtue he never had an opportunity to display while fighting on his own behalf.

In 1718, anxious for heirs to continue the House of Stuart, James began to look for a wife. He sued for the hand of a Russian princess, but was not successful, and then sent an ambassador to Poland — this was a young man by the name of Charles Wogan, who had almost lost his life in the '15 when he was only nineteen years old — to enquire whether one of the daughters of Prince James Sobieski would be interested in marriage and the prospect of becoming Queen of Great Britain. Wogan interviewed all three of the Prince's daughters: Casimire, 'astonishingly solemn'; Charlotte, 'beyond all measure gay'; and Clementina, 'sweet, amiable, of an even temper, and gay only in season'. Clementina made the most favourable impression, so Wogan entered into negotiations with her father, and an agreement was reached. As a result of this, Clementina and her mother soon afterwards set out for Italy, but the Court of St James's, determined to make trouble if it could, put pressure on the Emperor (who was Clementina's cousin) to prevent the marriage, and the two travellers were arrested at Innsbruck and confined in a convent. Wogan thereupon determined that he would rescue his future Queen. He began by recruiting for the expedition, and enlisted the help of three friends at Strasbourg, along with the wife of one of them and her maid, who was called Jeanneton. This party of six reached Innsbruck in April 1719, and Wogan proceeded to put into effect what must be the oldest and simplest plan of escape in the world; that is to say, he proceeded to substitute Jeanneton for Clementina. He seems to have encountered no great difficulty. And then, with the use of an Austrian passport which gave the party false identities, the conspirators made their way by coach, cart and the garrets of bad inns to the Austrian frontier and on to Bologna. What happened to Jeanneton? one is bound to ask. She deserves to be remembered, for she kept to her room in the convent for twenty-four hours, thus delaying discovery and may surely be said to have done as much for Prince Charles as Flora MacDonald did later. On this interesting question history has not much to say, but she is believed to have been able to return, unharmed, to her mistress in Rome.

James had no share in these proceedings, for he was part of the time in Italy and part in Spain, engaged in negotiations which led to the abortive rising of 1719. But a marriage by proxy was soon per-formed, and a second ceremony took place a few months later after James had returned from Spain. A medal was struck, with a head of Clementina on one side and on the obverse a representation of her in a chariot driving into Rome. She brought to the Jacobite court youth, beauty, gaiety and wealth (the last of these included the Sobieski rubies), and she acquired the right to sign herself 'Clem-entina R'.

James's hopes for an heir were not disappointed. Charles Edward was born towards the end of 1720, and in 1725 Clementina bore a second son who was christened Henry Benedict. These two children were brought up in Rome, in what were at best very difficult circum-stances. The life of an exile is never easy, especially that of a royal exile. There is a certain unreality about it, inherent in the contrast between present circumstances on the one hand, and on the other hand what was and what it is hoped will be again. Appearances have to be kept up as far as possible, lest claims begin to seem absurd. But keeping up appearances requires money, and this few exiles have. James, for all his dignity, was constantly and largely dependent on the King of France and on the Pope for the ability to maintain himself, his family and his little court in Rome. He was never extravagant. But in spite of all the support he received, he frequently seemed to be poor, or at any rate hard up, because of the generous help that he gave to numberless other Jacobite exiles less fortunate than himself. And the anxieties of this careful life were further complicated by endless plots, schemes and disappointments relating to the restoration of the House of Stuart. Dependence on others, and continual uncertainty about the future, were James's lot. He and his family had to live in a world of impoverished make-believe, of would-be grandeur and of few serious responsibilities.

Nor were these the only difficulties that the young princes had to grow up with, for James and Clementina did not live happily together. The reasons for matrimonial conflict are seldom clearly understood, and it is strange with what confidence historians explain what went wrong with James's marriage when some of them might scarcely be able to say what went wrong with their own. But we can be sure of two things. James and Clementina disagreed strongly about the education of their sons, especially about their religious education. Although both parents were Roman Catholics and both princes were brought up in that faith, James was sufficiently tolerant — and perhaps also sufficiently politic — to allow Protestant tutors to have some part in their upbringing; to this Clementina most strongly objected. And secondly, differences of temperament set a gulf between husband and wife. Clementina was young and inclined to laugh and be merry, whereas James, more than ten years her senior, was a melancholy, laborious man, indifferent to society and constantly immersed in a vast correspondence which he conducted for the most part in his own hand and which was all about schemes that were doomed to failure. There seems no doubt that James was an unsympathetic husband, and that Clementina's natural cheerfulness was soured in her gloomy home. To make matters worse, she disliked and distrusted many of James's closest advisers, and found that her elder son was not so much her own child as a pawn in political conspiracies. So James and Clementina quarrelled, their quarrels became public and were made a part of the ecclesiastical politics of Rome, and the unfortunate lady 'wept freely' and withdrew to a convent. After a time the marriage, such as it was, was patched up; but James hoped for some 'prudent means of separation', and was perhaps still hoping for this when his unhappy wife died in 1735.

Prince Charles was not yet six years old when these troubles began, and he was scarcely fifteen when his mother died. He must have been affected by many pressures and sadnesses, but from an early age he showed great promise and attracted much admiration. When not yet in his teens it was reported that 'he is most alert in all his exercises, such as shooting, the tennis, shuttlecock, etc.' and that 'he bore his part at the balls in the carnival as if he were already a man'. His formal education seems to have ended when he was thirteen. He was then fluent in English, French and Italian and spoke some Spanish; loved and understood music 'to a great degree', and was an excellent performer on the bass viol; danced very well; and possessed that magnetic charm of manner which was commented upon by almost everyone he met, friend and foe alike. But above all, Charles was an outdoor man. He enjoyed tennis and golf, but boating, riding and shooting were his favourite diversions. In his early twenties he often went out before daybreak and 'killed a great dale of game', displaying so much energy and such powers of endurance 'that nobody here can keep up with him, even a servant or two, that are clever fellows have more than enough to do to do it . . .' In all these matters he completely outshone his younger brother, although Henry also was a good shot and sometimes 'took the air on horseback at night after a day's strong fatigue'.[1]

In 1734 the Duke of Liria, son of the Duke of Berwick and a relative of the Prince, invited Charles to join the Spanish forces that were besieging the Imperial troops in Gaeta. To a youth of Charles's temperament this invitation must have been pure joy; and James, who was himself an old campaigner and who dreamed like many others that one day his son would lead the Jacobites to a great and final victory, gave the idea his blessing. War was a prince's business in the eighteenth century, and the siege of Gaeta, which was not a very desperate affair, although conducted in earnest, provided an excellent opportunity for Charles to gain some useful experience. He left Rome with a small retinue which included two of his tutors, James Murray, brother of Lord Mansfield, and Sir Thomas Sheridan, who was later to land with the Prince in Moidart; they remained at Gaeta for about two weeks. Both Liria and the two tutors were very anxious to keep Charles out of the line of fire, but he was conducted to the trenches, where, in Liria's words, 'he showed not the least concern at the enemy's fire, even when the balls were hissing about his ears'. Later he managed to enter a building which was a target for the imperial artillery and in other ways to get as close to the action as he possibly could. His friends and his

Spanish hosts were delighted with him. Never, wrote one of them,

> was any Prince endowed with so much vivacity nor appeared
> more cheerful in all the attacks. If he had been master of his own
> inclinations he never would have quitted the trenches, and was
> overheard to say that the noise of the cannon was more pleasant
> music to him than that of the opera at Rome.[2]

In short, Charles showed courage, staying power and enthusiasm,
and already exercised, even at the age of thirteen, that magic ability
to appear as the inspiring representative of a great cause that has
distinguished men as dissimilar as Nelson, Haig and Mountbatten.

Three years later, James sent the young prince on a short tour of
Italy, through Florence to the great cities of Genoa and Venice.
Everywhere he went there were 'splendid receptions', 'noble dinners' and long formal speeches. He was received with the honours
due to royalty, and came into close contact with the splendour and
decadence of the Italian city states. This experience must have made
the moth-eaten hangings and the worn-out furniture of his father's
house seem duller than ever, and the plotting and scheming that
went on there even more futile. Charles was temperamentally a man
of action, and he was brought up to lead a great cause. 'Had I
soldiers', he is reported to have said during this Italian tour, 'I
would not be here now but wherever I could serve my friends'. He
asked for permission to fight in Hungary and was refused. His
opportunity to live as he wished to live had still to come.

So Charles returned to Rome, and to wait. He continued to be
treated by those who surrounded him with the greatest deference.
He was styled the Prince of Wales, and visitors ushered into his
presence knelt down and kissed his hand; when he was received in
audience by the Pope, an armchair was provided for him, and the
Sacred Conclave yielded him precedence. But he was seventeen
years of age and old enough to understand the partial unreality of
his position. Clearly, the grandeur that surrounded him would soon
become a charade unless he and his friends could by their own
efforts 'repair the injustice of fortune'. This process Charles could
not initiate; but in or about the year 1740 a number of moves were
made and contacts established which were in due course to draw him
out of Rome and then on to the battles of 1745 and 1746.

These fresh developments depended largely on new Jacobite leaders, many of them young men like Charles himself, and many of

them destined to play a prominent part in the '45. Murray of
Broughton, sometimes described — and with good reason — as the
Judas of the cause, was one of these. Energetic and ambitious,
Murray was the son of a Peebles-shire baronet of no great importance. He studied for a time at Leyden, and then, in 1737, at the age
of twenty-two, he visited Rome. During that visit or a little later he
met Prince Charles who made a great impression on him. 'The eldest
son of the Chevalier de St George', wrote Murray, 'is tall, above the
common stature, his limbs are cast in the most exact mould, his
complexion has in it somewhat of an uncommon delicacy; all his
features are perfectly regular and well turned, and his eyes the finest
I ever saw.'[3] Murray on his part made a good impression on the
Prince, and an even better one on James. He was an ardent Jacobite,
well educated and possessed agreeable manners. He became a daily
guest at the Palace, and later, in 1740, having secured the complete
confidence of James, he became recognised as the King's agent in
Scotland. During that same year, when Murray was again in Rome,
Lord Elcho arrived in the city. He was the son of the Earl of Wemyss
(who had steadfastly refused to take the oath of allegiance to the
House of Hanover) and he naturally sought an interview with the
Chevalier. He, too, seems to have made a good impression, and like
Murray he was introduced to the Prince, being about the same age.
Murray and Lord Elcho now became constant in their attendance at
the Jacobite court.

In a short time some business of importance turned up. A group
of influential Scots Jacobites, meeting in Edinburgh, had formed an
association with a view to promoting the restoration of the Stuarts.
The Associators, as they came to be called, were seven in number,
and four of them were destined to play no great part in history; but
the names of the others are indissolubly connected with the '45.
Simon Fraser, Lord Lovat, chief of the Clan Fraser, is remembered
by Jacobites and Hanoverians alike as a double-dealer and a rascal
who caused trouble for everyone: at the age of eighty he ended with
his head on the block. The Duke of Perth was a very different
person. Not very much older than the Prince, he had been educated
in France, and was a man of much amiability and considerable
culture. In the early 1740s he was living at Drummond castle and
because he was a known Jacobite the government sought to arrest
him as soon as the Prince landed in Scotland. But he escaped, lived
concealed in the highlands until he was able to join the Prince at
Perth, and fought with him throughout the campaign. Donald

Cameron of Lochiel — 'the Gentle Lochiel' — was chief of the Clan Cameron. His father had been attainted and forfeited for his part in the '15, and had retired to the continent, leaving his son to head the clan. Lochiel was not a great highland magnate like the Duke of Gordon or Sir Alexander Macdonald of Sleat, but he ruled his territories in Lochaber with an absolute sway, and was acknowledged everywhere to be just, honourable and courageous. A man of education who managed his affairs in a business-like way, he was above all a highlander in the great highland tradition. His support for Charles, once given, never wavered. Without his support, the '45 would probably not have taken place.

The seven Associators, having agreed to take up arms and venture their lives and their fortunes to restore the House of Stuart, on condition only that France was willing to give them some initial military support, sent Drummond of Balhaldie, a close relative of Lochiel, to inform James about the Association and its members' intentions. The new development seemed well-timed, for the popularity of George II and his ministers was at a low ebb, and James therefore ordered Drummond to proceed to the French court in order to find out what help France might be willing to provide. Much talking now ensued. Cardinal Fleury and the other French ministers were in dilemma. If France gave military assistance to the Jacobites, this would almost certainly lead to a war with Great Britain, which Fleury still hoped to avoid. On the other hand, if James were given no encouragement he might look for help elsewhere or even reach an accommodation with the politicians in London, and in either case would no longer be available as an ally for France if war should come, as seemed likely. So the French procrastinated. And they procrastinated for so long, and seemed disposed to do so little, that James and his supporters began to suspect that the purpose of French policy was not to help in restoring the House of Stuart to the throne of Great Britain but only to use the Jacobites as a diversion, stirring up trouble for the British government at home; or at most to use Jacobitism as a tool to destroy the unity of Great Britain, by helping James to become King of Scotland while leaving the rest of the country in the possession of George II.

Whatever French intentions were, nothing was done in 1741 or in 1742; and in February 1743, John Murray of Broughton arrived in Paris in order to discover how matters stood. Many agents, both French and Jacobite, were exploring the chances of a rising at this time, for France and Great Britain were on the brink of war; but

Murray was exceptionally well placed to influence the course of events because besides having the full confidence of James he was also authorised to act as an envoy of the highland chiefs. He discussed matters at length with the French ministers, and then immediately left for Edinburgh in order to provide his friends there with an account of the Paris conversations. He seems to have been able to report that French help would be forthcoming 'as soon as an opportunity offered'; that the plan would be for French troops to land both in Scotland and near London; and that Louis 'had the interest of the Stuart family as much at heart as any of those gentlemen who had signed the association'. Murray must be given some of the credit for securing a firm statement of French intentions; and he carried conviction in Scotland also, because the chiefs responded by agreeing that a rising would take place to coincide with the arrival of French troops. Plans began to be made for 1744.

What was planned to occur in 1744 was very different from what actually happened in 1745, which was but a fragment of the original design. The 1744 plan was that the main French invasion force would consist of no fewer than 12,000 men under the command of Marshal Saxe, and that they would land somewhere along the Thames estuary, near London. A much smaller force of 3,000 men would simultaneously land in Scotland and would be joined by Lovat and the Frasers, the Camerons under Lochiel, the MacLeans of Mull, the MacDonalds, the MacLeods and other clans. This was a very ambitious scheme. Marshal Saxe was the greatest general of the age, and the numbers proposed to engage the forces of Hanover were very large. Indeed, 15,000 French troops made so formidable a host as to turn the Jacobites into very junior partners indeed, although the list of clans expected to rise was a very long one and included several which did not 'come out' in 1745. The very scale of the proposed operation had important consequences. First, because it looked like — as indeed it was — a piece of naked aggression by France against Great Britain, it was important for Louis to secure not only the support of James but if at all possible his presence or that of Prince Charles with the invasion forces; this would at least help to make it appear that the French aim was not simply to cripple Great Britain but was to restore the legitimate King to the British throne. So an invitation was sent to Rome which could presumably have been accepted by either James or Charles. James, however, showed no inclination to join Marshal Saxe, nor did he press Charles to go. And this also was probably because of the scale of French preparations — James did not wish to regain his kingdom as the afterthought of a French invasion. On the other hand, he could not stand completely aside — if this was the best opportunity that fate offered, it must not be rejected. So he left it to Charles to go or not; and, characteristically, Charles jumped at the chance. To get away from the priests and the petty intrigues of Rome and back to the world of action, which he had seen so briefly at Gaeta; to free his enslaved countrymen; and to restore his father and all his family to their rightful place in Great Britain and the world — such a prospect was the breath of life to Charles, the great adventure for which he must have been consciously waiting for at least ten years.

The first problem was to leave Rome without arousing any suspicions. The French invasion plans would be seriously endangered if the Whig ministers in London were given any ground for supposing that something was afoot; and the departure of Charles from Rome and his arrival in France would be a certain signal to the Whigs and their friends that they had better be on the alert. But for Charles to leave Rome without all the world hearing about it was no easy matter, for he was a prominent person in the city; and besides, English spies kept James and all those about him under constant surveillance, so that whatever happened in Rome was soon reported in London. The Prince, however, was equal to the occasion. He let it be known that he and his brother would go boar-hunting at Cisterna, not far from Rome, on 11 January, and a few days beforehand he sent on the horses and the baggage. Before first light on 11 January he left the palace — his brother Henry being still asleep — got into a postchaise that was waiting for him, and drove off towards Cisterna. He was accompanied by a companion named Dunbar and a servant, both of whom knew what was planned, and by a few other servants who did not. After a few miles Charles halted the chaise, and, saying that he preferred to ride, mounted one of the led horses and rode on ahead. On rejoining the chaise later in the morning he said that he had injured his foot in a fall, and had better proceed straight to Cisterna; but the others — excepting his own servant who was in the know — were ordered to go directly to Albano where Henry had been told, on waking, that his brother would be waiting for him. Charles then rode off, and when Henry duly arrived at Albano, Dunbar explained to him that Charles was on his way to France and that what now had to be done was to maintain the fiction that Charles was not to be seen because he was recovering from an accident. So Henry went boar-hunting without his brother, accounts of whose gradually improving health were occasionally handed out, and hampers of wild boar, purporting to come from both the Princes, were sent to Rome.

While this was going on, Charles, now in the guise of a Neapolitan courier on his way to Spain, was travelling north. At the Tuscan frontier he produced a passport supplied by the kindness of the Grand Duke, which gave him the identity of an officer in the Spanish service. As such, he rode through Siena, Castel Firentino and Pisa, and on reaching Carrara went on board a Maltese barque which awaited him. He reached Genoa, went on to Savona, where he paused briefly, and then boarded another vessel and sailed to Antibes. Once in France he posted night and day via Lyons to Paris, which he reached three weeks after his departure from Rome. He was made welcome by the ministers of Louis XV, and soon afterwards he was on the Channel coast, observing the preparations for the invasion of Britain.

It took the British several weeks to discover that Charles had left Rome and was now in France. By the time that this information reached them, however, they had already begun to realise that a French invasion attempt was imminent. For two months Louis had been remarkably successful in keeping his preparations secret, but the forces which should have been ready to sail on 20 January 1744 were not assembled on time, and the ensuing delay of several weeks allowed the British government to discover that an all-out military effort by France was planned, and gave the opportunity to take counter-measures. The country was almost devoid of troops, as usual, because almost the whole British army was on the continent supporting the interests of the Elector of Hanover; so if the 10,000 men that Louis was almost ready to send across the Channel had ever landed in the Thames estuary, not to mention the three battalions of the Irish Brigade who were destined for Scotland, there is not much likelihood that George II would have kept his throne. But luck and the British navy rescued George and the Whigs. Louis had ordered the Brest fleet to sail, with instructions to draw Admiral Norris and his ships out of the Channel; but the French did not encounter any British warships at sea and the French admiral concluded that the British fleet was still in Portsmouth harbour and that the coast was therefore clear. This information was sent to Dunkirk, and Saxe proceeded to embark his troops as fast as possible. On 23 February, a British frigate came into the Downs with the signal for sighting enemy ships flying at her mast-head, Sir John Norris at once beat down the Channel and at four in the afternoon came on the French fleet near Dungeness. Norris's move, which left the Channel clear, would have given Saxe his opportunity, had the weather been favourable. But a violent storm blew up, the transports at Dunkirk could not get out of the harbour, twelve vessels were lost, and the French fleet at Dungeness was scattered by the storm. One week later, before Louis' forces could re-group, a second violent storm struck the ships at Dunkirk, driving many ashore and causing further loss of life. With remarkable promptitude, Louis abandoned the idea of an invasion.

It appears that Prince Charles, who was certainly in Dunkirk during the critical days in February, actually put to sea on board one of the French vessels ready to set sail for the Thames. But whether this is the case or not, he must have believed more than once that he was within a day or two of entering London at the head of an army. The invasion seemed certain to take place, for there were 10,000 officers and men in Dunkirk, and the harbour and the approaches were crowded with shipping; and given the forces assembled, success seemed almost inevitable. But within two or three days of the second storm, Charles, who was given no say in the matter, was informed that the whole great enterprise was cancelled. Marshal Saxe returned at once to Paris, and the shipping and the troops began to disperse.

Few men engaged in great affairs can have experienced so sudden a transition from the pinnacle of confident expectation to the void of achieving precisely nothing — worse still, of being able to attempt precisely nothing. For Charles, of all men, it was a personal disaster and it affected the rest of his life. He was only twenty-three and not, like his father, accustomed to disappointment. And it was not only his own feelings that were involved, for his position, already difficult and insecure, became much more so. As long as the invasion was in prospect, he was a subordinate in the French plan but an essential part of it, and therefore he was given much consideration although he had to contend against being treated as one who, although important, merely took orders. But in the space of a few hours he sank from being a person of consequence to being no more than a slightly privileged spectator at the old endless game of European politics. The French no longer found him very interesting. It is true that he was allowed to remain in France. Shortly after his arrival the British secretary at the court of Versailles had tried to have him thrown out of the country, but had received an answer 'injurious and offensive'; and soon after the invasion débâcle, Louis declared war on Great Britain, which put Charles's presence on French territory beyond the scope of British diplomatic protest. But he had no role to play; he was in limbo. It was proposed to him that he should leave France and go back to Rome incognito, but this he scornfully rejected. He made a counter-proposal — might he not take part in the coming French campaign in Flanders? This was refused. By April the unfortunate Prince was back in Paris, where the French King did not receive him.

For over twelve months, starting in the spring of 1744, Charles led a very strange life. The French ministers and the French court acknowledged his existence — he was given a small allowance which does not seem always to have been paid, or not regularly — but they did not want to know about him; their behaviour was 'negligent and indifferent'. To begin with, he pressed whenever he could for a revival of the invasion project — there were memoranda and hints and semi-assurances, put out by one French minister or another, that an invasion would indeed be organised whenever a suitable opportunity presented itself. But as time went on, Charles placed less and less faith in these signs of French sympathy; he came to realise that whatever help France might give would be determined by what she expected to receive in return. He nevertheless remained in France, because his departure would have encouraged French indifference to the Jacobite cause; but for a while he lay very low. On returning to Paris, however, he made the acquaintance of a young banker named Aeneas MacDonald, who was later to accompany him to Moidart, and sometimes the two young men went out together on 'parties of pleasure'; they even attended two or three *bals masqués* at Versailles. But although he came to know the Prince well, MacDonald, by his own account, never heard him mention the names of any Jacobite agents, never heard him discuss any of their schemes, never even heard him allude to his own hopes or plans for the recovery of the throne. Charles had charm; but he was also tough, self-reliant and, when necessary, circumspect.

However quietly he lived, Jacobite agents soon sought him out. The diplomatic world was full of their comings and goings, and it would be a hard task to disentangle all their schemes. The basic trouble was that there were too many agents; and a secondary trouble was that they mostly disliked and distrusted one another. James's preferred and official representative was Daniel O'Brien, who had good contacts at Versailles. But James gave letters of credence to Francis Sempil, who was the son of a forfeited Scots Jacobite whom James had known in his youth, and who made a living out of exaggerating and retailing the wildest stories about the extent of Jacobite support in several countries. Drummond of Balhaldie, the original agent of the Association, was another tireless purveyor of fanciful Jacobite reports. Numerous discreditable stories were told of Balhaldie; that he had stolen the Earl Marischal's baggage at Sheriffmuir; that he had had to leave Scotland because of trouble over a note for fifty pounds; that he had falsely pretended to spend Jacobite money on buying arms in Holland; that he was 'always in a passion, a mere bully, the most forbidding air imaginable, and master of as much bad French as to procure himself a whore and a dinner'. Yet James was inclined to trust Balhaldie, and Sempil and Balhaldie were often in Paris trying to involve Charles in their schemes, until he saw through them. The Earl Marischal himself was another well-known Jacobite, of a very different kind. He had taken part in the '15 and the '19, but had become cautious and disillusioned and although Charles saw a good deal of him he did not like him. Sir Thomas Sheridan, Charles's tutor, was another 'adviser', and one whom the Prince trusted. And finally there was Murray of Broughton, destined to be the Prince's secretary and one of his confidants in Scotland. All of these men — and there were others — had access to the Prince, and most of them used the opportunity to advance their own opinions and interests by denigrating their rivals. Thus Balhaldie described Sheridan as 'pernicious and useless', Murray repeated the story about Balhaldie helping himself to the Earl Marischal's baggage, the Earl Marischal advised James that Sempil and Balhaldie 'impose, as far as they can, on all the world', while Murray was accused (quite unjustly) of proposing to Charles that he 'seat himself on the throne, and leave the King at Rome'. Through this welter of rivalry and faction, Charles had to find his way as best he could.

Of all the agents, Murray of Broughton was the most effective. He had the confidence both of James and of the highland chiefs, he did not disseminate gross distortions of the facts, and he knew what he wanted. In the summer of 1744 he travelled from Scotland to Paris in order to discover how matters stood and what might be done next, and he had a long conversation with the Prince. Charles no doubt told him that the French had not altogether given up the idea of invading Great Britain, and that he knew that he had friends in Scotland upon whom he could rely; and according to Murray he further stated his intention of going to Scotland 'with but a single footman' if he could find no other help. This was a far more desperate idea than any that had yet been suggested, but Murray undertook to find out the reaction of the highland chiefs. It was unfavourable, as Murray must have expected. The chiefs believed that no rising could succeed without at least a modicum of help from abroad, and only the Duke of Perth was in favour of the Prince coming to Scotland on his own. Murray accordingly wrote to Charles, explaining the chiefs' reaction, but this letter, which was sent off in January 1745, miscarried, as was often the case with secret Jacobite communications, and was returned to Murray three months later.

Charles in the meantime kept his own counsel, listening but not responding to endless rumours and suggestions put out by Jacobite agents and sympathisers, and hoping no doubt that France would soon decide to revive the invasion plan. But French policy at this time was not well directed and French intentions remained vague. As time went on Charles must have realised that he could not wait upon events for ever, as his father had been prone to do, and his inclination to action was strengthened in the spring by a change of company. He moved his lodgings in Paris, saw far less of Sempil and Balhaldie, and became friendly with a group of officers in the French service — men like Lord Tyrconnel, Lord Clare and Colonel Dillon, whose conversation, by comparison with what Charles had recently had to endure, must have been much more about campaigns and much less about intrigues. They no doubt encouraged him to do as they would have done, and to take matters into his own hands. And then, on 11 May, Marshal Saxe inflicted a serious defeat at Fontenoy on an army commanded by the Duke of Cumberland and swept on into the Low Countries, to take Tournai, Ghent, Oudenarde and, later, Ostend. George II and his troops were not invincible. And it was perhaps at this point that Charles made up his mind to go.

In taking this decision he was certainly not without friends and sympathisers. There were many Jacobites on the continent who supported the idea of a rising without promises of French help. Sir Thomas Sheridan was in favour, as were the Irish officers; Murray of Broughton, although he warned of the difficulties, had collected money in Scotland and — according to Lord Elcho — had secured promises of support from, among others, the Duke of Hamilton, the Duke of Perth, Lord Traquhair, Lord Pitsligo, MacLeod of

MacLeod, Keppoch and Lochiel. As for French help, that could not be depended upon; but Charles realised that if he waited for the French he might wait for ever, whereas if he took the initiative it was very likely that Louis and his ministers would see some advantage to themselves in his expedition succeeding, and would follow where he had led. And the support he set out with was not merely conditional and for the future. He could not sensibly begin without money and arms, and he could not begin at all without shipping. These were made available — but not by France. He was lent money by two Jacobite supporters who were bankers in Paris. He pawned his jewels in Rome and bought, in the Netherlands, twenty small field-pieces, 1,500 muskets, 1,100 broadswords, ammunition, some other weapons and supplies. The problem of shipping was more difficult, and crucial. France and Great Britain were at war, and it would have been extremely risky for the Prince to travel to Scotland in anything other than a fast, well-armed vessel. Fortunately, vessels of this kind were often used for privateering, which in the eighteenth century was an activity often combined with trade and carried on by mer-chant-shippers as a well-understood part of their business; and Charles counted among his acquaintance a number of merchants based at Nantes and St Malo, chief among them being Antoine Walsh. Walsh was a man of wealth and consequence, a shipowner who was familiar with privateering projects and who knew his way around the French Ministry of Marine. When the time came, he was able to provide the Prince with two ships, the *Doutelle*, a frigate with 44 guns, and a man-of-war (hired by Walsh for privateering pur-poses), the *Elizabeth*, with 68 guns.

Early in July, in a hot summer, the *Doutelle* lay at the mouth of the Loire, and there the Prince and a few companions went on board. They sailed for Belle-Ile, where they remained for several days taking in provisions, and were joined by the *Elizabeth* with one hundred marines on board, 2,000 muskets and 600 broadswords. On 16 July, both ships set sail for Scotland. No one in France, except those few whom the Prince thought that he could trust, seems to have had any idea of what was going on. Louis and his ministers; Sempil and Balhaldie; the host of English spies on the continent; even Charles's own brother and James himself had no idea. The voyage to Scotland was one of the most skilfully executed under-cover operations on record.

Before leaving, Charles wrote to his father from the Château at Evreux. The letter begins with an acknowledgement that his plans will come as a surprise; but what would have happened, he asks, if he had tried to persuade his father to let him go? The circumstances which make the venture advisable are not easily understood in Rome, 'and, had I failed to convince you, I was then afraid you might have thought what I was going to do to be rash, and so to have absolutely forbidden my proceedings'. Charles realised that his father was a very cautious man, and that caution was not going to recover the throne. It was, he believed — and there is every reason to think that he believed correctly — a case of now or never. To go to Scotland was 'the only way of restoring you to the crown'; for (whatever James might think) 'to return to Rome . . . would be just giving up all hopes'. Moreover, honour and reputation were also involved. He had received 'scandalous usage' at the French court, and although he had tried 'all possible means and stratagems to get access to the King of France' he had been unable to do so. His only course, therefore, if the world was not to despise him, was to show that he was not dependent upon the French, and could act alone. France would no doubt send some men or arms in due course, and that would be sufficient, 'there being a certainty of succeeding with the least help'. What he is about to do is in order 'to save my country and make it happy'. To risk everything is no more than his duty. 'Let what will happen, the hour is struck.'

By the time that this letter reached the Palazzo Muti the Prince was at sea on his way to Scotland and the first shots in his campaign had been fired. Only four days out of Belle-Ile the *Doutelle* and her escort were intercepted by HMS *Lion* one hundred miles off the Lizard, and a running battle ensued. The *Elizabeth* engaged the British man-of-war and prevented her from attacking the *Doutelle*, which crowded on sail and escaped to the westward. Neither of the other ships could follow her, for they were evenly matched; and when they disengaged some hours later with severe casualties on both sides, the *Elizabeth* was so badly damaged that she was obliged to make for Brest, and the *Lion*, also damaged, had no chance of catching up with the *Doutelle*. The Prince had slipped through his enemies' fingers, for the first but not the last time. Navigating round the west coast of Ireland, Walsh made a landfall on 2 August, and on a grey summer evening Charles saw the islands of the outer Hebrides low on the horizon, his first sight of Scotland. On 3 August, two and a half weeks after leaving Belle-Ile, the Prince landed on Eriskay and spent the night in a cottage. Two days later the *Doutelle* sailed across the Minch to Lochnanuagh, and Charles set foot on the Scottish mainland at Borrodale in Arisaig. The rising of 1745 had begun.

Notes and References

1. Letter dated 1/10/1742, from James Edward or his secretary.
2. Quoted in Ewald, op. cit., pp. 29–30.
3. Ibid., quoted p. 43.

8 THE DESCENT FROM THE HIGHLANDS

Arisaig, along with Moidart, Knoydart and North and South Morar, lies on the west coast of Scotland just south of Skye. Only a few years after the Prince was there, this part of the west highlands was described by one who visited it as follows:

> these Countries . . . are the most Rough Mountainous and impassable parts in all the Highlands of Scotland, and are commonly called by the Inhabitants of the Neighbouring Countries the Highlands of the Highlands. The People here have very little Corn Land and what they have by Reason of its steepness and Cragginess they are obliged to Dig with the Spade; but the People in these Countries breed prodigious Numbers of Cattle of all kind, especially a Sort of Wild Horses which sell very well at the Markets in the Low Country . . . They have also great plenty of Venison of all Kinds. The Inhabitants of this Large Tract of Ground are all Popish, Gentlemen and Commons . . .[1]

Remote and inaccessible, and surrounded on all sides by the territories of chiefs who had for generations fought for the Stuarts and who, as one highland gentleman put it, 'were never difficient or absent when the Roy[ll] family had the least to doe',[2] Arisaig was an altogether excellent place for the Prince to begin.

He had come to Scotland with only a small group of companions, among whom the most notable were the Marquis of Tullibardine, elder brother of the Duke of Atholl, Sir Thomas Sheridan and Aeneas MacDonald, the banker whom Charles had met in Paris and who was a brother of MacDonald of Kinloch-Moidart. At Eriskay the only person of importance who came to see Charles was Alexander MacDonald of Boisdale. This chieftain from the Outer Isles refused to assist him, and even suggested to the Prince that he should return to France; he further declined to advise his brother, MacDonald of Clanranald, to support the rising. But Charles remained determined, and although he was at this point 'single in his resolution of landing' he and his party sailed across the Minch to Lochnanuagh and landed at Borrodale in Arisaig. At Borrodale things at first went only a little better. Clanranald came on board the

Doutelle and, although for some time he hesitated, agreed to join the Royal Standard with all the men he had on the mainland. MacDonald of Keppoch came in, as did MacDonald of Glengarry and several minor chieftains such as Morar and Kinloch-Moidart; and messengers were despatched, Clanranald to Skye in order to summon Sir Alexander MacDonald of Sleat and MacLeod of MacLeod, and others to the south to summon the Duke of Perth, John Murray of Broughton and Lochiel. But the future looked almost hopeless when Clanranald returned with the news that neither MacDonald nor MacLeod would join their Prince. This was a heavy blow, because Sir Alexander MacDonald of Sleat could have brought eight hundred men into the field, and his family had moreover 'engaged in all the Rebellions at and since the Revolution', except the '19. But on this occasion he and his clan defected to the Hanoverians, while MacLeod went so far as to communicate the news of the Prince's arrival to the government's agents in Edinburgh. Even those who had accompanied Charles from France now urged him to return, but he refused. Nevertheless, there was no denying that his venture could go on only if he received the support of some notable chief, and therefore everything turned on Cameron of Lochiel, already summoned to Borrodale, 'a man of pretty good understanding, though of no learning, and esteemed by everybody to be in private life a man of strict honour'.[3] It is said that Lochiel had resolved not to join the Prince, which is likely enough because he had previously advised him not to come to Scotland unless with troops; but that on his way to Borrodale in order to tell Charles of his decision, he visited his brother, who urged him to write to Charles but not to see him at Borrodale, because 'if this Prince once sets his eyes upon you, he will make you do whatever he pleases'. Certainly this is what happened. Lochiel came to Borrodale and met the Prince. At first he advised him to go back. But the presence of Charles, son of James Edward, a direct descendant of the Stuart kings of Scotland, was too much for his previous resolution, and that day Lochiel joined the cause.

Having secured only this slender support, Charles wrote letters to the chiefs on the mainland, informing them that the standard would be erected at Glenfinnan at the head of Loch Shiel on 19 August, and requiring their presence on that date, or as soon as possible thereafter. A few days later the *Doutelle*, having discharged her stores and arms, stood out to sea, and Charles made his way to Kinloch-Moidart, where he remained for one week.

Even before the standard could be raised, the first shots had been exchanged on Scottish soil. All that summer there had been rumours flying through the highlands that the Prince had landed or would soon land; and the suspicion that something was afoot, and that the clans might soon make a move of some kind, began to worry the government commanders in Scotland. Their troops were strung along the Great Glen, from Fort William on the west coast to Fort George in Inverness, and the army and the government fondly supposed that this arrangement would overawe the clansmen and prevent them from deploying any force south of the Great Glen or even from attempting any kind of military operation whatever. They were soon to be disillusioned. When the governor of Fort Augustus heard reports of unusual happenings on or near the west coast, he decided to send two companies to reinforce the garrison of Fort William, and another three from Ruthven of Badenoch to escort provisions going to Fort Augustus. News of these plans was at once brought to Borrodale, and it was agreed that some of Keppoch's people should waylay the troops going to Fort William whilst others performed the same service for those on the way to Fort Augustus. The second part of this plan miscarried through no fault of the highlanders. MacDonell of Lochgarry, acting with great expedition, led a small force to the top of Corriearrack and lay in ambush for three days, waiting for the soldiers; but they never came, and Lochgarry had to be content with capturing the commander of the barracks at Ruthven, who happened to be crossing Corriearrack on his way to take command at Fort William, along with his horses, his baggage and his servants. It was a different story beside the lochs. The two companies attempting to reach Fort William set off early in the morning and were shadowed until they were within nine miles of the fort when MacDonald of Tiendrish with about fifty men launched the attack. The soldiers were driven back along the military road, but for a time the attack could not be pressed home, probably because the clansmen had very few firearms and could not use their broadswords against troops retreating along a road protected by a steep hill on one side and a dense wood on the other. But when open ground was reached at Auchendroon, where Tiendrish was joined by some of Glengarry's men, the highlanders gave 'one smart fire' and attacked sword in hand. The enemy thereupon surrendered immediately.

Two days later the Prince, now accompanied by John Murray of Broughton, left Kinloch-Moidart and proceeded to Glenfinnan at the head of Loch Shiel. This narrow loch is hemmed in by high hills and dark serrated ridges, the slopes of the hills are covered with rocks and heather, and innumerable little streams of very clear water run constantly into the loch. In this remote spot the Royal Standard was raised on 19 October by the aged Marquis of Tullibardine. It seems that only about six hundred men commanded by Clanranald and Keppoch gathered round the flag; these were joined later in the day by seven hundred Camerons under Lochiel. The prisoners taken at Auchendroon were also there, as was the solitary officer captured on Corriearrack, and Prince Charles addressed them all in a speech which most of his hearers, speaking only Gaelic, cannot have understood.

News of the Prince's arrival reached Edinburgh on 8 August in a letter to Cope, and was confirmed on the following day by a letter to the Lord President from the treacherous MacLeod of MacLeod. Many who learned the news were at first incredulous, for although it was known that the Prince had left France, the report which circulated was that he had come to Scotland almost alone, which seemed unlikely. The government was not alarmed and saw no great need for energetic measures. But Lord President Forbes, understanding the danger much better than the ministers in London, travelled at once from Edinburgh to Inverness in order to exert what pressure he could to prevent the clans from joining the Prince, and General Cope, who was in command of the usurper's forces in Scotland, began to collect stores and to assemble an army at Stirling. Cope's plan, which the ministers in London strongly approved, was simple; he would march into the highlands and nip the rising in the bud. But he hopelessly underestimated his enemy. He left Edinburgh on 19 August — the very day that the standard was raised at Glenfinnan — and marched to Stirling; on the following day, he marched to Crieff. But the Prince had friends everywhere; and before Cope was fifty miles from Edinburgh, news was brought to Prince Charles at Kinlochiel, not far from Fort William, that the General was on his way, and that his intention was to march through Dalwhinnie and on to Fort Augustus. There, or near there, Cope no doubt expected he would win as easy a victory as had been won by his predecessor, General Wightman, in 1719.

Whether or not Charles had studied the campaigns of 1715 and 1719 we do not know; but he certainly avoided the great mistake made on both these occasions, that of waiting to be attacked. Abandoning twelve out of his twenty swivel guns for lack of transport, he moved forward without delay towards Fort Augustus, and within a week of raising the standard he and his small force arrived at Invergarry. Here he received a message from Lord Lovat assuring him of his loyalty and urging him to march to Inverness where he would be joined by Lovat's clan, the Frasers, and by many others. But Charles knew better than to spend time merely adding to his numbers. He planned to drive south with all possible speed, raise the Atholl country, take Edinburgh, and unite his followers not in the highlands but in the heart of the lowlands of Scotland. Such a success had never been achieved before, even with much larger forces; but Charles was a man of drive and confidence, always in favour of attack, and he realised moreover that if he could take Edinburgh he would add enormously to his support. He was kept well informed about the movements and even the intentions of Sir John Cope, and when he learned that Cope had reached Dalwhinnie with a view to marching over the Corriearrack he at once sent some of his men with orders to make a forced march and if possible to seize the head of the pass before Cope could reach it.

The lumbering battalions south of the mountains had meanwhile taken almost a week to travel from Stirling to Dalwhinnie, and when they arrived there they did not like the prospect. Cope had expected to be joined on his march north by Whig clans, but none appeared — 'not one single man having joined him since he set out'; instead, a number of highlanders belonging to the Black Watch and to Lord Loudon's regiment deserted, taking their arms with them, along with some Atholl men. To make matters worse, minor acts of sabotage were a daily occurrence — sacks of corn were ripped open and their contents lost on the road, stores disappeared and animals were stolen — and the 'inhabitants of the mountains' failed to provide any help with transport.

The Corriearrack is never a hospitable place, and the sight of it from Dalwhinnie, fifteen miles away, in October, was not encouraging; 'the south side is extremely steep, and, when seen from a distance, seems to rise almost perpendicular like a wall', and it was quite obviously no place for regular troops, but the natural habitation of 'mountaineers' and wild highlanders. It began to seem to Cope and his men that they had walked into a trap, or were about to do so. The government troops numbered only about 2,000 men; the cavalry had been left at Stirling, and although there were guns there were no expert artillerymen to bring them into action; food was scarce. What had seemed easy in Edinburgh now began to look extremely dangerous. Cope, indeed, did not really know what he was doing, and still less did his political masters in London. He had been led to believe — quite possibly by Jacobite sympathisers, who understood the situation — that if he remained in the low country Prince Charles would have time to assemble considerable numbers of men and might become difficult to defeat; so the best plan was to advance into the highlands and disperse the insurgents immediately: whereas the truth was that as long as Charles remained confined to the highlands he would have difficulty in keeping the clansmen together, both for want of money and for want of military success; whereas if Cope and his soldiers marched into the hills, the highlanders might quite possibly be able to use their knowledge of the terrain and their skill in mountain warfare either to defeat the regular troops or to slip past them and advance into the lowlands; whereupon the course of events would become unpredictable.

While Sir John lost men, Charles gained them. At Invergarry Castle he was joined by two hundred and sixty Stewarts of Appin under Ardshiel, and on the following day at Aberchalder, near the north end of the Corriearrack, by four hundred Glengarry MacDonalds, the MacDonalds of Glencoe, and some of the Grants of Glenmoriston. All told, Charles now had between 1,500 and 2,000 men and his forces thus almost equalled in number the government army, about whose movements scouts and deserters kept him well informed. By contrast, the enemy's intelligence was poor. Cope held a Council of War at Dalwhinnie, to try to decide what to do next, and at this council he informed his subordinate commanders that more than 3,000 armed clansmen opposed them on the Corriearrack, some entrenched on the pass itself and several hundred lying in ambush on its southern approaches, and that the enemy had twenty swivel guns which had no doubt been positioned to fire into the zig-zag path up the mountain. He therefore did not believe that the northward advance could continue. This assessment of the situation is very revealing. Its wild inaccuracy must in some part be attributed to the care taken by the native population to provide greatly exaggerated reports about the Prince's numbers — the House of Hanover had few sympathisers in the mountains. As for the swivel guns, this information came from the officer captured on the Corriearrack a week before and then released; he had seen the guns at Glenfinnan; he did not know that when Charles advanced he had decided to leave the guns behind; and those who did know the true facts kept the knowledge to themselves. Thus Cope campaigned in

Gaelic darkness. And on the basis of all the misinformation carefully supplied, the Council of War readily agreed that they should all change their minds about going to Fort Augustus, and march to Inverness instead.

Poor Sir John Cope! He has suffered much censure and scorn for his Scottish campaign, but it never had much prospect of success. He might have done well enough against the Earl of Mar. But the Prince was too quick for him, and too well informed. As soon as he was north of Perth Cope found himself in strange, hostile country, close to an adversary whose swift and well-calculated movements made his original plan far too dangerous to be attempted, and he was forced onto the defensive. Those who were wise after the event maintained that when Cope could not get over the Corriearrack he should not have gone to Inverness but should have 'stayed somewhere near Dalwhinnie' and disputed the passage to the south. But it is not easy to see how he could have stayed for long, short of food in hostile country; nor how he would have been able to pin down an agile and more numerous enemy who knew their way perfectly across a country almost devoid of roads, and whose morale was excellent.

So while the general turned his army round and prepared to retire towards Inverness, Charles made ready to ascend the pass and fight the enemy. The highlanders were under arms by seven o'clock on the morning of 8 October, and the ascent began. It was six miles to the top, and Charles sent forward Lochgarry and Murray of Broughton to reconnoitre. They arrived at the head of the pass and found it unoccupied, save for a few deserters from Cope's army, who told them that the soldiers had left Dalwhinnie for Garvemore on the previous day; and before the bulk of the highland army reached the top of the pass, news came that Cope was definitely on the road to Inverness. The Prince and his men immediately set off down the traverses and reached Garvemore by noon. A Council of War was held to consider what should be done. But it was evident that they were too late to catch or intercept the Hanoverian army. Even if they cut across country they would not be able to get between the enemy and Inverness and bring Cope to battle on favourable terms, so it was wisely decided not to carry the pursuit any further. The small army that was marching about in Scotland on behalf of the House of Hanover was of minor importance by comparison with the capture of Edinburgh and the attraction of further support to the Royal Standard. Charles had his priorities right, and he stuck to them.

From the summit of Corriearrack, therefore, the Prince led his men southward by an easy route. The pass of Killiecrankie was not occupied by the enemy, and the Atholl country was loyal to the Marquis of Tullibardine and the Stuarts. At Blair castle, a fortress since the thirteenth century, the Jacobites halted for two nights, and the Atholl tenants came forward to welcome Tullibardine, who had been an exile since 1715. 'Men, women and children came running from their houses, kissing and caressing their master, whom they had not seen for thirty years . . .'⁴ A few days afterwards the army entered the flat and fertile area of Strath Tay. Lochiel occupied Perth, and when Charles arrived there later in the day his father was proclaimed James VIII of Scotland.

On this march south Charles had gained several important recruits, notably Lord Nairne and Colonel John Stuart. But he hoped for many more, and one of the most important was Lovat. It was Lovat's overriding ambition to become Duke of Fraser and Lord Lieutenant of Inverness-shire, and he had made a bargain with James that these honours would be conferred on him if, when the day came, he supported the cause. But as he was actuated solely by self-interest, Lovat had no intention of committing himself to either side until it was clear to him that the Jacobites were going to win or lose. He therefore sent a messenger to the Prince at Invergarry asking that the King's promises should be fulfilled, but at the same time regretting that his age and infirmities made it impossible for him — for the time being — to raise his clan. A commission was made out for him as Lieutenant-General; but he continued to temporise. If ever a man played both sides of the street, it was Lovat. In a letter to the Lord President he referred to his 'zeal and attachment for His Majesty's person and Government', and described Charles as 'that mad and unaccountable gentleman'; but he was more honest in advising Lochiel at much the same time that he had been 'ower rash in going out ere affairs were ripe', and he corresponded with both sides for several weeks longer.

While Lovat played for time, men of higher principles joined the Prince. One of these was James Drummond, third Duke of Perth, honourable, loyal and an ardent Jacobite. He had been brought up in France, but owned extensive properties in Scotland and was actively engaged in their development, including the 'improvement and inlargement' of the town of Crieff. He had, it was said, 'an overfondness to speak broad Scots' and was 'rather over-tedious in his discourses', but he was a man of unquestionable courage, 'the most exemplary, humanely, and universally beloved'. He brought a good number of men with him, and although he was quite wanting in experience, Charles appointed him Lieutenant-General, a rank which he shared for a time with Lord George Murray. With Perth came the Oliphants of Gask, father and son, unswervingly loyal, whose lands had been held for several centuries against the annual gift of a white rose, and Lord Ogilvy, eldest son of the Earl of Airlie, who had been 'out' in the '15. Ogilvy, who was only twenty, had met Charles in France where he had gone to extend his knowledge of soldiering and war, knowledge which he was to put to very good use in the service of the Prince. He subsequently brought from Angus a regiment of six hundred men.

But perhaps the most important of all those who joined the Prince in the early months of the rising was Lord George Murray, son of the first Duke of Atholl and younger brother of the Marquis of Tullibardine. Lord George was a man of the world, educated, experienced, well-informed. Born in 1694, he had served from 1712 to 1715 in the 1st Royals, had taken part in both the '15 and the '19 (fighting alongside his elder brother, and after the defeat at Glenshiel had fled abroad, serving for some years in the Sardinian army. He was pardoned in 1726 and returned to Scotland, and shortly before the '45 was appointed Sheriff-Depute of the Regality of Atholl, thus assuming a recognised responsibility in public affairs. Moreover, his eldest son held a commission in one of the government regiments, and he himself visited Cope when the latter paused at Crieff on his march north. It therefore seemed almost certain that he would remain quietly at home and let the rising take its course — especially since he believed that the Prince, having landed with little money and few supporters, 'made the attempt seem desperate from the beginning'. And yet, when the highland army entered the Atholl country, he made up his mind to engage, declaring in a letter to his younger brother, the Duke of Atholl, that 'a principle of (what seems to me) honour, and my duty to King and Country, outweighs everything'.[5] But the Jacobites were not convinced. If Lord George was so anxious to help the House of Stuart, why had he lived quietly in Scotland for almost twenty years, even taking public office under the Whigs? Why had he not come forward as a friend as soon as Charles had landed? Why had he visited Cope at Crieff, and what had passed between them? Was it not suspicious that even his own brother, the Marquis of Tullibardine, doubted his sincerity in the cause? His conduct in declaring for King James was certainly surprising, and we can say no more than that his motives, like most men's, were probably mixed. Loyalty to James Edward, whom he had first met during the '15, must have played a part; so may a revival of his old ambitions for military glory.

In any case, Lord George's arrival in the Jacobite camp was an event of the first importance. He was an excellent commander; but he was also a divisive personality. Recognising his military talents, Charles at once appointed him a Lieutenant-General, along with the Duke of Perth — an appointment which Lord George's experience and past services amply merited. More than this, he served throughout the campaign, in effect and as far as circumstances permitted, as commander of the army; for he possessed, in the words of the Chevalier de Johnstone,

> a natural genius for military operations, and was indeed a man of surprising talents, which, had they been cultivated by the study of military tactics, would unquestionably have rendered him one of the greatest generals of the age. He was tall and robust, and brave in the highest degree, conducting the Highlanders in the most heroic manner, being always the first to rush sword in hand into the midst of the enemy. He used to say when he advanced to the charge, 'I do not ask you, my lads, to go before, but merely to follow me' . . . He slept little, was continually occupied with all manner of details, and was altogether most indefatigible, for he alone had the planning and directing of all our operations; in a word, he was the only person capable of conducting our army.[6]

But the authority that Lord George was called upon to exercise brought him into repeated conflict with others among the Prince's entourage. He was a general of outstanding ability — there is no question about that; but he was also haughty, outspoken and irascible; and those who disliked him were able to insinuate to the Prince (and to anyone else who would listen to them) that he had joined the rising for what he could get out of it, or even that he was a secret servant of the Whigs. He made enemies, mostly of men of inferior capacities, who envied him; but before long he also alienated Prince Charles, who, when the rising was over, 'could not help averring that he had had much to bear from the temper' of Lord George Murray. It was, indeed, Charles's prime misfortune to have attracted a very mixed company to his standard. No doubt many good causes have disreputable supporters, and in adversity any man may find himself in dubious company. But a man who is young, and poor, and yet who might regain a throne, is sure to find among his companions both the best and the worst in human nature. Charles had with him men such as Lochiel and Lord Pitsligo, men with whom Lord George could work on the best of terms. But there were others, less admirable. Lord Elcho, by his own confession, was educated at Winchester 'with a taste for pleasurable vice', and his subsequent career demonstrates an unnatural streak of vindictiveness. Sir John MacDonald, after his arrival in Scotland, lost no time in insulting his hosts, and was widely regarded as 'drunk or mad, if not both'. O'Sullivan, whom many Jacobites came to regard as Charles's evil genius, had been educated for the Church and was in priest's orders; but he deemed himself an expert in military matters, having served in the Corsican army, and at the outset of the campaign Charles appointed him Quartermaster General. For this appointment Lord George Murray considered O'Sullivan 'exceedingly unfit', and when all was over observed that he had 'committed gross Blunders on many occasions'. These two were in constant conflict throughout the campaign. Murray of Broughton, who also disliked Lord George and who, after the failure of the Rising turned King's evidence, seems to have been of a jealous disposition and undoubtedly saw his friendship with Charles as a means to make his way in the world. These and others sought above everything to advance their own interests, and to stand well in the Prince's esteem.

Charles thus had to conduct his campaign not only with an army but in the company of a self-seeking court as well; and managing this court was no easy matter. There was too much intrigue and too much malice, and Lord George Murray was often the target of both. But he himself was not the type of man to take notice of malicious gossip, to engage in backstairs intrigues, or to ingratiate himself with others. He knew his worth, was haughty and condescending, called a spade a spade, and was apt to state his opinions in such a way as to make enemies of his friends or even — on more than one occasion — to mortify the Prince. Thus, almost from the beginning, suspicion and dissension permeated the Jacobite camp.

These weaknesses, however, were not evident as long as things were going well, and they were going very well at Perth. The Prince remained there for a week, and then continued his march south, intelligence having been received that Cope was on his way to Aberdeen, and that he had made arrangements for transports to be collected there so that his army could be moved as rapidly as possible to the Firth of Forth. It had dawned on the General that his precipitate move out of the highlanders' way at the Corriearrack had left the capital unprotected and that his best chance of doing anything effective was to get back to lowland Scotland as soon as he could. His expedition to the highlands — which was to have nipped the rising in the bud — had reduced the Whigs in Edinburgh to a state of the utmost alarm and despondency. News that their protector was stranded at Inverness whereas the Prince had reached Blair Atholl, on his way to Edinburgh, made them realise the seriousness of their position, and several left Edinburgh for London or for their residences in the country without further delay.

The most effective steps that the Whigs could take at this stage were being taken by Duncan Forbes, the Lord President, who was a protégé of the Duke of Argyll and a loyal servant of the Whigs. Forbes was at Culloden House, near Inverness, writing letters — 'my eyes are almost out, and . . . it is not possible for me to write one line more with candlelight'. He had two tasks to carry out. The first was to persuade as many chiefs as possible that they should not join the Prince — no easy task for an Edinburgh lawyer, working against highland loyalty and the natural celtic inclination to battle. He had some successes, but equally he failed in some notable cases. Cluny Macpherson, in spite of blandishments and promises from Forbes, was won over for the Prince. Lovat, who was a personal friend of the Lord President and with whom Forbes kept up a very frequent correspondence, allowed his clan to march in spite of everything that the Lord President could say, and may even have had some knowledge of the attempt by two hundred of his own clan to capture Forbes at Culloden House on 15 October. But if Lovat deceived the Lord President, Forbes himself was not very scrupulous about the methods he employed. Having persuaded MacIntosh of MacIntosh not to join the Prince, Forbes put it about that the reverse was the case and that the MacIntosh clan was about to march, intending in this way to silence those of their neighbours who were pressing them to 'come out'.

Forbes's second task was to find some loyal Scots Hanoverians, and to grant them commissions as officers in eighteen 'independent companies' which the government proposed to raise in the highlands. The idea was that these companies would be able 'to hinder more men to be raised for the Pretender's service' and that they might also, in the words of Lord Stair, 'go and live at discretion in the countries which the rebels have left' — intimidating the population, no doubt, and probably also helping themselves to cattle and provisions. Forbes had a hard time of it putting this idea for what might euphemistically be called a 'citizens' army' into practice. The trouble was that he had to bestow the commissions on men who knew the highlands and who could be counted upon to show zeal for King George's service, and such men were far from easy to find; as an Under-Secretary in London expressed it, this was a time when all over the country 'zeal is no epidemic'. So great were the difficulties, indeed, that the Lord President met with several refusals and worse. He offered a commission to Lovat, who temporised as usual. Lord MacLeod, son of the Earl of Cromarty, refused a commission; and then the father joined the son, much to the Lord President's mortification, and the pair of them travelled south to enlist with Prince Charles, taking with them between one hundred and two hundred of their followers. Another rebuff came from Mackenzie of Fairburn, who declined to bear arms against the House of Stuart because 'this small mealing I possess was given my predecessor by King James V in free gift . . . the case is conscience with me'. There were many other consciences which stirred, although there were some which failed. In time, eighteen independent companies were formed, at any rate on paper. They were small in size, and the whole force probably never amounted to 1,800 men at any time. It was always poorly armed. Forbes repeatedly asked his masters in Whitehall for arms, money and credit, but the response he received was tardy and limited. Some historians attribute this to a failure on the part of the Whig politicians to realise the seriousness of the situation; but it may equally have been that they realised only too well the doubtful sympathies of those whom they were asked to arm. Men recruited into the independent companies deserted with depressing frequency, taking their weapons (if they had any) with them; and both men and weapons sometimes turned up a few weeks later in the forces of the Prince. The truth is that the government did not dare to trust even those who declared themselves its friends.

This attempt to recruit an army in the north went on through September and into October; and it seemed for part of this time as if nothing else was happening. The contest between Prince Charles and the Whigs was for some weeks a silent one, and everyone lived on the tiptoe of expectancy. The Prince and his men were somewhere in central Scotland — they crossed the Corriearrack on 28 August — and they were advancing on Edinburgh. General Cope was on the move between Inverness and Aberdeen — he actually arrived in Aberdeen on the same day that Charles entered Dunblane — and was known to be waiting for ships to take him south; but for the time being he was no more able to influence events in lowland Scotland than to influence them on the still undiscovered prairies of North America. George II had arrived back in London from Hanover on 31 August. And Duncan Forbes persevered with his campaign of propaganda and persuasion from Culloden House. On 12 September Charles left Dunblane, and on 13 September he reached the Forth. Here he at last came in sight of the enemy, for one of the regiments of dragoons which Cope had left behind on his march north was stationed on the south bank, at the Fords of Frew, west of Stirling. This was where the highlanders intended to cross. As soon as they appeared on the north side of the river, the dragoons withdrew, and Charles and his men waded over, unopposed. They were now only some forty miles west of Edinburgh.

It might be supposed that the government would have been able to make at least a show of defending the capital of Scotland. But the two great non-events of the rising of 1745–6 were the battle for the Corriearrack and the defence of Edinburgh. Just what happened in Edinburgh during the week or so that preceded Charles's entry into the city will never be accurately known. So great was the confusion and so many were the cross-purposes of those involved that the citizens at the time could not understand the sequence of events and historians ever since have been unable to explain them to everyone's satisfaction.

What might be described as the official Whig story goes something like this. The defence of the city was in the hands of the Lord Provost and the magistrates, and when they realised that Charles was advancing closer every day and that Cope was unlikely to come to their rescue, they resolved to put the city 'in a proper state of defence'. They decided to repair and strengthen the walls — for Edinburgh was a walled city — and to raise a regiment of 1,000 men, to be paid by voluntary subscriptions from the citizens. They were advised, however, that they could not raise a regiment without royal warrant, so an application was immediately made to London. A week later, a number of citizens petitioned to be allowed to train as volunteers for the defence of the city, arms to be obtained from the castle. The Town Council agreed that this should be done, and the volunteers forthwith set about their training. The warrant from the King authorising the raising of a regiment duly arrived, and a professor from the University (who could be expected to understand the art of fortification) undertook to supervise the strengthening of the town walls, upon which were now mounted several cannon brought up from armed vessels lying in the harbour at Leith. All seemed to be going well and a determined resistance to the Jacobites was to be expected. On 15 September the highlanders entered Linlithgow, and the dragoons who had fallen back at the Fords of Frew fell back a second time and halted at Corstorphine, just west of Edinburgh. A daring plan was now put forward. It was proposed that the dragoons at Corstorphine, along with another regiment of dragoons at Leith, should be joined by three hundred or four hundred men from the city (most of them the newly-trained volunteers) and that this combined force would attack the highlanders as they marched from Linlithgow. The plan was accepted, for the authorities were determined to resist, and some of the volunteers were sanguine enough to hope that the two regiments of dragoons assisted by three hundred or four hundred amateur soldiers 'might break the force of the rebel army; and leave to the Highlanders, if victorious, a bloody and fatal victory'. But when the ordinary citizens saw some of their young relatives and friends about to leave the town in order to join the dragoons in this desperate venture, they were seized by 'an universal consternation'; their panic was communicated to the volunteers; the Lord Provost wavered in his resolution; the captain of the volunteers received no orders; and the whole scheme collapsed.

This version of events is not very flattering to the citizens of Edinburgh or to their principal representative; but the truth almost certainly is that nothing very like it ever took place. The attempt to strengthen the walls, for example, can hardly have been intended very seriously. To achieve anything worthwhile would have taken weeks or even months, and that nothing was achieved is shown by the prompt abandonment of the idea of defending them as soon as the Prince approached. A regiment of 1,000 men was to be raised; but such was civic enthusiasm that the regiment seems never to have exceeded one hundred and eighty, apart from officers; there were either no more men to be found, or no more subscriptions. As for the volunteers, many of them were, according to one of their number, 'very young men', at least as anxious to impress the ladies as seriously fired with 'ardour for arms and the field'.[7] The evidence is, that those who were genuinely prepared to fight — and when it came to the bit fewer than two hundred offered to leave the town and join the dragoons — were college students or young blades of an adventurous disposition who were foolish enough to think that fighting the highlanders would be good sport, not unlike roaming the streets after dark and twisting the door-knockers on or off the front doors of the houses of respectable citizens, which was a form of entertainment to which patrician youths in Edinburgh were much given in the eighteenth century. The parts played by the Lord Provost and the captain of the volunteers are also open to two interpretations. Are we to believe that the Lord Provost was so utterly incompetent that he thought that he could repair the town walls in three weeks, raise a regiment of 1,000 men and then that he could halt the Jacobite army by sending out two hundred or three hundred raw recruits to meet it — an idea, incidentally, which he was 'very much against' less than twenty-four hours after he had agreed to it? Did the captain of the volunteers finally dismiss them because he received no orders to march, or was his captaincy, as some thought, merely a device to attract attention to himself — for he was a local politician standing for election during these very weeks? The evidence is that if the city fathers had really wanted to resist, there would have been far more serious activity and far less shilly-shallying than actually took place. The proposed 'defence' of Edinburgh was no more than a charade. The great majority of the citizens welcomed the approach of the Prince, the return of the Stuarts, and the early advent of King James III. Had it been otherwise, a population of 50,000 would have produced many more than two hundred men willing to march in the cause of preserving Edinburgh for the Whigs, and these men would have found leaders to help them.

The final failure of resistance puts the matter almost beyond doubt. On Monday 16 September the Jacobite army resumed its advance towards Edinburgh, and a message was sent requesting entry into the city. The Lord Provost sat down to consider the matter, or affected to do so. But before he had got very far, the two regiments of dragoons, which had been moved into a position between Edinburgh and Corstorphine, were observed just north of the town, riding in no very orderly manner to the east, away from the city and away from the enemy. It was their third retreat. This was bad news for the Edinburgh Whigs, and it was worse still when they discovered that the precipitate flight of the dragoons, who retreated all the way from Corstorphine to Dunbar, had been caused by a small party from the Jacobite army who had approached them, looked them over, and then fired their pistols at them. If a few pistol shots produced a retreat of thirty miles, and a retreat, moreover, which left the road to Dunbar 'strewed with swords, pistols, and firelocks', what would be the effect of an assault by the whole highland army? The answer was obvious at least to the Justice Clerk, the Lord Advocate and the Solicitor, who quit the town forthwith and left the Lord Provost to do what he could or would. Any talk of defending the city was now drowned by 'noise and clamour'. The volunteers gave up their arms because it had become obvious that no good could result from keeping them, and the magistrates sent a deputation to Charles asking that hostilities should be delayed so that they could have time to think. This was yet another piece of make-believe, for there was nothing to think about. The Prince, nevertheless, returned a courteous answer, saying that he wished only 'to be received into the city, as the son and representative of the King his father, and obeyed as such when there'; but adding that he had to have an answer before two o'clock in the morning. This should have settled the matter, and would have done so had not news arrived just then that the egregious Cope had reached Dunbar, and would land his troops in the morning. This put the Lord Provost in a terrible dilemma. If he surrendered the town and a battle took place and Cope won it, he could expect to end up, at the very least, in the Tower. If, on the other hand, he refused to surrender the town and Charles either took it or defeated Cope and then took it, he would probably be hanged in the Grassmarket. So he prevaricated, praying, no doubt, that the battle would come first and that he could place his bets afterwards. A second deputation was accordingly sent to the Jacobite camp, asking for yet more time. But Charles was not to be imposed upon twice, and the deputies were sent packing. When their coach returned to Edinburgh and passed through the Nether Bow port at two in the morning, eight hundred highlanders under Cameron of Lochiel stepped through the scarcely guarded gate and took possession of the city. Not a shot was fired. Thus ended the Gilbertian 'defence' of Edinburgh in which nothing was lacking save common sense and sincerity of purpose.

Notes and References

1. *The Highlands of Scotland in 1750*, ed. A. Lang (Edinburgh, 1898), pp. 67–8.
2. 'Lochgarry's Narrative', in W.B. Blaikie, *Itinerary*, p. 113.
3. Murray of Broughton, State Papers, Domestic, 22 August 1746.
4. Murray of Broughton, quoted in Lang, op. cit., p. 77.

5. Letter dated 3 September, in K. Tomasson, *The Jacobite General* (Edinburgh, 1958), p. 20.

6. Chevalier de Johnstone, op. cit., pp. 32–3.

7. Carlyle, op. cit., p. 135.

9 PANIC IN LONDON

Charles came to Holyrood on the morning of 17 September. Tall and handsome, with brown eyes and a fair complexion, he wore a short tartan coat without a plaid, a blue bonnet, and on his breast the star of the Order of St Andrew. The Earl of Perth rode on his right, Lord Elcho on his left; and the King's Park was full of people, for most of the citizens of Edinburgh had left town to see this extraordinary young man. Even the Whigs 'acknowledged that he was a goodly person';[1] while the Jacobites — not least the ladies among them — fell immediately under the spell of his magnetic personality. Charles had the gift of projecting an aura of royalty and command. He was physically very fit and an excellent horseman; he looked every inch a prince; and he had the manner of a very distinguished and well-bred person. It might be said that what tens of thousands of people in the twentieth century saw in Lord Louis Mountbatten, thousands of people in the eighteenth century saw in Prince Charles Edward.

Having allowed himself to be seen by the crowd, Charles rode the short distance to Holyrood Palace, where he gave orders for his father's proclamation. At midday this was read by the Heralds and Pursuivants at the old Market Cross, with all due ceremony. James VIII was declared King, and a Commission of Regency read in favour of Prince Charles. The very large crowd that had gathered round the Market Cross cheered, and a number of ladies in nearby windows 'strained their voices with acclamation, and their arms with waving white handkerchiefs in honour of the day'.[2]

Meanwhile, Cope was landing his far-travelled troops at Dunbar. They were joined there by the dragoons from Corstorphine, the flight of the latter being concealed from the new arrivals as far as possible, which suggests that their own morale was none too high. But at least they had got back. Their movements were promptly and fully reported in Edinburgh, and the Jacobites knew that there was no time to lose. A battle was now inevitable. The Jacobite army had increased in number to about 2,500, of whom only 1,500 were armed with both swords and muskets. Cope's numbers were much the same (the highlanders were well-informed; when they prepared for the battle they believed Cope's army to number about 2,700), but he had the important advantage of possessing several cannon, and his six hundred horse outnumbered by over ten to one the small body of cavalry with Prince Charles. Cope left Dunbar on 19 September and marched to Haddington, and on the next day Prince Charles put himself at the head of his army and marched eastward through Musselburgh and Tranent, lying all night on the high moorland to the east of the village.

Cope was not a great general but he was not nearly as incompetent as many historians make out. Informed on the morning of 20 September by Lord Loudon, who had been sent to reconnoitre, that the highland army was marching towards him, he chose a stretch of open, flat ground between Seaton and Prestonpans as the field of battle, and drew up his army there, facing west. His choice was a good one, for the position was well protected on three sides, by park walls, the huts and clutter of small villages and the sea; and to the south by soft, boggy ground, full of springs, and broken up by 'small enclosures, with hedges, dry stone dykes and willow trees'. The area thus protected was admirable for the combined action of infantry and cavalry, and it was on the strength of this combined action, which Charles could not match, that Cope confidently expected victory. Indeed, the Jacobite leaders were a good deal dismayed when they first saw the position that Cope had taken up: 'it was chosen with a great deal of skill. The more we examined it, the more we were convinced of the impossibility of attacking it; and we were all thrown into consternation, and quite at a loss what course to take'.[3]

That night the highlanders wrapt themselves up in their plaids and lay down to sleep, with the intention of attacking next morning along the awkward line of a wagon road that led through the morass, as best they could. But from this they were saved by the son of a local laird (the father had been 'out' in the '15) who knew the country 'exceedingly well'. Contacting Lord George Murray, he explained that there was another passage through the boggy ground, not readily discoverable, where the army 'might easily pass, without being seen by the enemy, and form without being exposed to their fire'; and he added that he would be willing to lead the way. Lord George, at once realising the importance of this information, awakened the Prince, who was lying on the ground nearby, and a short Council of War was held. It was agreed to use this local knowledge, and surprise the enemy; and before dawn the highlanders began to move. They came down by some low ground, their march at first concealed by darkness and then, when day began to break, by a frosty mist. They moved silently, accustomed to concealment along winding tracks, and when at length challenged by an outpost of dragoons they made no answer but marched on. The whole army successfully passed the morass, entered the level ground where Cope had drawn up his men, and formed into two lines, the Prince taking his place between the first and the second line. The dragoons meanwhile rode back to give the alarm, and Cope lost no time in reforming his troops so as to face the highlanders, now unexpectedly close by, and to the east. He had just sufficient time to complete this manoeuvre before the highland charge began.

Charles's men had no advantage at the start of the battle. The ground between the two armies was an extensive cornfield, newly reaped, flat and level, and without shelter. The highland infantry was unsupported by artillery or horse, and the men had to make a simple frontal attack. No one at that moment knew what the highlanders could do against regular troops. Before the battle, MacDonald of Keppoch, who had served in the French army, had said to the Prince, according to Home,

> that as the country had been long at peace, few or none of the private men had ever seen a battle . . . but he would venture to assure his Royal Highness, that the Gentlemen would be in the midst of the enemy, and that the private men, as they loved the cause, and loved their Chiefs, would certainly follow them.[4]

And so it was. The details may be argued about, but the general course of events is abundantly clear. The battle was hardly a battle at all, for it lasted only a few minutes. The speed and ferocity of the highland charge completely unnerved Cope's troops. The stubble of the cornfield 'rustled under the feet of the Highlanders as they ran on, speaking and muttering in a manner that expressed and heightened their fierceness and rage';[5] and yet, although their movement was very fast, it was uniform and orderly; 'every Front Man covered his Followers, there was no Man to be seen in the Open . . .' The Camerons bore down on Cope's artillery, firing as they advanced, and the Hanoverian artillerymen took to their heels. An officer managed to fire some of the guns, which seemed to make the highland line waver; but they kept coming on 'at a great pace'. A squadron of dragoons moved to support the artillery, were fired upon, and immediately fled. The second squadron moved forwards, refused to charge, fell into confusion under fire, and likewise fled. The soldiers, staggered to see the cannon already taken and the dragoons put to flight, fired without orders and therefore without co-ordination or much effect. The highlanders threw down their muskets, drew their swords and ran on. None of the soldiers even attempted to load a second time, and not one bayonet was stained with blood; they scattered in the utmost confusion, and only about two hundred men escaped, besides the dragoons. Victory was complete.

The battle of Prestonpans was a signal triumph of loyalty, courage and morale. Cope had a better balanced force, with better weapons, and he fought on ground of his own choosing. But his hired soldiers were no match for clansman who fought with the courage born of absolute loyalty and conviction. Those who were 'ready at all times to die for the head of the kindred' were not easily withstood in battle, when led by their chiefs and fighting on behalf of a direct descendant of the Stuart kings.

The Prince and his bodyguard advanced onto the field within two or three minutes of the first shots being fired, but saw 'no other enemy . : . than those who were lying on the ground killed and wounded, though we were not more than fifty paces behind our first line, running always as fast as we could to overtake them, and near enough never to lose sight of them'.[6] The Hanoverian army was virtually destroyed. According to Charles's own account, 'all ye fut [were] killed, wounded or taken prisoner, and of ye horse only to hundred escaped like rebels, one by one'. This seems to be not quite accurate, for some two hundred foot soldiers also escaped, most of them taking refuge in Edinburgh castle, and after the battle Cope managed to collect together about four hundred and fifty dragoons at the west end of the village of Prestonpans. This was all that remained of his army. The cannon, the tents, the baggage and the army's money all fell into the hands of the highlanders, whose losses seem to have been not higher than thirty dead and seventy wounded. Cope and his remnants left the field and rode without delay over Soutra and through Lauder, and managed to reach Coldstream, fifty miles to the south, by evening. The next day they proceeded to Berwick-on-Tweed, where they paused at last behind its formidable fortifications.

That only two or three hundred Hanoverian troops were killed was due to the prompt action of the Prince himself, along with the Duke of Perth and Lord George Murray. They exerted themselves to stop what might have been a considerable slaughter; and Charles 'remained on the field of battle till midday, giving orders for the relief of the wounded of both armies, and preserving . . . every appearance of moderation and humanity'.[7] A young follower of the Hanoverian army, coming up with surgical instruments, was kindly received by Lochiel, 'who was polished and gentle'.[8] The prisoners were also well treated, which apparently surprised some of them. The officers 'were deeply mortified with what had happened, and timidly anxious about the future, for they were doubtful whether they were to be treated as prisoners of war or as rebels'.[9] In fact, Lord George Murray himself found them quarters and provided them with food of his own, and he arranged likewise for a supply of army biscuits to be brought up from Cockenzie for the other prisoners.

After the battle, Charles and his army returned in triumph to Edinburgh. The highlanders were in high spirits, and they celebrated the occasion by marching through the town and firing pretty frequently into the air. This uninhibited behaviour nearly produced a disaster, for one of these stray bullets slightly wounded a lady of a Jacobite family, who was looking on from a window above the street. But because she was a Jacobite no harm was done, for, as she is reported to have said, 'Thank God, the accident happened to me, whose principles are known. Had it befallen a Whig, they would have said it was done on purpose'. Charles, on the other hand, was thoughtful and even melancholy. He had won a remarkable victory, and he was no doubt anxious to follow it up as soon as possible. There was, indeed, some talk during the first few days of marching southward immediately and pressing home the advantage already gained, before the Hanoverians could bring over further contingents of the British army in Flanders. But attractive as this blitzkrieg idea was, it had to be abandoned. The highland army was very small, and was for a time reduced below 2,000 men because many returned to the highlands with booty, and to attend to their little pieces of land; and besides, it was thought that the appearance in England of so small a force would discourage English sympathisers from declaring themselves, and joining the Prince. It was therefore decided to remain some time in Edinburgh and gather additional strength before starting the next stage of the campaign; for Charles, this decision, wise as it probably was, no doubt went against the grain.

For a time, therefore, Charles lived at Holyrood Palace, as his forefathers had done before him, exercising his authority as Prince

Regent. In order to carry on business in the proper fashion of royalty he appointed a Council to meet every day at Holyrood at ten o'clock in the morning; its members included Lord George Murray, the Duke of Perth, Murray of Broughton, Sir Thomas Sheridan and all the highland chiefs. Messengers were sent to France with accounts of the recent battle — accounts which caused astonishment in the French capital and euphoria among the Jacobite exiles living there. Other messengers went to Skye, to acquaint Sir Alexander MacDonald and MacLeod of MacLeod that a great victory had been won and that their failure so far to join the standard would not be held due 'to any failure of loyalty or zeal for His Majesty's cause'. The response of these chiefs was to consult with Lovat, who said 'it was a victory not to be paralleled in history; and that as sure as God was in heaven, his right master would prevail'; and who at once concocted a scheme that a number of clans who had so far remained at home (including his own) would soon meet near Corriearrack and march to join the Prince at Edinburgh. But this meeting of the clans never took place. Sir Alexander MacDonald and MacLeod of MacLeod were faint hearts who at the end of the day 'resolved to stay at home, and not to trouble the Government'; and so Lovat sent his secretary to acquaint the Prince that although he had hoped to come to Edinburgh at the head of 4,000 or 5,000 men, this was now impossible, and all he could do was to send his clan under the command of his eldest son. But even in this Lovat procrastinated and the Frasers did not march from Castle Downie until after the Jacobite army had left Edinburgh, and even then they got no farther than Perth.

Charles made light of this disappointment, although it was a severe one; and it was to some extent counterbalanced by the arrival of other new supporters. Lord Elcho had joined him just before the fall of the city, and now Lord Kilmarnock and Lord Balmerino joined, as did MacPherson of Cluny, who came in advance of his clan. Gordon of Glenbucket, who had fought under the Earl of Mar in 1715, arrived from Aberdeenshire about the same time, with four hundred men, and shortly afterwards came Lord Pitsligo from Banffshire, attended by numerous gentlemen from the north-east, along with their servants well armed and mounted. Pitsligo also had fought in the '15, when Liria had judged him to be 'of considerable understanding and knowledge of the world . . . cultured, likeable, zealous for the King, and capable of giving very good advice'. He was a man of high principle. He left Aberdeen for Edinburgh after the battle of Prestonpans, leading his men forward with the words, 'Oh Lord, Thou knowest our cause is just. Gentlemen, march'. Also at the beginning of October, several ships arrived from France at east coast ports, bringing arms and ammunition.

The time spent at Edinburgh was thus not wasted, and the levees and balls at Holyrood Palace were only a small item in the Prince's routine. How he passed the month of October was recorded by an officer in his army, whose account Home gives as follows:

> The Prince Regent in the morning before the Council met, had a levee of his officers, and other people who favoured his cause. When the Council rose, which often sat very long, for his Counsellors frequently differed in opinion with one another, and sometimes with him, Charles dined in public with his principal officers. After dinner he rode out with his life guards, and usually went to Duddingston, where his army lay. In the evening he returned to Holyrood House, and received the ladies who came to his drawing-room: he then supped in public, and generally there was music at supper, and a ball afterwards.[10]

Charles's stay in Edinburgh and his conduct there have been much censured by Hanoverian historians. He is represented as having wasted valuable weeks, and having passed his time in idle and frivolous amusement. In fact, the whole period was spent in building up the Jacobite forces and planning ahead. The anxieties of Charles and his commanders were numberless; and a young Whig who saw the Prince 'beheld his countenance thoughtful and melancholy . . . he seemed to have no confidence in anybody, not even in the ladies, who were much his friends . . .'[11] This is an interesting observation, for it agrees entirely with what has already been said about dissension and distrust in the Jacobite high command and in the council. Problems were inevitable, if only because the members of the council varied in age, nationality, religion and social background. Several spoke French, or Gaelic, better than they spoke English; some had military experience and some had none; a few — but only a few — understood the political background. The reconciling of conflicting ambitions and advice was the Prince's crucial problem, and he was destined never to solve it. Already, after only seven or eight weeks in Scotland and on the morrow of a remarkable victory, he and his advisers could not agree. Their differences, which were to become much more serious later in the campaign, were at this stage mostly about when to cross the border and in which direction to march. Should they wait for more Scots supporters (such as Lovat) to join them? Should they wait for further encouragement, or arms, or men, to come from France? Should they wait for assurances that the English Jacobites were ready to rise? Or should they move at once and take time by the forelock? Should they make for Carlisle, or march on Newcastle? In every campaign questions like these arise, and fateful decisions have to be taken. Surrounded by men of many divergent interests, not all of whom were worthy of his trust, anxious to succeed but unskilful in the arts of securing agreement, it is little wonder that the Prince appeared, to those who saw him, thoughtful and melancholy.

Towards the end of October the arguments and the waiting came to an end; it was resolved by a very narrow majority that the army would march, and advance towards London through the north-west of England. The force that set off at the beginning of November to cover the three hundred and fifty miles between Edinburgh and London was far stronger than that which had fought the battle of Prestonpans. Total numbers were now about 5,500, of whom five hundred were mounted. The clan regiments, six in all, were the backbone of the army; the Camerons, MacPhersons, MacDonalds of Clanranald, MacDonalds of Keppoch, the Appin Stewarts and the men of Glengarry. Each regiment was commanded by the chief, or his son or brother (according to the situation of the clans), and in battle each chief stood between two of his closest relations. The front rank of each regiment consisted of gentlemen of the clan, better armed than those in the ranks behind. These regiments totalled about 2,200 men. Seven other regiments were of the nature of feudal levies, or were composed of men who had chosen to serve under some well-known Jacobite leader, such as Gordon of Glenbucket. The cavalry was in several groups, none of them large, but this arm included many gentlemen 'of familly and fortune . . . extremely well mounted', and there was a troop of light horse whose role was to reconnoitre the country and bring back intelligence. Furthermore, there was now a train of artillery which consisted of General Cope's field-pieces, taken at Prestonpans, and some Swedish guns which had been brought over from France. Thus Charles's army had not only increased in size, it had also become much better balanced and much more like a modern fighting force of the mid eighteenth century. Yet it was still very small — in 1715 Mar had been at the head of perhaps 10,000 men, and armies which numbered 30,000 or 40,000 were far from uncommon — and its strength in cavalry and artillery was disproportionately little. It was, indeed, having regard to its strategic objectives, a force of almost miniscule size which crossed the border on 8 November and spent its first night in England, and its weaponry did nothing to compensate for its size. But there was nothing deficient in the Jacobite army's morale, or in its expectations.

Once on the march, a great deal depended on the military talents of Lord George Murray, for it was he who had command of the army — although not, unfortunately, sole and undivided command. The initial problem was how to neutralise the army commanded by Field Marshal Wade. This venerable gentleman — he was 72, which was at any rate thirteen years younger than the commander of Edinburgh castle — had been put in charge of the northern army based on Newcastle, after fighting a singularly unsuccessful campaign in Flanders in 1744. Some Jacobites were in favour of disposing of Wade just as they had disposed of Cope, but Lord George preferred to slip past the Hanoverian forces in the north. It did not prove difficult. He and the Prince took part of the army by Lauder to Kelso, which convinced Wade that all he had to do was to await their arrival near Newcastle, for they seemed to aim in that direction; they then, one day later, took the road to Carlisle, and in a short time joined their comrades who had gone direct from Edinburgh. By the time that Wade realised what was happening, Charles was nearer London than he was, on the other side of the hills, and was preparing to besiege Carlisle. Carlisle was a fortified town, and the castle a place of some strength; but its defences had been for long neglected. The siege began, but almost at once word came that Wade had marched from Newcastle, so the Jacobite army moved to Brampton, looking forward — no doubt — to attacking regular troops in the hills. But it was soon discovered that Wade had not marched, the siege was resumed, and a few days later the city and the castle capitulated. That very day Wade and his army — which out-numbered Prince Charles's by about two to one — left Newcastle, and they had got as far as Hexham when they learned that Carlisle had surrendered — so they went back to Newcastle. The meaning of these Hanoverian manoeuvres is not clear, but the obvious inferences are that the Field Marshal was not a fast mover, and that his urge to do battle with the conquerors of Cope was by no means overwhelming.

The Jacobites could now look back on a series of uninterrupted successes — the passage of the Corriearrack, the entry into Edinburgh, the battle of Prestonpans, the siege of Carlisle. Yet within themselves they continued to be plagued by faction and disunity. The surrender of Carlisle was negotiated by Murray of Broughton and the Duke of Perth, and this arrangement caused Lord George Murray to resign as Lieutenant-General. He objected to the prominence given to the Duke of Perth, partly because he was a Roman Catholic, and he objected on all sorts of grounds to Murray of Broughton. Prince Charles was disposed to accept the resignation — Perth and Murray of Broughton were his friends, of his own age, and Lord George, against whom his mind had already been poisoned, was a relative stranger. But he misjudged the situation. The Scots commanders — men like Ogilvy, Lord Elcho and Lochiel — would trust no one but Lord George to lead the army, and the Prince had to give way. Murray of Broughton was henceforth excluded from the council, and the Duke of Perth agreed to serve under Lord George.

Such quarrels are not uncommon in high commands; but the Jacobites could not afford to quarrel, for they were a small force engaged on an almost commando-style operation where everything depended on unity and speed. Lord George was imperious, touchy and difficult to deal with; but he was a first-class commander, incomparably better than the Duke of Perth, and he knew it. The Prince should never have appointed the Duke of Perth to a senior position; but his misfortune was that he had very little experience of handling men, and was naturally disposed to prefer those of his own age, or those whom he had known previously or those who, like himself, were familiar with the wider worlds of Paris or Rome. Moreover, when trouble broke out, his youth and lack of experience made it difficult for him to exercise his authority to the full. On this occasion matters were smoothed over, because the Duke of Perth very handsomely resigned his commission and agreed to subordinate himself to Lord George; but relations between Lord George and the Prince became very strained, and trouble was stored up for the future.

A second cause of disunity was the problem of what to do after taking Carlisle. A Council of War was held, and three different courses were advocated. Some proposed to march across the hills to Newcastle and secure the north of England — and probably bring in more support — by defeating Wade; which should not have been impossible, although his numbers were twice those of the Jacobites.

Many of the chiefs, however, were in favour of returning at once to Scotland. They disliked remaining in or advancing further into England with so small an army, especially when the active support of English Jacobites, which they had been led to expect, had in no way materialised. They also felt that they had been betrayed by the French, who had not yet landed and who had not even detained George's troops on the continent; they were uneasy being so far from home; and perhaps they felt that it was enough to return the Stuarts to the throne of Scotland. But the Prince was not a man for half-measures, and he pressed the argument for advancing directly on London. He believed that the English Jacobites, who talked so much of their loyalty and some of whom had visited his father and himself at Rome, would take to arms if he made a sufficient show of force in England, the further south the better. He also believed that Louis XV was his friend and would soon provide him with substantial support. Louis had in fact sent an envoy to Edinburgh in order to learn more about the Prince's progress; and this man, the Marquis d'Eguilles, had brought Charles an encouraging letter from the King of France and himself assured Charles that a landing by French forces in England would soon take place. Moreover, shortly before the Jacobite army left Edinburgh, a Franco-Jacobite alliance came into existence with the signing of the Treaty of Fontainebleau. This treaty promised French assistance by force of arms in Charles's war against the common enemy, 'the Elector of Hanover'. Help was to be given by Louis' Irish Brigade, and it was emphasised that Louis intended to support a Stuart restoration by every means in his power, including military assistance and intervention. The Prince was therefore justified in assuring his followers that they were not alone in their fight against the English government, and that they could expect to see very shortly a French invasion force in England, and a rising — or several risings — by the English Jacobites. These arguments did not persuade everyone. But Lord George Murray, who 'spoke at some length', comparing the advantages and disadvantages of the various proposals, concluded that if his Royal Highness was set upon advancing farther into England the attempt should be made, and assured the Prince that if he went forward the army would follow him. The chiefs, however reluctantly, gave their consent. And so it was decided.

Leaving two hundred or three hundred men to garrison the castle of Carlisle, the army marched south in two divisions, Lord George Murray commanding the first, and the second, following one day behind, commanded by the Prince. They advanced through Penrith, Shap, Kendal and Lancaster, and within a week reached Preston. Here another council was summoned, at which Charles held out further hopes of being joined by English supporters; a few gentlemen and 'common men' did indeed join the army at this point from Wales, and these newcomers encouraged the hope that Sir Watkin Williams Wynn — a leading magnate in North Wales — and other prominent sympathisers would shortly declare for the cause. Thus encouraged, the army pressed on to Manchester, which in those days was a fair-sized country town. Here several gentlemen, along with two hundred or three hundred other citizens, joined the Prince, and were formed into the Manchester Regiment under the command of Mr Francis Townley, a gentleman of good family in Lancashire, and a Roman Catholic. There were acclamations, bonfires and illuminations, and with this small show of support the army moved on to Macclesfield, which they reached on 1 December.

The Prince and his men were now almost two hundred miles from Edinburgh, and not very much more than one hundred and fifty miles from London. They knew, however, that the Whig government was at last alive to the dangers of its situation and was taking active steps for its own preservation. Troops had been rushed back from the continent, two regiments were ordered over from Ireland, and the Dutch were reminded that they had a treaty obligation to make 6,000 men available if the Hanoverian dynasty were threatened. Efforts were even made to organise the militia, and this was actually done in several counties; but when brought together, these antiquarian units made so wretched a show that the army commanders declared that they would rather do without them; and when the Prince marched into Lancashire the militia was hastily moved out of his way to Liverpool, and disarmed. Thus, even if Charles found disappointingly little support, he found no trace of a 'people's resistance'; indeed, large numbers of the aristocracy and gentry, who were supposed to be 'the king's friends', abandoned their seats at the Prince's approach and left the local population to accept whatever might befall. The slow-moving armies of Hanover meanwhile struggled with problems of their own. Wade, left behind at Newcastle, was at last on the move, and was supposed to be making for Manchester. But his supply arrangements were abysmally inadequate even by the standards of the eighteenth century and his men suffered accordingly, for want of both food and shelter. Remonstrance was useless and advice fell on deaf ears, because, as one of his own officers said, 'the Marshal is infirm and peevish . . . both in body and mind, forgetful, irresolute and perplext, snappish and positive sometime at the expence of good breeding'. By the time that Charles reached Manchester, Wade had crawled no further south than Ripon, and posed no threat. What the Prince had to deal with was the third army sent out to stop him and his supporters in their campaign to liberate their country. This force, for the most part consisting, like Wade's, of troops hastily recalled from the task of supporting Hanoverian ambitions on the continent, was at first commanded by Sir John Ligonier. But when Ligonier fell ill, the King appointed his son, the Duke of Cumberland, to the command. Cumberland had commanded in only one campaign, in which he had been soundly defeated at the battle of Fontenoy, and the case for his appointment was therefore far from overwhelming. But kings move in a mysterious way and Cumberland thirsted for glory: so, on 21 November, when the Prince had reached Penrith, Cumberland was put in command of Ligonier's army strung out from New-castle-under-Lyme almost as far south as Coventry.

Like most generals of little imagination, Cumberland decided that the first thing to do was to await the arrival of more troops — in spite of the fact that he already greatly outnumbered the forces opposed to him. But while he waited, it became clear to him that he might be waiting in the wrong place. Charles's unopposed and rapid advance through Lancashire had brought him to the point where he could choose either to press on towards London or turn westward and advance into Wales, where it was known to him and to others that he might very likely gain substantial new support. If he turned west his first objective would be Chester, which Cumberland was too far south to protect; so detachments of the Hanoverian army were hastily sent north to hold the bridges over the Mersey at Warrington and Stretford, and thus delay any move that the Jacobites might make on Chester. But it at once became clear that the Prince was advancing so rapidly that he could reach the bridges long before Cumberland could come to the support of the detachments sent to hold them; and so the order was given to make both bridges unusable.

The scene was now set for a battle of wits between the Hanoverians and Lord George Murray. Cumberland, with his forces strung along the upper reaches of the Trent south of Manchester, was trying to prevent the Jacobites from approaching any closer to London, and at the same time to stop them from getting into Wales. There was no certain way of doing this, because, as Sir John Ligonier explained, between the Hanoverians and the Mersey there lay 'a ridge of impracticable hills called Bow hills which separate this part from Derbyshire. On the other side of the mountain is the great road from Lancashire by Buxton to Derby. If we move up to the Mersey, they may behind that mountain march into Derbyshire; if we remain here in order to prevent that, I fear they may get into Wales.'[12] Lord George exploited this dilemma with consummate skill. He first sent troops forward to repair the bridge at Stretford, on the route to Wales. Cumberland, informed about the work at Stretford, became more and more convinced that Wales was indeed the Prince's objective. The Hanoverian army began to move forward, hoping that if by any chance their inexperienced commander had guessed wrong, the breaking up of the road between Derby and Buxton, recently carried out, would slow down a Jacobite advance to the south. Meanwhile, Lord George moved westward from Macclesfield with about half the army, entering Congleton on the afternoon of 2 December. This move succeeded admirably, for it convinced the Hanoverians that the Jacobites were either making for Wales or marching to meet them — convinced them so thoroughly that they actually chose a suitable field of battle near Newcastle-under-Lyme. But from Congleton Lord George turned east and marched expeditiously across the 'impracticable hills' to Leek, where he joined Prince Charles, who had gone there direct from Macclesfield with most of the army. The Jacobites then proceeded to Derby, never even using the Buxton road which had been so painstakingly broken up. Cumberland waited on his chosen battlefield at Stone. He waited through the early hours of 3 December. At last it dawned on him in the slowly gathering light that he had been outwitted and outmanoeuvred. Prince Charles reached Derby on 4 December, having gained a day's march on the enemy; and there was every prospect that he and his army would reach Northampton and then London before they could be intercepted. Cumberland's army had been left behind, and the soldiers in it, by Cumberland's own account, were exhausted; his troops 'had scarcely halted six hours these ten days, had been without victuals for twenty-four hours, and had been exposed to the coldest nights I ever felt without any shelter'. It is not surprising that at this point he advised the Whig government to assemble on Finchley Common whatever forces could be mustered.

Everything now depended upon the Jacobite leaders' appreciation of the position. They were only one hundred and thirty miles from London and they knew that any forces between themselves and the capital must be of an ill-balanced and improvised nature. A Council of War was held, and it immediately became evident that few if any of the officers and chiefs were in favour of advancing any further. At least four arguments in favour of a withdrawal to the north were put forward, although we do not know how much importance was attached to each. There was the consideration, most obviously, that the small Jacobite army was opposed by three other armies, and outnumbered by each of them: Cumberland, with at least 9,000 men, was only some thirty miles to the west; Wade, advancing south, had reached Wetherby with over 5,000 foot soldiers and almost eight hundred cavalry; and at Finchley an army of sorts was assembling, which was reported (with gross exaggeration) to number 30,000. In a sense, therefore, the Jacobites were or appeared to be surrounded by superior forces. Secondly, the premisses upon which the advance on London had been based seemed not to have been well founded. Where were the English Jacobites whose help had been so often and so confidently predicted? Admittedly, a few hundred had joined the standard on the march south, but thousands had been expected. Where, in particular, was Sir Watkin Williams Wynn, one of the greatest Jacobite supporters, whose sphere of influence the Jacobite army had passed very close to south of Manchester? And thirdly, where were the French? Louis XV was to have sent an expedition to England, but none had appeared. Instead, Lord John Drummond had arrived from France with his regiment of the Royal Scots, along with some piquets of the Irish Brigade, all first-class troops; and more were expected. But these forces had landed in Scotland, and were therefore of no immediate help to the Prince. Indeed, this addition of strength caused some confusion, because the information received at Derby was that a very large force of approximately 4,000 men was now assembled in Scotland, some from France and some recently arrived from the highlands; and many argued that the best course was to return north, and join this second and still growing army. It was further represented to the Prince that to remain near London was to invite a battle with Cumberland, in which the Jacobites would certainly be victorious, but there would be losses; and an army diminished in size would then have to fight a second battle only a few days later against whatever forces might be found on Finchley Common; the final outcome would then be doubtful. Better, surely, to retire to the north, intact and in good order, and await or contrive a better opportunity for battle.

Prince Charles would have none of it. One of the best attested facts about the '45 is that he never wavered in his passionate desire to advance on London — he 'always obstinately insisted'. What his arguments were, we do not know for sure. We do know, however, that he believed that large numbers in England supported him ('his Irish favourites to pay court to him had always represented the whole nation as his friends');[13] that he was convinced that the highlanders could never be beaten in battle; and that this faith was reinforced by a conviction that British soldiers, fighting for whatever cause or whatever ruler, would never fight seriously or for long against the House of Stuart. These arguments may have pleased his commanders, but they could not convince them; and Charles's credibility must in any case have been low as a result of his often belied statements or even promises of English risings and a French invasion. The Duke of Perth took no part in the debate, 'resting his head against the fireplace and listening to the dispute without uttering a single word; but at last he declared himself loudly of the opinion of the other chiefs'.[14] Lord George Murray also took the view that retiring north was the course of wisdom, and that it was indeed absolutely necessary; and at the end of the day Charles, in his own words, 'could not prevail upon one single person'.

According to Hanoverian historians, the retreat from Derby was 'inevitable'; or, if not inevitable, was one of the few thoroughly sensible moves that the Jacobites made. These historians are bound to approve the decision taken at Derby, of course, because the road from Derby led to Culloden. But was Charles so certainly wrong? Three armies in the field against him sounds bad. But the assemblage at Finchley consisted mostly of the 'trained bands', who were notably untrained, and who would almost certainly have fled at the mere commencement of a highland charge, while the regular troops who were to stand alongside them were less numerous than the Prince's army. As for the venerable Wade, his leaden-footed attempts to close with the Jacobite army, and the near-starvation conditions in which he kept his troops, made it very unlikely that he posed a serious threat to Prince Charles. And as for Cumberland, he had been manoeuvred out of the way; and his strenuous but largely unsuccessful efforts to catch up with the Jacobites on the march to Scotland suggest that he could not have prevented them from reaching London, had they decided to try. The situation was therefore by no means hopeless. To have gone on, and not back, would certainly have been very risky. But war even more than life is full of chances. There is really no saying what would have happened if Charles had got his way.

One is bound to ask why the decision went the way it did. Charles's loss of credibility must have been a vital factor, and this loss was to some extent his own fault. He forecast risings in England and a French invasion often and with confidence, doubtless because he believed that these would take place. But nothing had been definitely arranged. His sudden and almost secret departure from France; the lack of all consultation with either his father or Louis XV; the whirlwind nature of his campaign; his faith that hints and half-promises from his friends would produce action at the right time (a sure sign of political inexperience); all these meant that there was no political planning behind his campaign, and that he had to trust to his star and simply keep going at all costs. He had made a start such as no one else could have made and he had to keep the initiative. Perhaps he instinctively realised this when he tried, and failed, to persuade the chiefs and the others at Derby.

Yet the blame was not all theirs. Even today it must be found surprising that so many men who visited James Edward and his family at Rome, who corresponded with him and professed their loyalty to him, stood idly by and did nothing to help their Prince in the autumn and winter of 1745. The English Jacobites — who unquestionably existed — seem to have been something between cautious and pusillanimous. They were good at drinking the King's health; but as James Ray said of them, 'no people in the universe know better the difference between drinking and fighting'.

As regards the French, too, Charles was unlucky. A French landing, even a small one, would have made all the difference — and a landing was actually planned. All that the Prince knew, while at Derby, was that Louis XV had promised help and had in fact sent men and supplies to Scotland in November. But Louis was devious, secretive, indecisive. He had no great wish to assist the Stuarts, but he calculated that they might provide a useful diversion in his war with England. So he dreamed of an invasion which would take place soon after the English Jacobites had shown their strength and resolution by rising against the Whig government. The trouble with this scenario was that the English Jacobites proposed a different one; they would rise against the government soon after the French landed. This was the impasse that Charles aimed to solve by marching to London; and well before the battle of Prestonpans he took the trouble to tell Louis that that was what he was going to do. Had the French King possessed one quarter of Charles's imagination and resolution he would have acted then — he could even have agreed to a request made in August by the Earl Marischal for 4,000 men to sail for Scotland immediately. This would have had a decisive effect. But Louis was no more accustomed to moving fast than Marshal Wade. It was not until Charles had taken Edinburgh that Louis finally decided that here was an opportunity too good to miss. And by the time he had got together troops and transports and a commander for the expedition and they were all ready to set off, the Jacobite army was back in Scotland. Even so, the French preparations made a significant impact, and had the Jacobite leaders known more about them, they might have been persuaded to march on, from Derby to London. For during the final month of 1745, fears of a French invasion haunted ministers in the capital. They knew that an invasion force was being assembled in Dunkirk, but they could not guess where or when it might land. The arrival of the Prince and his men at Derby was almost the last straw. There took place, in the words of Fielding, 'a panic scarce to be credited' — a Whig panic more than anything, for there were many in London who knew that they had nothing to fear from the Jacobites. Charles's army had committed no outrages in England — the Prince and his commanders saw to that. Even the *London Gazette* was obliged to admit that 'the rebels behaved tolerably well on their march southwards'. But stories of rape and destruction were assiduously spread around. The monied interest took fright as usual, and the Bank of England suddenly found itself short of ready cash; and a rumour went about that the King was packing his bags while the Duke of Newcastle tried to decide 'whether he should not instantly declare himself for the Pretender'. These stories were without foundation; but that they were circulated and in part believed shows how unstable the situation had become. Firm news of a French landing might well have turned them into reality.

The moment of crisis at Derby was therefore a moment of crisis in Whitehall as well. When the government discovered that the Jacobite army had left Derby and was moving north, an almost audible sigh of relief went up from the Whig ministers. The French threat remained; but now there could be no fear of its being co-ordinated with the movements of Prince Charles, and the government knew that it could count on very wide support for a struggle simply against France. The Jacobites in retreat, moving away from London and the south coast, could, ministers imagined, be quickly disposed of.

As usual, the Whigs and the Hanoverians had got it wrong. Cumberland's idea was that Wade should march across to Lancashire and intercept the Prince; but by the time that Wade reached Wakefield the Prince was north of Manchester, whereupon the Marshal decided that the best he could do was to go back to Newcastle. Undismayed, Cumberland remained confident that he himself could catch up with the Jacobites, having already set off in pursuit with all his cavalry and 1,000 foot soldiers mounted on horses procured locally. But even this 'flying corps', which sometimes covered twenty-five or thirty miles a day 'over a most dreadful country', proved unable to close the gap until the Jacobite army had reached Clifton, just south of Penrith. It was here that Cumberland discovered that he was not pursuing a panic-stricken mob fleeing before him, as he seems fondly to have imagined, but a mobile, well-led and formidable enemy.

On the march north the Jacobite rearguard was always commanded by Lord George Murray. Having with them the artillery and the ammunition wagons, which frequently broke down, the rearguard was often well behind the main body of the Jacobite army, and on the day that the Prince reached Penrith, Lord George was obliged to halt for the night at Shap, among the bleak hills of Westmoreland. Setting out very early the next morning, the highlanders had not gone far when bodies of horsemen appeared on the ridges of the nearby hills, shadowing the marching column and keeping out of musket-shot. Information about this was at once sent forward to Penrith. Arriving near Clifton, Lord George found two hundred or three hundred horsemen drawn up between him and the village, but they galloped off as soon as the highlanders, throwing off their plaids, ran to attack them; and the rearguard entered Clifton. Word was received shortly afterwards, however, that the Duke of Cumberland, with (it was reported) 4,000 horse, was only one mile away, and Lord George, rather than withdraw into the gathering darkness, decided to fight a rearguard action that evening. He hoped, indeed, to do more. The broken nature of the country suited the highlanders' way of fighting and made the use of cavalry difficult; and given sufficient men there was a good chance that he would be able to position them so as to attack the flank of the dragoons, already drawn up on Clifton Moor. He therefore sent Colonel Roy Stuart to

Penrith, with a request for the immediate assistance of 1,000 men. But Charles, whose distrust of Lord George was now reinforced by a cordial dislike, perhaps partly because of the latter's outspoken opposition to any advance south from Derby, refused. Instead, he sent a small force sufficient only to help save the rearguard from annihilation, coupled with an order not to engage the enemy, but to retire at once to Penrith. Compliance with such an order could only have resulted in the destruction of most of the rearguard by Cumberland's troops, and Murray therefore ignored it; according to Home, 'Lord George Murray desired Colonel Stuart not to mention this order to any other person'.[15]

The sun had now set, and it was beginning to grow dark. Cumberland was poised to attack over the moor and along the road into the village of Clifton, and he no doubt expected that his dragoons would drive the highlanders before them. On each side of the road, however, there were fields enclosed by hedges, ditches and stone walls, and Lord George positioned his regiments along these defences, with only the Glengarry regiment on the road (which was, no doubt, a wide and ill-defined track quite unlike a modern road). The action about to take place was one that Lord George could not afford to lose, for he was fighting it against orders. 'Day-light was gone; the night being dark and cloudy, the moon sometimes was overcast, and at other times shone bright . . . Lord George Murray went backwards and forwards, speaking to every commanding officer, and giving him particular directions what to do . . .'[16] In the semi-darkness a body of men was dimly seen coming from the moor. These were dragoons, dismounted because of the mud, the ditches and the darkness. The highlanders advanced to meet them, taking advantage of the walls and hedges. The dragoons fired, the fire was returned, and then Lord George drew his sword and led his men forward, running upon the dragoons before they could load a second time. The soldiers fled back to the moor as best they could, accompanied by others who had attempted to advance along the road. Significantly, during their flight they were fired upon by other highlanders concealed behind the hedges. The conflict lasted no more than a few minutes, and even the Hanoverian losses were not heavy.

This encounter at Clifton has been a great deal misunderstood and misrepresented — it has even been dismissed as unimportant. Yet the facts speak for themselves. Cumberland's objective was to overtake and destroy the Prince's army before it could unite with the

3,000-strong force under Lord John Drummond in Scotland. But having at last overtaken the rearguard and launched an attack, his troops were so roughly handled that the action lasted for only a few minutes and was never resumed. Hanoverian historians emphasise that Cumberland (whose exact whereabouts during the fighting do not seem to be known) was able to enter Clifton later that night and remain there. But this he was able to do because Lord George, having rested his men for a few hours, moved on to Penrith with all the artillery, all the ammunition wagons and all the baggage. The measure of Cumberland's failure is, after all, quite simple; after the check he received at Clifton, he never again saw any part of the Prince's army until the battle of Culloden four months later. Yet his intention had been to prevent the Jacobites from re-crossing the border as a fighting force.

Secondly, what happened at Clifton is very instructive in demonstrating the gulf that separated the military abilities of Lord George Murray from those of Cumberland. Cumberland, it is clear, could only fight a set-piece battle. He understood the idea of lines of men facing one another, in full view, advancing one against the other, firing; orthodox, simple and stupid. But it is hard to imagine what he thought was going to happen when he sent his dragoons forward, on foot, still wearing their boots, across Clifton Moor in the intermittent moonlight. The only rational explanation for his order would seem to be that he expected the highlanders to run away; and if that was his idea, he was very soon undeceived. Lord George, on the other hand, made full use of the natural advantages of the ground, gave his men the kind of action in which they excelled — and, incidentally, led them himself. It was a type of warfare which was beyond the capabilities of the Hanoverian army; sudden, unexpected, intelligent; and Lord George was to demonstrate it again, in Scotland, in 1746. Had Charles sent the 1,000 men asked for, Clifton might have been as conclusive as Prestonpans, with incalculable consequences.

Experiencing no further trouble, or the threat of any, Charles and his army reached Carlisle on 19 December, almost exactly four weeks after they had left that town on their way south. There they received further news about the men and supplies sent from France and about the size of the army collected under Lord John Drummond, and it was agreed to march on to Scotland and to join forces there. Possibly with the idea of facilitating his re-entry into England at a later date, Charles left a garrison of about four hundred men — including the Manchester regiment — to hold the town and the castle; but both had to be surrendered ten days later, Cumberland having brought over siege artillery and gunners, Dutch as well as English, from both Whitehaven and Newcastle on Tyne. The best terms that the unlucky garrison could get were 'that they shall not be put to the sword but be reserved for the King's pleasure', which was not much security, considering that Cumberland had already had four prisoners hanged in sight of the castle 'as a specimen of what the rest may expect'. Meanwhile, the Jacobite army crossed the border and, dividing into two columns, followed two separate routes to Glasgow. The lowland regiments, under Lord George Murray, entered the city on Christmas day, and Charles, at the head of the clans, arrived on the following afternoon. A day or two later he reviewed the whole army on Glasgow Green. Its numbers were still small, but he was perhaps not unwilling to let the world see with what an exiguous force he had penetrated almost to London; he could say, moreover, that he had brought back with him almost all the men whom he had taken across the border on this remarkable sortie, for the number of those killed while in England seems to have amounted to no more than forty.

Notes and References

1. Home, op. cit., p. 100.
2. Ibid., p. 102.
3. Chevalier de Johnstone, op. cit., p. 35.
4. Home, op. cit., p. 108.
5. Ibid., p. 118.
6. Chevalier de Johnstone, op. cit., p. 37.
7. Home, op. cit., p. 122.
8. Carlyle, op. cit., p. 157.
9. Ibid., p. 157.
10. Home, op. cit., p. 139.
11. Carlyle, op. cit., p. 163.
12. Speck. op. cit., p. 87.
13. Elcho, op. cit., p. 340.
14. Chevalier de Johnstone, op. cit., p. 60.
15. Home, op. cit., p. 149.
16. Ibid., p. 150.

10 TRIUMPHS AND TRAGEDY

From the time that Prince Charles landed at Arisaig until his departure fourteen months later, the life of Scotland was continuously divided and disturbed. This was just as much the case when Charles was in England as when he was north of the border, for during that time also he acted as Prince Regent, exercising his authority over a country in which neither magistrates nor judges were free to act, and in which, for a good part of the time, most but not all men under arms were subject to his control.

Before he marched south early in November, Charles had appointed Lord Strathallan as commander in Scotland. Strathallan at that time had with him, in and around Perth, only a few other gentlemen and a handful of French-Irish officers, with their men; but a month later he was joined by Lord John Drummond who arrived from France with a force of about eight hundred men, landed at Montrose, Stonehaven and Peterhead; and by the time that Charles re-crossed the border, a considerable army had collected, with its headquarters at Perth and Dunblane. This army consisted mostly of highlanders and of men from the north-east of Scotland. The Frasers under the Master of Lovat had at last appeared, Lovat himself having escaped from 'protective custody' early in December. At much the same time, Lord Lewis Gordon · came in with a good many men from Aberdeenshire; Lady MacIntosh had raised her clan despite the fact that her husband was with the government; Lady Fortrose had done almost as much in the same circumstances; Lord Cromarty and Lord MacLeod joined with a MacKenzie regiment; while MacDonald of Barrisdale, young Glengarry and the elder Lochiel brought fresh recruits from the west. All told, this was a respectable force, probably numbering not much less than 4,000 and Lord John Drummond assumed its command.

In spite of their numbers, the Jacobites did not have complete control in Scotland. The wheeling and dealing of the Lord President was not without effect on those who could not decide where their loyalty lay, and he had managed, although with much difficulty, to assemble not more than 2,000 men under arms (or supposedly under arms) in different parts of the country. The most numerous of these bands was under the command of Lord Loudon, who, along with the Lord President, made his headquarters at Inverness. Late in December, a clash took place between some of Loudon's men and those under Lord Lewis Gordon, who had fixed his headquarters at Aberdeen, in his own country. Rash enough to take the offensive, Loudon sent MacLeod of MacLeod from Inverness with five hundred or six hundred men (most of whom came from the Isle of Skye) to harass the Jacobite forces around Aberdeen. The move was not a wise one, for there is ample evidence that many of these west highlanders were, to say the least, half-hearted in their opposition to the Prince. The result was as might have been expected. Lord Lewis, informed of MacLeod's whereabouts, marched his men to attack the enemy, encamped near Inverurie. The action began by moonlight, and there was firing for some time by both sides; but when the Jacobites advanced to close with their opponents, MacLeod's men 'did not stand the charge', but precipitately left the field and escaped as best they could. Few men were killed on either side, but Lord Lewis took some prisoners, and MacLeod retired across the Spey, once more leaving all the country from Aberdeen to the Spey in the undisputed control of the Prince.

This skirmish at Inverurie, as it came to be called, was not very important in itself, although it freed a substantial part of the country from Hanoverian control; but it again demonstrated the moral superiority of the Jacobites over their enemy, and showed how easily they could extend their influence within Scotland.

Moves were now set afoot to unite the Prince's forces. Stirling was the rendezvous, and the main army marched from Glasgow on 3 January. Reaching Bannockburn, they encamped in the villages roundabout, and were soon joined by the army under Lord John Drummond, as well as by Lord Lewis Gordon's men from Aberdeen. The Hanoverian forces made no attempt to intervene, nor could they have done so. At this point, Charles had at his disposal about 8,000 armed men, most of whom had been in action, either at home or on the continent, and several able and experienced commanders. Had this force been available when he set off for London, there is almost no doubt that he would have reached his objective.

The first task was to take possession of the town of Stirling and to lay siege to the castle. This operation was of some importance to the clans, because men going to or returning from the highlands could not with safety take the natural and easy route through Stirling as long as it was held by the Hanoverians. The town presented no difficulties, it was not fortified. The Prince agreed to the conditions of surrender, and the gates were opened. Reducing the castle was a much more difficult matter, however, and the siege was most incompetently conducted by a Monsieur Mirabelle, a French engineer who had come to Scotland with Lord John Drummond.

> It was supposed that a French engineer, of a certain age and decorated with an order, must necessarily be a person of experience, talents, and capacity; but it was unfortunately discovered, when too late, that his knowledge as an engineer was extremely limited, and that he was totally destitute of judgment, discernment and common sense.[1]

Trenches were opened on 10 January, and six pieces of artillery, carried over the Forth from Perth to Stirling, not without a good deal of trouble and difficulty, arrived on 14 January. But on the evening of 16 January the siege was called off and orders were given for the whole army to be reviewed next morning at break of day on a moor just east of Bannockburn.

The reason for this change of plan was the rapid build-up of Hanoverian forces in Scotland and a new threat of attack. Cumberland was back in London, 'highly pleased and satisfied', in his own words, with what he had accomplished. The King and the ministers in London had to find a new army and a new commander, and it says a good deal about them that their first choice was Marshal Wade. Luckily for them, Wade declined. Major-General Huske was then considered. Time was to show that Huske was a man of genuine ability, but the government preferred seniority to ability and chose Lieutenant-General Hawley, who had an evil reputation for 'discipline' and whose 'first exploit' on taking up his new command was to have gallows erected in Edinburgh and Leith. The build-up of Hanoverian forces continued, and by the middle of January Hawley had assembled in Edinburgh twelve regiments of foot, five regiments of dragoons (including the two that had so distinguished themselves at Prestonpans), and a miscellaneous collection of other troops. It had been hoped to include at least some of Lord Loudon's men; but Lord Lewis Gordon at Inverurie had put paid to that idea. Nevertheless, Hawley was full of confidence. He had superiority in numbers, and the same unreasoning contempt for the Prince's army as was shown by Cumberland. The latter referred to Charles's men as 'that despicable enemy' and forecast that 'they

will retire to Perth upon the first appearance of the king's troops';
while Hawley described them as 'rascally scum' and expected that
on his approach 'they will go off or else they are mad'.

These opinions were soon put to the test. Huske, who had been
appointed second in command, led the Hanoverian advance guard
from Edinburgh to Linlithgow on 13 January. Lord George
Murray, who had been holding Falkirk as the advance post of the
Prince's army, marched five battalions and some cavalry to
Linlithgow, but retired on Huske's approach and then fell back on
the main body of the army at Bannockburn. Huske moved forward
to Falkirk, where he was joined by Hawley on 16 January, and the
whole army encamped in a field at the west end of Falkirk. Well-
informed about all these moves, the Jacobites were drawn up on
Plean Moor, two miles to the east of Bannockburn and only seven
miles away from their enemy.

When Hawley failed to advance from Falkirk, the Jacobites
waited no longer but once again manoeuvred so as to take full
advantage of the lie of the ground and to surprise the Hanoverian
forces. Instead of marching straight towards the enemy, the Prince's
men marched south, crossed the River Carron and the main roads,
and then swung round to reach the high ground above Falkirk, only
about a mile from the enemy camp. This position of vantage the
vanguard reached early in the afternoon. The surprise achieved by
this march was almost complete, for Hawley's men had earlier seen
a party of Jacobites on the high road to the north, 'with standards
and colours displayed', and had concluded that it was from this
direction that the Prince in due course would come. Not until one
o'clock was the discovery made that the whole Jacobite army was on
the march, and when informed of this Hawley 'said that the men
might put on their accoutrements, but there was no necessity for
them to be under arms'.[2] Whether this *sang-froid* communicated
itself to his officers and other ranks we do not know; but it was sadly
misplaced, for he had not the faintest idea what was going on. An
hour or so later, horsemen 'came in upon the spur' and reported that
the Prince's army was about to cross the Carron and seemed to be
making for the high ground near Falkirk. This alarming news was
passed on to the commander, who was now enjoying a leisurely
lunch at near-by Callander House; and when he at last returned to
the camp and realised how serious the situation was, he hastily
ordered three regiments of dragoons to take possession of the high
ground at which the Jacobites were evidently aiming, and ordered

his infantry to follow the dragoons as fast as possible.

This order must have been given some time between two and three o'clock in the afternoon — a winter's afternoon. No sooner had the Hanoverian infantry set off than a violent storm of wind and rain broke out and blew directly in the faces of the soldiers, who were marching up hill with their bayonets fixed, and who could not protect their muskets and powder from the rain. They made heavy work of it. But the dragoons were a good way in front, and so it became a sort of race between the Jacobites and the dragoons, which of them should first reach the top of the hill. In the event, both sides arrived so nearly at the same time that neither could take advantage of the other, but the Prince's army had the advantage of the ground. And when the dragoons halted, watching the Jacobite army form into two lines, Hawley's infantry regiments continued to mount the hill until they, likewise, could form into two lines.

The scene, now set for the battle of Falkirk, was peculiar in several respects. The dragoons were strung out in front of their own infantry over a great distance of ground so that they faced two-thirds of the Jacobite front line. The ground behind the dragoons sloped away, so that most of the Hanoverian infantry were standing on the declivity of the hill, those on the left wing being so far down the slope that they could not be seen by those standing in the front line of the Jacobite army. The Hanoverian regiments on the right wing were more on a level with their opponents, but were separated from them by a ravine or gully which ran due north, becoming deeper and wider as it went down to the low ground west of Falkirk. There were no cannon on the hill, for the Jacobites had made such speed to reach the high ground before the dragoons that they had left their artillery a mile behind them; while Hawley's cannon were 'stuck fast at the bottom of the hill'. Finally, the storm of wind and rain continued, the darkness increased, and conditions became so bad 'that nobody could see very far'.

Lord George Murray commanded the right wing of the Prince's army, and from where he stood he could not see any infantry behind the dragoons. He therefore ordered two officers on horseback to go as near the dragoons as possible, in order to check what enemy infantry were in the field; they returned with the report that they could not see any; and Lord George immediately led his men forward to the attack, with his sword drawn. At this precise moment the colonel of the dragoons received an order from General Hawley to attack the Jacobite army; and the dragoons moved forward. Lord

George allowed them to come very close, and then gave the order to fire. This fire, withheld until it was deadly, had such effect that an onlooker 'saw daylight through them in several places', and all three regiments of cavalry fled in confusion, many horsemen plunging through their own infantry. Then, in spite of an order from Lord George to stand firm, the greater part of the right wing of the Jacobite army rushed forward after the dragoons. Down the slope of the hill, in the rain and semi-darkness, they came on Hawley's infantry, still drawn up in two lines. Both sides fired, and then the Jacobites threw down their muskets, drew their swords, and fell upon Hawley's luckless regiments of foot. What happened next is best described in the word of a Hanoverian historian who was present at the battle:

all the regiments in the first line of the King's army gave way, as did most of the regiments of the second line. It seemed a total rout; and for some time General Hawley did not know that any one regiment of his army was standing . . . The disorder and confusion encreased, and General Hawley rode down the hill.[3]

But things did not go so well on the Jacobite left wing, where the highlanders under Lord John Drummond faced the enemy across the ravine. Each side fired on the other, but a charge was impossible; and the fire of Hawley's better-equipped troops had such effect that the Jacobites, after losing a good many men, fell back a little; and those who had set off in pursuit of the dragoons, hearing so much noise of battle behind them came back to the higher ground where they had first stood. There they expected to find the second line of the Prince's army. But the second line was nowhere to be found, for most of the men in it had joined the chase; and those who had not done so, hearing the continuous firing across the ravine and unable to see what was happening, concluded that the Hanoverians were getting the upper hand and that the best thing they could now do was to make their escape. Thus large numbers of Hawley's men were fleeing eastward, while a good number of Prince Charles's men were in flight to the west. And in the centre of the battlefield 'there was a considerable space altogether void and empty' except for those who had returned from the pursuit, 'and were straggling about in great disorder and confusion, with nothing in their hands but their swords'.[4]

The battle had thus far lasted for only about twenty minutes; and the fighting was, in fact, at an end. Lord George Murray, who had kept a body of men together on the extreme right wing, moved to the centre of the field where Charles and the Irish piquets joined him from the rear, and all moved forward to the brow of the hill. At the same time, the few Hanoverian regiments which had stood their ground behind the protection of the gully, moved off down the hill, covered by one of the regiments of dragoons which, once more venturing forward, hastily retreated when seeing the body of men around Charles and Lord George. The storm of wind and rain continued as violent as before, and night was coming on. What was left of Hawley's army made their way back to the camp that they had left only an hour or two previously, set fire to their tents, marched through Falkirk and did not halt until they reached Linlithgow, seven miles away. They left behind them seven cannon and a great quantity of ammunition, provisions and baggage, and on the following day, Hawley and his men retreated a further seventeen miles to Edinburgh.

For a short time the Jacobites were not sure that they had won a victory. Their army was in complete disorder, 'dispersed here and there with the different clans mingled pell-mell together, whilst the obscurity of the night added greatly to the confusion'. Some men had left the field, thinking that all was lost, and others had dispersed to find shelter from the weather, for the rain was incessant. Many commanders could not find their regiments, and for a time even the Prince's whereabouts were unknown to many if not most of his senior officers. But Lord Kilmarnock, who knew the country, went forward to reconnoitre, and returned with the news that the Hanoverian army was on 'the great road to Edinburgh . . . panic-struck and flying in the greatest disorder as fast as their legs could carry them'.[5] Charles, who had remained on the field of battle, went down to Falkirk and occupied the quarters which earlier that day had been occupied by Hawley, and sent back orders that the army was to assemble at Falkirk next morning by break of day.

Three battles had now been fought, and this was the third successive Jacobite victory. They had annihilated Cope's army at Prestonpans, frustrated Cumberland's blundering designs at Clifton, and now had driven Hawley from the field with the loss of approximately three hundred killed and seven hundred taken prisoner, at a cost of only about forty men killed. The Jacobite military superiority appeared to be overwhelming. Admittedly, Hawley had contributed a good deal to his own defeat. It is not easy to see why, when the Prince's army was found to be approaching the hilltop, he should have tried to get there first. He did not succeed; and had he remained where he was it would have been difficult to attack him with any advantage. It is even more difficult to understand the order which he gave for seven hundred or eight hundred dragoons to advance in the teeth of a storm and attack 8,000 foot drawn up in two lines. The officer who received the order is reported to have said 'it was the most extraordinary order that ever was given', and this was certainly not far off the mark. When the dragoons attacked, their chances of success were about the same as those of the Light Brigade at Balaclava; the difference is that the order given to the Light Brigade was misunderstood, whereas that given to the dragoons was not. At the same time, Hawley made these mistakes having been put in a position to make them by his opponents. The Jacobites' march to the hilltop was a bold and surprising move which seems quite to have destroyed Hawley's coolness and presence of mind — if he ever had any; the dragoons were scattered by an army properly deployed and handled; and Charles's men followed up their advantage with an immediate and overwhelming infantry attack. Thus the Jacobites won the battle through a display of both intelligence and courage.

Yet their victory was a curious one. The only person to whom it seems to have given much satisfaction was General Cope, who is said to have 'offered bets to the amount of ten thousand guineas, in the different coffee-houses in London, that the first general sent to command an army against [the Prince] in Scotland would be beaten, as he himself had been at Prestonpans';[6] so Cope presumably made some money and looked less foolish than he had done for several months. The Whigs, of course, were aghast. Veteran troops who had fought at Dettingen and Fontenoy had been obliged to scramble back to the comparative safety of Edinburgh.

> At no time, from the beginning to the end of the Rebellion, were the real friends to the Constitution of their country more dejected, or more apprehensive, than they were when they saw the troops return from Falkirk, who had marched against the rebels a few days before, as they thought to certain victory.[7]

As for Hawley, he went so far as to profess himself broken-hearted; although he attributed his defeat entirely to the 'scandalous cowardice' of his troops and recommended that a number of them should be shot. On the Jacobite side, also, there were recriminations. Lord George Murray maintained that none of the Hanoverian infantry would have escaped if, on the Jacobite left wing (which was — or was supposed to have been — commanded by Lord John Drummond), the second line had been brought forward to out-number or outflank the regiments of Hawley's right wing, who ultimately retreated in relatively good order. Lord John Drummond and others blamed Lord George Murray for holding back some regiments from joining in the pursuit of the dragoons and attacking the infantry. And stories went round that O'Sullivan, the Prince's adjutant-general, had kept out of harm's way at Falkirk, and had done nothing when he might have done much. Thus the personal rivalries and animosities — always apt to surface in an irregular army composed of men and officers with widely differing back-grounds — continued to bedevil the Prince's campaign. And these conflicts were especially noticeable and severe after Falkirk because of the widespread feeling that a chance had been lost. The Hanoverian army was depleted and to some extent demoralised. Had Hawley's men been pursued, as one of the Jacobites wanted 'with the rapidity of a torrent', had the highlanders 'kept contin-ually at their heels, and never relaxed, till they were no longer in a condition to rally',[8] the Prince's control of Scotland might well have become absolute, and Whiggism north of the border would have quietly died. But there was no pursuit — perhaps it was not pos-sible, for the Prince's men were scattered and weary, and on the day after the battle the wind continued to blow and the rain to pour down in torrents.

Nevertheless, there was no point in the Jacobites remaining at Falkirk, and a decision had to be taken about what to do next. Even if the defeated enemy could not be pursued immediately, Charles could have allowed his men a short rest and then followed the wreck of Hawley's army into Edinburgh. For some time after their defeat, the Hanoverians were in a poor state to resist; the defensive walls of the Scottish capital were no stronger than they had been four months earlier; artillery (some of it Hawley's) was available to the Jacobites whereas none had been available in September; and a great many citizens would have welcomed the Prince's return. Re-possession of the capital would not have been very difficult, and many of Charles's advisers urged this course. Once in Edinburgh, Charles would have been in a strong position and there is no saying how the war would have gone. Forces sent from England could have been successfully harassed by guerrillas operating from the wild hill country of Cumberland, Northumberland and the south of Scotland. The Jacobite position would have looked good at Versailles, and supplies from France would probably have been landed in increasing volume along the east coast of Scotland. The Whig ministers in London might soon have tired of the whole affair. And an independent Scottish kingdom might have been set up.

It is true, of course, that Charles was not *persona grata* with everyone in Scotland. But what king, prince or politician is ever welcome throughout the whole of his domain or electorate? As a direct descendant of the Stuart kings, Charles was naturally looked up to by all patriotic Scotsmen. He was the born leader of an independent Scotland, and for the concept of an independent Scotland there was much support. The Act of Union had been passed only thirty-eight years before Charles began his campaign, and its unpopularity had, if anything, increased during that period. The purpose of the Act was to bring Scotland under the control of the Whig ministers in London. As long as the old Scottish Parliament existed, Scotland had almost complete management of her own affairs, in spite of the union of the crowns, and it was rather obvious in 1707 that an 'incorporating union' would transfer that management to London and lead to the gradual erosion of Scotland's identity as a nation. It had therefore been necessary to buy off the more influential sections of opinion in Scotland, and as a result of this the Act was from first to last a political job, in the worst sense of the phrase. Scottish traders and investors were offered free access to the English market and to English colonies, notably in North America; the existing rights of large numbers of the Scottish nobility to administer justice within their domains were guaranteed; the Scottish Kirk was given formal assurance that its privileged position in Scotland would be maintained; and a substantial bribe in the form of a quarter of a million pounds was offered to 'compensate' those who had lost money in the disastrous Scottish project for colonising the isthmus of Panama, the Darien Scheme. These and other provisions, along with various forms of localised bribery and corruption, secured the passage of the Act, in spite of a large number of petitions from a variety of corporate bodies against it. It was an unpopular measure, and the way it worked — or was worked — made it more unpopular still. Few of the expected economic advantages appeared. The linen and woollen manufactures languished, east coast ports declined, taxation increased, and the quarter of a million pounds compensation was tardily paid. Because the Scots Parliament in Edinburgh disappeared, many of the Scots nobility removed to London, leaving the capital of Scotland poorer in every way. After a while, the Scots Privy Council was quietly abolished, although the Act of Union had seemed to guarantee its continuance. No wonder that the Act was a strong encouragement to moves for renewed Scottish independence.

But Prince Charles's bid for a throne was not the ideal vehicle for Scottish nationalism for one very important reason: Charles was a Roman Catholic whereas the great majority of Scots were Presbyterians. The Kirk was a very powerful force in Scottish life, and not a single minister of the Kirk was known to support the Jacobite cause; on the contrary, the ministers condemned it, and although many of them may have been nationalists at heart, they seem mostly to have felt that the Union gave the Kirk a measure of security that it would lose under a Stuart regime. Thus although Charles announced the abolition of the Union and guaranteed religious freedom in Scotland, this was not enough to bring the whole of Scotland to his side. Large numbers loved the man but feared his religion; with the result that the Scots Roman Catholics and Episcopalians who almost unanimously gave him their support were joined by only a proportion of the nation's Presbyterians. It is thus possible that Charles might have improved his position by one simple step; he might have given up his allegiance to Rome. In the opinion of one who later became a minister of the Kirk, if he had been willing 'to venture to the High Church of Edinburgh and take the sacrament . . . this would have secured him the low-country commons, as he already had the Highlanders by attachment'.[9] It may be so, and it may be that the allies he would have gained in this way would have outnumbered whose whom he might have lost. But a political manoeuvre of this kind — and a cynical one at that — was not in the Prince's nature. He was not a political animal, and he was not — like his great-uncle Charles II — a cynic. Perhaps this was his greatest misfortune, for is not a little cynicism necessary in life, at least in situations of conflict and the government of men?

However that may be, Charles did not return to Edinburgh and he did not change his religion. A most surprising course of action was settled upon. It was decided that the next step should be to resume the siege of Stirling castle. What discussions led to this decision, and who was in favour of it, we do not know, but to opt for a renewal of hostilities at Stirling does not seem to accord with the Prince's character, for he was always in favour of enterprise and action, and the siege of Stirling could be expected to prove little of either. There is some suggestion that he was persuaded by the afore-mentioned Monsieur Mirabelle, 'who promised to reduce the castle in forty-eight hours'; but its possession was of no geat consequence, and it is not easy to believe that Monsieur Mirabelle exercised so much influence in the counsels of the Prince. In any event, the failure to press on to Edinburgh after Falkirk was as critical a mistake as the failure to press on to London from Derby. Not to pursue a beaten enemy was a gift to the Hanoverians; it was indeed, as one of Charles's own officers said, 'the beginning of our calamities'.[10]

So the Prince returned to Bannockburn and the siege was renewed. Gun positions were prepared, a good many lives being lost in the process, and after a week the gunners opened fire on the castle. The cannonade was of short duration, for the guns of the castle commanded the positions chosen by Mirabelle and the firing from the castle was so destructive that in a very short time the besiegers' battery had to be abandoned. And then, before anything else could be attempted, word was received that the Duke of Cumberland was about to join the Hanoverian forces at Edinburgh, which had now been reinforced by two crack infantry regiments who had seen service overseas, and who had behaved 'remarkably well on every ocassion'.

As it was expected that Cumberland would not stay long in Edinburgh but would very soon march to the attack, Charles ordered Lord George Murray to prepare a plan of battle, and the sick and wounded, along with the women, were evacuated to Dunblane. The Prince approved Lord George's plan, which was submitted on 28 January, and preparations appeared to be almost complete. Then, on the morning of 29 January, Charles received a document signed by Lord George Murray and seven great chiefs, including Lochiel, Keppoch and Clanranald. This document read as follows:

> We think it our duty, in this critical juncture, to lay our opinions in the most respectful manner before your Royal Highness.
>
> We are certain that a vast number of the soldiers of your Royal Highness's army are gone home since the battle of Falkirk; and notwithstanding all the endeavours of the commanders of the different corps, they find that this evil is increasing hourly, and not in their power to prevent: and as we are afraid Stirling Castle

cannot be taken so soon as was expected, if the enemy should march before it fall into your Royal Highness's hands, we can foresee nothing but utter destruction to the few that will remain, considering the inequality of our numbers to that of the enemy. For these reasons, we are humbly of opinion, that there is no way to extricate your Royal Highness and those who remain with you, out of the most imminent danger, but by retiring immediately to the Highlands, where we can be usefully employed the remainder of the winter, by taking and mastering the forts of the North; and we are morally sure we can keep as many men together as will answer that end, and hinder the enemy from following us in the mountains at this season of the year; and in spring, we doubt not but an army of 10,000 effective Highlanders can be brought together, and follow your Royal Highness wherever you think proper. This will certainly disconcert your enemies, and cannot but be approved of by your Royal Highness's friends both at home and abroad. If a landing should happen in the meantime, the Highlanders would immediately rise, either to join them, or to make a powerful diversion elsewhere.

The hard marches which your army has undergone, the winter season, and now the inclemency of the weather, cannot fail of making this measure approved of by your Royal Highness's allies abroad, as well as your faithful adherents at home. The greatest difficulty that occurs to us is the saving of the artillery, particularly the heavy cannon; but better some of these were thrown into the River Forth as that your Royal Highness, besides the danger of your own person, should risk the flower of your army, which we apprehend must inevitably be the case if this retreat be not agreed to, and gone about without the loss of one moment; and we think that it would be the greatest imprudence to risk the whole on so unequal a chance, when there are such hopes of succour from abroad, besides the resources your Royal Highness will have from your faithful and dutiful followers at home. It is but just now, we are apprised of the numbers of our own people that are gone off, besides the many sick that are in no condition to fight. And we offer this our opinion with the more freedom, that we are persuaded that your Royal Highness can never doubt of the uprightness of our intentions. Nobody is privy to this address to your Royal Highness except your subscribers; and we beg leave to assure your Royal Highness, that it is with great concern and reluctance we find ourselves obliged to declare our sentiments in so dangerous a situation, which nothing could have prevailed with us to have done, but the unhappy going off of so many men.[11]

Charles, when he had read this document, 'struck his head against the wall till he staggered, and exclaimed most violently against Lord George Murray'.[12] He replied at once to this letter, expressing himself as 'extremely surprised', which is wholly understandable in view of the fact that Lord George only the day before had not in the least talked of retreating but instead had produced a plan of battle. But in spite of his surprise Charles opposed the chiefs' arguments with some very good ones of his own. Is it reasonable, he asked, 'that the Conquerors should flie from an engagement, whilst the conquer'd are seeking it?' To retreat will 'raise the spirits of our Ennemys and sink those of our own People', and sooner or later a battle must take place. And if we 'continue our flight to the Mountains', there will be no more help from overseas for an army that dare not stay to receive it. On the basis of this reply a discussion took place, at which there were present the Prince, Sheridan, Keppoch, Cluny and probably some others. After this discussion Charles wrote once again to the chiefs. They had no doubt 'heard great complaints', he wrote, 'of my Despotick temper'. But his case was, that he could see 'nothing but ruin and destruction to us all in case we should think of a retreat'. He reiterated the arguments that he had advanced already. And finally he concluded with these words:

> After all this I know I have an Army y[t] I cannot command any further than the chief Officers please, and therefore if you are all resolved upon it I must yield; but I take God to witness that it is with the greatest reluctance, and that I wash my hands of the fatal consequences w[ch] I foresee but cannot help.[13]

This is a most revealing correspondence. That Charles foresaw the disaster that was to take place is of course remarkable. But equally remarkable is the apparent sudden discovery by Lord George and the chiefs that so many men had 'gone off' that immediate retreat to the highlands was imperative. Are we to believe that the commanders of the army thought on 28 January that they could fight the Hanoverians and on 29 January that they were in the most imminent danger of destruction and must escape at once? It seems unlikely, but that is what, in effect, the Prince was told. It is little wonder that he 'exclaimed most violently against Lord George Murray', whom he already disliked and distrusted. And perhaps this is the essential tragedy of the '45. The Prince had the will, the fire and the magnetism to succeed, and in Lord George Murray he possessed a commander ready to give everything to the cause and with more than the requisite military ability; but there was no sympathy or understanding between them. The letters quoted above indicate an almost total breakdown of communications. Lord George, when he submitted the plan for the battle that never took place at Bannockburn, must have known very well that the battle was not going to take place. Yet he had to collect the signatures of seven chiefs before he could begin to persuade the Prince that such was the case. Relations had long been bad, and it seems likely that these relations were worsened in the course of angry debates about where to go after the victory at Falkirk. Charles always tended to consult only his old friends and acquaintances, principally Sheridan, O'Sullivan and Murray of Broughton, whom, along with a few others, he had known in Rome and Paris. He also got on well with the French and the Irish officers, although he never seems to have realised that several of them were adventurers and intriguers, quite unworthy of the military ranks to which he so promptly advanced them. With the Scots, on the other hand, he never made much meaningful contact. Although they comprised nine-tenths of his army and were splendid fighting men — as the Prince readily acknowledged — he no doubt found most of them strange of speech and strange of manner. In these circumstances, rivalries and animosities were ever the curse of the Jacobite army, and Charles, although he never wanted for courage and energy, was too young, too inexperienced and sadly too 'foreign' to compose his followers' quarrels. His was indeed an army 'which it was not an easy matter to command'.

The Prince's arguments in favour of staying to fight at Bannockburn were good; but the arguments against were compelling. The Hanoverian army had been considerably reinforced, whereas large numbers of Highlanders, most notably the MacDonalds of Glengarry, had gone back to their homes, and weariness and sickness, at the end of a campaign conducted in very bad winter weather, had taken their toll; at a general review on 1 February, just before the withdrawal began, 'there was hardly the appearance of an army'. The men crossed the Forth at the Fords of Frew and marched north, some going to Perth but the clans and most of the foot to Crieff. It was then decided to fall back on Inverness in three divisions: Lord George Murray and Lord John Drummond were to take the cavalry and the lowland regiments by the coast road through Montrose and Aberdeen; the Prince would go by 'the Highland road' through Aberfeldy, Blair Atholl and Strathspey; while Lord Ogilvy's regiment and the Farquharsons were to travel through their own country, up Glen Clova and then over the hills to Braemar and on to Speyside.

These movements were executed rapidly but in good order. The Prince reached Dalnacardoch on 10 February, and Moy Hall near Inverness, the seat of the MacIntosh, on 16 February, being received by Lady MacIntosh. Lord George Murray passed through Aberdeen and most of his men were on their way to Inverness by 11 February. If Cumberland thought that it would be an easy matter to catch the Jacobite army somewhere in the lowlands he was mistaken. When he passed through Stirling on 4 February Charles was already near Aberfeldy, and when he reached Perth on 6 February the Prince was at Blair Castle, in the heart of the Atholl country. Arrived at Perth, Cumberland gave up the pursuit. He contented himself with sending out garrisons to a number of places which he deemed to be in need of protection — these were as far apart as Fort William on one side of the country and Dundee on the other — and then, leaving most of his army at Perth, he returned to Edinburgh in order to consult with his brother-in-law, the Prince of Hesse, who had just arrived with 5,000 Dutch and Hessian troops in thirty-six transports, escorted by four warships. A Council of War was held, and the general opinion of those present was 'that the war was at an end', on the ground that the Jacobite army was already breaking up and that Charles and his advisers would never risk a battle against an army commanded by the Duke of Cumberland. Some of this was no doubt simple miscalculation and some was flattery; but it is surprising that after six months experience of being repeatedly outmanoeuvred and defeated in battle, the Hanoverian establishment should continue to underestimate their enemy to such an absurd degree. It is to his credit that Cumberland insisted on hearing the opinion of Lord Milton, 'who knew the country of the Highlands, and the Highlanders, better than any person present'; and Lord Milton said that as the government troops could not follow the highlanders into their 'wild and unaccommodated country' during the winter months, he believed that their army would in due course re-form, 'and risk a battle before they gave up the cause'.[14] Immediately after this meeting Cumberland returned to Perth and continued the build-up of his forces.

The forces of the Prince were now for the most part in their own country and their guard was no doubt relaxed. North and west of the Highland Line they were virtually unopposed, the only government supporters in the whole region being the 1,000 or 2,000 men whom Lord Loudon and Lord President Forbes had been able to get together and to arm, and these the Jacobites did not take too seriously; Loudon and his men constituted, indeed, no great fighting force. But cunning and the element of surprise can sometimes accomplish much, and Lord Loudon decided — unluckily for him — to see what he could achieve in this way. Learning that Charles was still at Moy Hall and had only a small number of men with him, he decided to launch a sudden night attack, capture or kill the Prince, and bring the war to an end. Loudon marched from Inverness in the evening of 16 February, as soon as night had fallen, at the head of 1,500 men. Lady MacIntosh was informed of this plan several hours before Loudon left Inverness — drunken talk by officers in an ale house is sometimes given as her source — and she accordingly instructed five or six of her servants, well armed, to keep watch on the road from Inverness, and to give warning if they should see a body of men approaching Moy. From Inverness to Moy Hall (burned down many years ago) was a distance of only eight miles, and Loudon and his troops were still three miles from the Hall when Lady MacIntosh's servants discovered them, marching along the road. Waiting until they were very close, the MacIntosh men fired out of the darkness, one after the other, and then, running here and there, called on the MacDonalds and the Camerons to advance at once, and took especial care to repeat the dread names of Lochiel and Keppoch. This was quite enough for Lord Loudon's army. Panic-stricken by the shouting, the darkness of the night, and a few musket-shots, they turned and ran. In the scramble to escape, many were knocked down and trodden upon, and their panic continued until they were almost back in Inverness. One man, it is said, was killed by the Jacobites, but hundreds were put in danger of their lives by the terror of their comrades. This was the rout of Moy, in which the supporters of the House of Hanover fled before a phantom army.

On the following day Charles collected 2,000 or 3,000 men and prepared to advance on Inverness, which Loudon and the Lord President had been using as their headquarters for many months. Their coming was expected. Lord Loudon, having had his fill of adventures, discreetly embarked his army — a good deal reduced by desertions — and crossed by the Kessock Ferry to the Black Isle; the Jacobite army entered Inverness unopposed. They were soon joined by the forces under Lord George Murray, who in marching north had taken the precaution of leaving garrisons at Elgin and Nairn in order to prevent Loudon from joining Cumberland — a move now beyond Loudon's reach unless by sea. At the same time the castle of Inverness surrendered to the Prince, providing a good supply of ammunition and provisions.

Charles was now secure from the possibility of immediate attack, and he could still expect reinforcements and supplies to reach him through any of the east coast ports north of Aberdeen. In a month or two Cumberland would no doubt show his hand. In the meantime, there was Lord Loudon to be dealt with. At the beginning of March, a force under the Earl of Cromarty marched north followed later by reinforcements commanded by the Duke of Perth and Lord George Murray. Loudon had remained in the Black Isle for only one day before crossing the Cromarty Firth and making for Tain, and four days later he retreated still further north, crossing the Dornoch Firth into Sutherland and setting up his headquarters in the town of Dornoch itself. Tain, on the south side of the Firth, was at once occupied by the Jacobites. Charles's men had thus compelled Loudon to cross two firths and retreat over fifty miles in the course of a week. But bringing him to action was not so easy, for he had seized all the boats he could lay hands on in order to prevent an attack by sea, and had established entrenched positions at the likely crossing places further up the Firth and along the river. While he waited, he received an order from Cumberland to join him at Banff. To do this, Loudon would have required a small armada, which would presumably have been unescorted, to transport his men across sixty miles of open sea; or, if he went by land, he would have had to fight his way past the entire Jacobite army. Flexibility of intellect was not one of Cumberland's strong points; he was, indeed, virtually devoid of military imagination, and both Loudon and the Lord President had to explain to him, as politely as they could, the near impossibility of complying with his instructions. But their letters had scarcely reached the commander-in-chief, now at Aberdeen, when the Duke of Perth achieved what was thought impossible, and brought eight hundred men across the Dornoch Firth in fishing boats — boats which Loudon had been unable to find. The fishermen of the north-east were no doubt far more ready to co-operate with the Jacobites than with the Hanoverians; and the operation was facilitated by a thick sea fog which hung over the water for two days. There was a skirmish near Dornoch, which resulted in the capture of some sixty or seventy government troops, and after this feeble attempt at resistance Lord Loudon's army 'separated', or, in other words, ceased to exist as a fighting force. Loudon, the Lord President and MacLeod of MacLeod made off as fast as they could to the west, taking a few hundred men with them. They crossed through Strathoykell to Ullapool, and ultimately escaped to Skye. A few others, officers and men of Loudon's own regiment, went north to the remote safety of Caithness. Thus the highlands were effectively cleared of all government troops, and the danger that Charles might be attacked from the rear while facing Cumberland was eliminated.

Lord George Murray had had a hand in the early stages of the offensive against Loudon, but he returned to Inverness before the Duke of Perth led his men across the Dornoch Firth. This was because he planned an operation against the government troops in Atholl, which was his own country. He left Inverness with the Atholl brigade on 15 March, and went to Badenoch, where he was joined by Cluny with 300 MacPhersons. At dusk on 16 March Lord George and Cluny led their little force of seven hundred highlanders, not one of whom knew what was intended, from Dalwhinnie to Dalnaspidal where Lord George halted, and explained his plan to the clansmen. This was, to divide his force into numerous separate detachments, each of which was to attack one of the posts in Atholl occupied by the enemy, before daylight, and as near as possible at the same time; after carrying out the attacks, all detachments were to return to the Bridge of Bruer, two miles north of Blair, where Lord George and Cluny would await them. The detachments set off immediately, many of them having a good way to go, and it seems that most of them were in position to attack before daylight, according to plan. Lord George and Cluny went to the Bridge of Bruer, and waited. But before any of the detachments returned, a highlander came from Blair and informed Lord George that Sir Andrew Agnew, commander of the government forces in Atholl, had learned that attacks had been made on his posts and that he was now in the vicinity of Blair at the head of a substantial body of men. Lord George and Cluny had only about twenty-five men with them at the Bridge of Bruer, and several members of the party were inclined to take to the hills at once and make their way back to Drumochter by tracks best known to themselves. But Lord George refused, knowing that if this were done his raiding parties would fall into the hands of the enemy as they returned, one after the other. It was daylight, but the sun was not yet up. Noticing a lengthy turf wall that had been built near the bridge, Lord George drew his men up behind the wall, at such distances from one another as would make them seem a large number, and to add to the effect the colours of two regiments were flown in their front. The pipers, both those of the Athollmen and those of the MacPhersons, were ordered to keep a watch on the road from Blair, and as soon as Sir Andrew's men appeared 'to strike up with all their bagpipes at once'. The soldiers came in sight just as the sun rose, the pipers began one of their noisiest pibrochs, and Lord George and the clansmen drew their swords and brandished them above their heads. The effect was as Lord George had hoped. Sir Andrew halted his men and gazed awhile at the spectacle before him; then he prudently turned round and marched back to the Castle of Blair.

Almost as soon as this ruse had succeeded, the raiding parties began to return, and made their reports. It emerged that success was complete. No fewer than thirty posts had been attacked between three and five o'clock in the morning, and all had been taken. At Bun-Rannoch, where a funeral wake had been taking place, 'the party entered the house without a shot being fired, and made all prisoners'; at Kinnachin, the sentinel raised the alarm and the defenders fired from the windows of the house, but the raiders broke in, killing one man and making the rest prisoner; only at Blair was there sufficient resistance to allow the officers to escape from the house, and it was they who had alerted Sir Andrew. The Jacobites lost not a single man and the Hanoverians only three or four; but some three hundred soldiers were taken prisoner, and Lord George, well pleased with the whole affair (from which Lord Loudon might have learned how to conduct such an operation) proceeded to lay siege to the Castle of Blair.

While these offensives were in progress north and south of Inverness, greatly extending the area under Charles's control, a less successful one was going forward at the other end of the Great Glen. This was the siege of Fort William. Charles seems to have had a fondness for sieges — perhaps a consequence of his childhood introduction to war at the siege of Gaeta. He had insisted on besieging Stirling castle, and now he sent General Stapleton, with some excellent troops, and the French gunners who had failed at Stirling, to take Fort William. It required three weeks to bring the cannon down the Great Glen; but the project was in any case doomed from the start. Fort William, strongly garrisoned, and built on the seashore from which side it was defended and supplied by two sloops of war, could not be taken. The siege lasted for only two weeks, and the defenders, who made several sallies, lost only six men.

In the meantime, Cumberland continued to build up his forces, now centred on Aberdeen. He was in hostile country — 'every dispatch of mine must be filled with repeated complaints of the disaffection of this part of His Majesty's dominions' — and his inclination to brutality and contempt for the law (which the rest of his army evidently shared) was already in evidence. On the march north from Manchester he had imprisoned any stragglers from Charles's army, fearing reprisals if they were shot out of hand. 'I did not care to put them to death', he wrote. 'But I have encouraged the country people to do it as they may fall into their way.' Once north of the border he was all in favour of what he called 'military execution'. His aim was 'crushing this band of robbers' or, as one of his aides put it more frankly, 'to . . . extirpate the Race if we are not stopt by lenity'. While still at Aberdeen he issued orders 'that all provisions, cattle, forage or arms which shall be taken from rebels shall be given to the people' (and who would the people be but his own men?) and that 'all methods' should be used 'for disarming the disaffected people in the hills, and even that they should be destroyed if they resist'. This savage attitude persisted, and spread. Late in March a detachment was sent up Glenesk with orders 'to destroy all them . . . in arms and to burn the habitations of all those who have left them and are with the rebels'. Such action was illegal, but what happened was, not surprisingly, much worse. The officer in charge burned down a meeting house, stole provisions from a man who was merely 'suspected of harbouring and holding intelligence with the rebels', and set fire to a house which turned out to belong to 'a good and loyal woman'. Hawley himself pillaged Callander House and was surprised when the matter was taken up in a court of law. Supposed to be defending the constitution and thereby the rights of all citizens, the Hanoverian army was soon notorious for murder, theft and arson.

Cumberland remained in Aberdeen for almost six weeks. During that time he was reinforced by a regiment of light horse, a regiment of foot, and other units, bringing his effective strength to over 7,000 men; and he had ample supplies of provisions, ammunition and transport, as well as being generously equipped with artillery. In addition to all this there were the 6,000 Hessians, foreign mercenaries, who had been brought to Leith early in February, and who later saw some service. But Cumberland was careful not to be seen to depend on them at Culloden.

It was now well into March, 'and as the cold wind of the spring, that dries the ground more than the heat of summer, had blown for some time, and made the rivers fordable',[15] it seemed to everyone likely that Cumberland would soon leave Aberdeen and march towards Inverness. In fact, his first move was to send a small force under General Bland northwards from Strathbogie to Keith, not far from the Spey. This was no doubt to test the Jacobites' defences. They responded by attacking Bland and his men in the early hours of 20 March, and to such effect that almost all of them were either killed or made prisoner. Once again success was virtually complete. The friends of Hanover 'were grieved and astonished when they heard of so many attacks made by an enemy, of whose attacks they never expected to have heard any more', and the outcome of the war once again began to seem doubtful. But this was the last Jacobite triumph. The war was entering its final disastrous phase, during which good fortune entirely deserted the Prince and his friends.

On 8 April, Cumberland left Aberdeen and advanced along the coast road towards the lower reaches of the Spey. This was not the shortest route, but by taking the coast road Cumberland no doubt felt safer, being accompanied by a number of transports offshore, and by several men-of-war. Charles, stationed at Inverness, had already called in his commanders and their troops from Fort William, Ross-shire and Atholl, where Lord George's siege of the castle of Blair had to be called off just when it seemed to be on the point of succeeding. There was nothing hasty about the Hanoverian advance, but it was conducted at a reasonable speed and on 12 April the army cautiously approached the Spey. Halting, the troops formed into three divisions, one on the high road and the other two spaced out half a mile and one mile to the north, nearer the sea and the ships. They advanced, and without encountering any opposition, crossed the river at three separate fords, all near Gordon Castle. They then encamped on the north-west side of the river, opposite Fochabers.

This failure to dispute the passage of the Spey was a major Jacobite blunder and a most surprising one. The Spey is a wide and fast flowing river, and it was a natural obstacle to Cumberland's advance. Charles had sent Lord John Drummond and the Duke of Perth forward to the river, presumably to guard the fords, which were all well known, and to obstruct a crossing by the Hanoverians. According to accounts, a trench and some other earthworks had been made, and when Cumberland approached there were as many as 2,000 of Charles's men on or near the west bank, as well as most of the Jacobite cavalry. We do not know why nothing was done. Even if the Jacobite numbers are exaggerated (as may well be the case), and even allowing for the fact that Cumberland's troops crossed at three separate places, and a crossing could probably not have been prevented, it remains the case that losses could have been inflicted on the Hanoverian army, perhaps quite severe losses, at a relatively small cost. For the first time the Jacobites failed to make good use of the lie of the land — failed, indeed, to make any use of it whatever. Had Lord George been present, it is unthinkable that some sudden attacks would not have been launched at the fords. To do the Jacobite commanders justice, there may have been some confusion in their orders — it is even said that they were 'under orders to retreat without coming to an action'. This makes no sense, because if there was to be no action at all it was pointless to send more than a few scouts to observe the river crossing. But there may have been orders to avoid any major action — and their indecision as to what would constitute a major action might bring on the failure to launch an attack of any kind. It is certainly plausible that Charles (or Lord George) wanted to avoid risking serious losses at this stage. The Jacobite army was still to some extent scattered, partly because provisions were scarce at Inverness, and was significantly out-numbered by Cumberland's forces. Had the whole army been assembled in time, Charles might have marched to the Spey and fought a battle in favourable circumstances. But this could not be done. Cumberland's unopposed advance was a serious setback for the Jacobites at a critical time, both morally and strategically.

Once across the Spey, Cumberland continued his steady progress, from Fochabers to Alves, from Alves to Nairn. At Nairn, which is only about fifteen miles from Inverness, his men came upon the rearguard of the forces commanded by Drummond and Perth; and a party of the Irish piquets, stationed at one end of the bridge, fired upon Cumberland's grenadiers at the other; shots were exchanged, but without much loss on either side, and the piquets then withdrew in good order, covered by the cavalry. The grenadiers followed for several miles, and both sides were again very close when Charles suddenly appeared with his first troop of guards, and the MacIntosh regiment. These forces immediately deployed, which was quite enough for the grenadiers, who promptly marched back to Nairn and rejoined the main body of the army, encamped on flat ground to the west of the town.

At dawn on 14 April Charles left Inverness, taking with him all his available troops, and after giving orders that those who were still to reach Inverness should follow him with all speed to Culloden, three miles east of Inverness on the high road to Nairn. Charles had resolved to fight, and to fight at once. He had assumed effective command of the army, for his relations with Lord George had reached breaking point; and his orders were issued after discussion, not with Lord George and the chiefs, but with his favourite advisers such as O'Sullivan, Sheridan and a few of the Irish officers; for no Council of War was held after the retreat from Falkirk. The Prince's determination to give battle is not easily explained. It is possible that his French and Irish advisers found the idea of retiring to fight in the mountains strange and alarming, and that they, like the aged Sir Thomas Sheridan, were weary of campaigning and hoped for a miracle. Charles himself was by no means exhausted and he feared nothing; but he was always ready to fight without calculating the odds, he still believed that his men were irresistible, and he despised the idea of retreat before a Hanoverian army. He took the wrong advice, and in three days, 14 to 16 April, the Jacobite cause was irretrievably ruined by a series of tragically mistaken decisions taken by the Prince, under the influence of a small coterie of sycophantic admirers.

What was decided, was to fight at the wrong time and in the wrong place. The timing was wrong because the army was considerably below strength. When Charles marched from Inverness to Culloden, Lochiel and Keppoch, with their regiments, had not returned from the siege of Fort William, although they were 'expected every hour'; Lord Cromarty and several other chiefs were in Sutherland with at least seven hundred men; and Cluny and the MacPhersons were still in Badenoch. In these circumstances it was folly to advance towards the enemy and move further away from badly needed reinforcements. But Charles was resolved to attack the carefully assembled forces of Cumberland — the expression he used, according to Lord George, was 'had he but a thousand men he would attack them'.

Secondly, the choice of Culloden Moor invited defeat. The sensible plan, proposed by Lord George, was to retire to a strong ground on the other side of the water of Nairn; where, if the Duke of Cumberland should attack us, we were persuaded we could have given a good account of him; and if he did not venture to cross that water, and come up to us there, we proposed (if no opportunity offered to attack him to advantage) to retire farther, and draw him up to the mountains, where we thought, without doubt, we might attack him at some pass or strong ground.[16]

This was no mere visionary scheme. Lord George had a particular place in mind, and two senior officers sent to view it confirmed that it was 'a very strong Ground . . . such as the Highlanders would have liked very well, and would have thought themselves in a fair way of Victory had the Duke of Cumberland ventur'd to have passt the water of Neirn in their Sight, and atact them there'. As for the idea of the Hanoverian army pursuing the Jacobites into the Monadhliath Mountains, it invites the supposition that large numbers of the government troops would never have been seen again. Cumberland was no commander for rough country, whereas the highlanders were masters of mountain warfare. The government troops would have been exposed to continual harassment, outposts would have been picked off as they had been picked off in Atholl, and one mistake by Cumberland might have resulted in a highland charge down a hillside as devastating as at Killiecrankie. But Charles would not retire into the hills. One of the arguments was that Inverness and such provisions as could be obtained there must not be given up. But Lord George did not agree with this, on the ground that supply for the army could be arranged in other ways. And even if control of Inverness was to be regarded as essential, there were other places where a battle might be fought, and to much greater advantage than on Culloden Moor. Lord George's 'strong ground on the other side of the water of Nairn' would have suited the Jacobite army and would have made the use of Cumberland's cavalry, and possibly also his artillery, impossible. But O'Sullivan, on the Prince's orders, inspected this ground, condemned it as unsuitable, and chose Culloden Moor instead; a location which, according to Lord George, not one single Jacobite soldier would have approved, being ideally suited for orthodox warfare and especially for the use of artillery.

Charles was at Culloden on 14 April, and was joined that evening by Lochiel and his regiment. The army spent the night among the whins and trees of Culloden Wood. Next morning they were drawn up in order of battle, but Cumberland did not advance to meet them and at about two o'clock the men were stood down. The position seemed less desperate than on the preceding day, because Keppoch and his regiment had now rejoined the army, as Lochiel had done the evening before. But the outlook remained very unfavourable. These additional troops were badly in need of rest, the army was still outnumbered by the Hanoverians, and food was extremely scarce. Charles now put forward a new plan. This was, that they should march as soon as darkness fell, and make a night attack upon Cumberland's army encamped at Nairn. This proposal at first met with a cool reception. The Duke of Perth and Lord John Drummond expressed their dislike of it, and Lochiel, who was a man of few words, observed that if they waited for twenty-four hours the army would be stronger by at least 1,500 men. But Lord George supported the Prince. He knew that the Prince would not wait; he knew that the bleak alternative was to fight 'on that plain moor'; and he knew, as he explained to the others, that a night attack would completely nullify Cumberland's overwhelming superiority in cannon and cavalry. So it was agreed, provided that the attack could be launched not later than two o'clock in the morning.

This 'desperate attempt' sealed the fate of the Prince's army. A night attack is of all things in war the most difficult to carry out successfully. It requires expert knowledge of the country, first-class leaders and highly-trained men in tip-top physical condition. The Jacobites had local guides and good officers; but the men were exhausted and hungry. They had marched and fought for six months and more with little rest, through an especially bitter winter; and the supply position was so bad that on 15 April (and not only on that day) their ration was one biscuit each. Only by a miracle could men in such miserable straits have made a successful night attack on an enemy seven miles away.

That evening, when the officers had got their men together, it was found that large numbers had gone to Inverness and adjacent villages in search of shelter and provisions — 'to shift for themselves' as Lord George later put it — and he estimated that at least 2,000 were absent in this way. The officers could not recall them, and for this reason there was talk of abandoning the idea of a night attack. But the Prince 'continued bent on the thing', and ordered Lord George to march immediately, at the head of the line.

Lord George had formed a well-thought-out plan of attack. Two miles short of their objective, the army was to divide. One third of the men, led by Lord George, would turn south and cross the river Nairn, march along its south bank so as to avoid enemy outposts, then recross and attack from the south east. The remainder of the army, led by Lord John Drummond, would march in a more or less direct line and attack simultaneously from the west. This plan, which was kept a closely guarded secret, 'if it had been executed as it was projected, would, in the opinion of some of the bravest officers in the Duke's army have proved not a little dangerous'.[17] But it could not be done. Avoiding tracks and houses, the men plodded and stumbled in the darkness across wet and difficult ground, which made progress slow. The van did not do too badly, but Lord George 'had not marched half a mile till I was stopped by a message, that the [rear] half of the line were at a considerable distance, and ordered to halt till they should join'. Lord George did not halt, but he slowed down. Even so, when still three miles from Nairn, he received a message that there was a gap in the line half a mile long, and 'the men won't come up'. So Lord George halted. It was now two o'clock in the morning, and would be broad daylight before an attack could be launched. Many of the men 'had left the ranks, and had laid down, particularly in the wood of Kilraick. This must have been occasioned by faintness for want of food, for it could not be weariness in a six miles march'.[18] A consultation among the officers followed, and all agreed that as surprise was no longer possible, the attack could not take place. The van turned back. And Charles, who thought that this was contrary to his orders, 'was extremely incensed; and said Lord George Murray had betrayed him'.[19]

Most of the Prince's men who had set out on the previous evening were back at Culloden, or near it, by five o'clock the next morning. And it is good evidence of their state that those who did not at once lie down to sleep made their way to Inverness in search of food.

The Jacobite army was now trapped. It was too late to withdraw (and in any case the Prince would never have done so); and loyalty to their chiefs and to the House of Stuart prevented men from melting away into the hills, as they might have done. About eight o'clock Charles, who lodged at Culloden House, was informed that Cumberland's army was in full march towards him. Orders were given immediately. Weary men turned out to fight, and were drawn up almost exactly where they had been drawn up the morning before; but far more weary now than then. The army was in two lines, with a body of reserve; Lord John Drummond commanded on the left, Lord George Murray on the right. Charles placed himself on a small eminence behind the right of the second line, with Lord Balmerino's cavalry and some of the Irish horse. The cavalry, much diminished in the course of the winter, was of little account; and the entire army probably did not amount to 5,000 men.

Cumberland had begun to form his army at daybreak, and the march towards Inverness had commenced an hour or two later. His men were in three columns, with the cavalry in front and rear, and they came in sight of the Jacobite army about noon, at a distance of two miles and a half. The Hanoverians advanced to the moor — an experienced French officer with the Prince remarked that 'he had never seen men advance in so cool and regular a manner' — and deployed into two lines, with cavalry on each wing. The cannon were placed in the intervals between the battalions, sixteen guns in all, and the battle began with an exchange of artillery fire. The Prince had twelve guns, of mixed calibre, but they were 'very ill-served' and did negligible damage to Cumberland's army; the Hanoverian artillery, on the other hand, 'did great execution, making lanes through the Highland regiments', and several shots were directed at the body of horse with Charles who 'had his face bespattered with dirt; and one of his servants who stood behind the squadron, with a led horse in his hand, was killed'.[20]

Cumberland's cannonade lasted for between fifteen and thirty minutes and virtually sealed the fate of the Jacobite army. 'When our cannon had fired about two rounds I could plainly perceive that the rebels fluctuated extremely and could not remain long in the position they were in without running away or coming down upon us.'[21] Because Cumberland had the wind and the weather behind him, Charles expected him to attack. But the Duke was not so foolish. The smoke from the Hanoverian guns drifted forward and increasingly obscured the view of the Jacobites; and when Cumberland's gunners switched to grapeshot the destruction in the clan regiments became so terrible that a few men broke ranks and fled. Charles still gave no order, perhaps because he could not see what was happening; and the highlanders 'impatient of sufferin. . . . grew clamorous to be led on to the attack'.[22] They had no advantage of ground; and because of confusion in drawing up the army — occasioned by haste, and by the usual differences between Lord George and O'Sullivan, who liked to think that he was in command — the regiments on the right wing had almost no room to move, jammed between their comrades in the centre and a turf dyke which protected the flank. The men were hungry and dejected, and to make matters worse O'Sullivan had not given the place of honour on the right to the MacDonalds, whose turn it was to occupy it; this they deeply resented.

At last, with or without orders from the Prince, the attack began. The Jacobite centre led the charge, 'coming up very boldly and fast all in a cloud together, sword in hand'. But heavy and continuous fire by well-trained troops made them incline to the right, and although they still came on they also partly impeded the charge of the right wing, led by Lord George. In spite of grapeshot and musket fire, some directed from the flank by men of Wolfe's regiment, the right and centre succeeded in breaking through the Hanoverian front line and fell upon the regiments in the second line. But Cumberland's great superiority in numbers allowed him a second line almost as strong as his first. The attacking clans 'were got close together', and for some moments were quite exposed. The second-line Hanoverian regiments:

> allowed them to come very near, and then gave them a terrible fire, that brought a great many of them to the ground, and made most of those who did not fall turn back. A few, and but a few, still pressed on, desperate and furious, to break into Sempill's regiment, which not a man of them ever did, the foremost falling at the end of the soldiers' bayonets.[23]

This heroic and desperate charge, failing against modern weapons and greatly superior numbers, decided the day. The men on the Jacobite left wing, starting at a greater distance from the enemy and having to cross some boggy ground, 'came running forward in their furious way', as a Hanoverian officer put it, 'firing their pistols and brandishing their swords', and drew fire from the regiments opposite them; but seeing their comrades to the right plunge into the smoke and then reel back, and Cumberland's cavalry begin to move forward to outflank them, they did the only thing they could, and fell back also. Lord John Drummond tried to steady the line, but once again Hanoverian cannon fire 'made a frightful carnage' and the Jacobite withdrawal was turned into absolute flight. Some, of course, stayed to fight to the end. Keppoch, already wounded, pressed forward and was killed by another musket shot. MacLean of Drimmin, missing two of his sons, turned back to look for them and was killed. Lochiel, advancing at the head of his regiment, had fired his pistol and was drawing his sword when he fell, wounded by grapeshot in both ankles. Most of the chiefs who commanded the principal attacking regiments were killed, 'and almost every man in the front rank of each regiment'. Lord George, at the head of the Athollmen, 'lost his horse, his periwig, and bonnet . . . had several cuts [by swords] in his coat, and was covered with blood and dirt'[24] when he emerged from the smoke to try to bring up reinforcements. But it was too late; the battle was irretrievably lost, and had been lost even before the first shots were fired.

When it was clear that the Jacobite army was in retreat, the Hanoverian regiments were ordered to stand where they had fought, and dress their ranks. The pursuit was left to the cavalry. The Jacobite left wing, which had not been heavily engaged, had no protection on its flank and was attacked by Cumberland's troopers almost at once. Some considerable bodies of men kept together and were able to move towards the centre of the second line, where they were covered by steady fire from the Irish piquets, but many regiments on the left and centre disintegrated, and men attempting to escape singly or in small groups were ruthlessly cut down. The Jacobite right wing retreated in better order, protected by a long wall on its flank, and also by the courage and discipline of Lord Ogilvy's battalions, who several times faced about in square formation and fired on Hawley's cavalry. At one point there was danger of encirclement, for substantial numbers of Hanoverian cavalry succeeded in entering and crossing the walled enclosures of Culloden House, which protected the Jacobite flank, and placing themselves in a position to cut off the retreat. Most fortunately, Lord George, who had previously studied the ground and had concluded that some such movement might take place, at once ordered most of the Prince's cavalry to a strong position which guarded the line of retreat. This force cannot have numbered one hundred and fifty, and they were opposing between four hundred and five hundred well-mounted and well-armed dragoons. But some time passed before the dragoons decided to risk an attack, and during this time most of the men of the right wing made their escape. These actions — by FitzJames's Horse, a squadron under Lord Elcho, and two battalions commanded by Lord Ogilvy — saved the army from destruction. The Hanoverian cavalry was conspicuously reluctant to attack any Jacobite units that held together and were clearly resolved to fight. Instead, they 'contented themselves with sabering such unfortunate people as fell in their way single and disarmed'.

Charles, before he left the field, appears to have made an attempt to rally some of the retreating regiments. From the position which he occupied he can have seen almost nothing of the battle, and he was evidently incredulous when he saw the clansmen 'repulsed and flying'. But there was nothing that he could do. Dazed by the turn that events had taken, he was led away to safety by Sir Thomas Sheridan and other close advisers, escorted by a body of cavalry.

Meanwhile, the main part of Cumberland's army, once again in order of battle, resumed its progress across the moor. The whole body of infantry, still supported by cannon, moved relentlessly and indivisibly, like a steam-roller, 'always firing their Cannon and platoons in Advancing'.[25] Pursuit was left to the dragoons, and therefore 'their was not so many people kill'd or taken as their would have been had they detach'd Corps to pursue'.[26]

But there was enough slaughter without that. Wounded men or stragglers overrun by the army found no mercy. As for the dragoons, they were out for revenge. Some of those at Culloden had fought and run at Prestonpans, one of the regiments had sustained losses in a skirmish with the Jacobites only a few weeks before, and Charles's whole campaign had turned the Hanoverian army and the dragoons in particular into something of a laughing stock. When they triumphed at last, their brutality was remarkable even for the eighteenth century. Fleeing men:

> were pursued by Kingston's Light Horse, and mangled terribly, while the Soldiers, warm in their Resentment, stabbed some of the wounded. A Party meeting others at Culloden House brought them forth and shot them . . . The Troops were enraged at their Hardships and Fatigues during a Winter campaign; the habit of the enemy was strange, their Language was still stranger, and their mode of Fighting unusual; the Fields of Preston and Falkirk were still fresh in their Memories.[27]

These words were written by Cumberland's biographer, and while admitting the facts they are also an apologia. A battlefield is of course not a scene of restraint, and every age has its atrocities; but those committed on Culloden Moor surprised even contemporaries. The pursuing horsemen 'cut down everything in their way', so that 'for near four miles from where the pursuit began, the ground is cover'd with dead bodies'. Many of Charles's men, fatally wounded, 'crawled off and died in the woods', rather than wait to be murdered. The blame for all this was put on Cumberland. But the evidence is that Cumberland was responsible only to the extent that he probably turned a blind eye to what was going on. The real responsibility belongs to the Hanoverian government, its servants and supporters. It was they who, refusing to recognise the highlanders as members of a civilisation at least as old as their own, habitually referred to them as savages or animals. Henry Pelham, in the seat of government, called them 'animals'; the Duke of Richmond called them 'vermin'; Sir John Ligonier called them 'those wild beasts'; they were also referred to as 'wolves and tygers', 'barbarians', 'rebellious savages', and even the Merchant Company of Edinburgh could do no better than think of them as 'the barbarous inhabitants of the more remote parts of the country'. Like the Jews under Hitler, the highlanders were regarded by the rulers of the country as less than human. It is therefore not surprising that they were hunted down by the soldiers at and after Culloden as if they were wild beasts; or that Hanoverian society salved its conscience afterwards by trying to shift the blame for what had happened onto 'Butcher' Cumberland.

Culloden was a very fatal battle. The Hanoverian army may have lost one hundred men — the official figure was fifty — but the Jacobite losses were variously estimated at from 2,000 to 4,000. The latter figure is certainly too high.

Before the killing was over, Charles crossed the river Nairn at a ford some three miles from the moor, and then, after dismissing his cavalry escort, he proceeded west to Gortleck. He took with him only a few companions, who included Sir Thomas Sheridan, Lord Elcho and O'Sullivan. At Gortleck he for the first time met Lovat, who knelt and kissed his hand. After supper, and after changing his clothes, Charles travelled all night, and early next morning reached Invergarry, near Fort Augustus.

This was on 17 April, and was the beginning of the Prince's extraordinary wanderings through the west highlands and the Hebrides. For five months and two days he remained a fugitive, hunted by literally thousands of soldiers, who were supported at sea by numerous men of war. He travelled almost as far south as Kinloch Rannoch, and as far north as Glen Affric. He left the mainland for the Hebrides on 26 April, and did not return until 8 July; during this time he was in South Uist, North Uist, Benbecula, Lewis, Raasay and Skye. His situation whilst on South Uist seemed at one time:

to be altogether desperate; a number of men in arms, said to be 1500 or 2000, were marching backwards and forwards through the Long Island in search of him; and the Long Island was surrounded on every side by cutters, sloops of war, frigates, and 40-gun ships; a guard was posted at every one of the ferries; and nobody could get out of the island without a passport. In this perilous state, Charles remained from the first week of June to the last; but, informed by the Islanders of every movement of the troops, he often passed and repassed them in the night, and his hair-breadth escapes were innumerable.[28]

From these dangers he escaped, disguised as Flora MacDonald's maid. Later, he was trapped in Moidart, seemingly caught behind a line of sentinels 'placed so near one another, in the day time, that nobody could pass without being seen: and when it began to grow dark, fires were lighted at every post, and the sentinels crossed continually from one fire to another . . '.[29] But the Prince and two companions crept up the channel of a small burn, 'and watching their opportunity passed between the sentinels'. He was never alone; 'and from the beginning to the end of his wanderings, never told the people whom he left whither he was going; nor those to whom he came, whence he had come'. He usually travelled at night and rarely had a roof over his head. Many of those who travelled with him, or who helped him on his way, were taken prisoner within a day or two of parting from him. Without great personal courage and outstanding powers of physical endurance, Charles could not have survived. He finally came to the country owned by Cluny and Lochiel, where after a time he learned that two French frigates had arrived at Lochnanuagh near Borrodale, to carry him to France. He sailed on 20 September, and never set foot in Scotland again.

As for the army, it began to break up as the battle ended. Apart from those who fled as individuals or in small groups, the Jacobites left the field in two bodies. The smaller of these, which included Lord John Drummond's regiment and the Irish piquets, marched straight to Inverness. There they surrendered, most of them securing honourable terms, because they owed their allegiance legally to the King of Spain or to Louis XV. The greater part of the army, however, amounting to perhaps 1,500 men who were kept together by Lord George Murray, escaped towards Badenoch and the west. At Ruthven they were surprised to learn that the Prince was even then on his way to Glengarry; and on the following day they received their commander-in-chief's final order: 'Let every man seek his own safety the best way he can.'

No one supposed that this was going to be easy. The day after the battle Cumberland ordered a detachment 'to march directly and visit all the cottages in the neighbourhood of the field of battle and to search for rebels . . . the officer and men will take notice that the public orders of the rebels yesterday was to give us no quarters'. It is virtually certain that no such orders were ever issued; but they were believed to have been issued, and Cumberland used this belief to encourage his men to spare no one. Search parties were soon sent far and wide with clear instructions. Brigadier Mordaunt was despatched along Loch Ness 'to destroy all the rebels he finds there'; Lord Loudon went from Skye to Fort Augustus with the aim of destroying whatever he could find 'belonging to all such as are or have been in the rebellion' and with orders 'to seize or destroy all persons you can find who have been in the rebellion or their abettors'. The official policy, at least for a time, was that those who voluntarily came forward and surrendered their arms would be allowed to return to their homes, only gentlemen being detained. But although many Hanoverian officers behaved correctly, others were not to be trusted — General Bland, for example, ordered that those who 'did not come in immediately' were to be shot, adding that 'prisoners would only embarrass him'. In the later phases of this mopping-up operation, when the Hanoverians had set up their headquarters at Fort Augustus — 'in the very centre of their fastnesses' — atrocities multiplied. At the end of May four raiding parties were sent into the wildest and most inaccessible parts of the highlands, where they apparently felt free to commit every kind of outrage. Men were shot out of hand, women stripped and raped, and whole families, their houses destroyed and their cattle taken, fled to the hills where the younger and weaker often died of hunger and exposure. During the whole summer, looting, theoretically allowed only by specific order, was widespread — one report was to the effect that no fewer than 20,000 animals were brought to Fort Augustus in a month or two and sold, animals upon which poor families had largely depended for their meagre existence. So vicious and barbarous was the behaviour of the troops that even communities that supported the House of Hanover were attacked. Cattle belonging to tenants of the Duke of Argyll in Morven were seized, and in Kintail Lord Fortrose himself protested that his tenants were taken prisoner, 'their houses plundered and burnt to ashes, their wives and daughters ravished, the whole of their cattle violently carried away . . .'[30]

Of those who actually fought with the Prince, most suffered for it. Supposing the total of his followers at one time or another to have reached as high as 10,000, possibly one fifth and perhaps as many as one third were killed in battle; between 2,000 and 3,300 men. The number of the wounded is not known. Over 3,400 Jacobites were taken prisoner, during or after the campaign. All were held to be guilty of high treason, and very few were acquitted. The commonest sentence was transportation to the colonies for life — or, more probably, for death. Over one hundred 'common men' were hanged, and the eight officers of the Manchester Regiment who had surrendered to the mercy of the House of Hanover at Carlisle were hung, drawn and quartered. Many prisoners escaped hanging or transportation because they died before the courts had finished with them, or perhaps had even seen them; brought to London in over-crowded hulks or kept in insanitary gaols, hundreds succumbed to typhus, pneumonia, erysipelas, dysentery and other maladies, not unmixed with starvation and ill-treatment. The government (some-times represented as lenient) was especially anxious to make an example of those in high position. Because most of the chiefs were killed at Culloden, few were available for execution. But Lords Balmerino and Kilmarnock had been captured at Culloden, Lord Cromarty had been captured in Sutherland the day before the battle, and Lord Lovat had been discovered by Cumberland's men hiding in the vicinity of Loch Morar early in June. Lord Cromarty escaped execution, thanks to his wife's intercession, but the other three were executed on Tower Hill. Lovat, eighty years of age, met his death with the utmost fortitude, as did Kilmarnock, whose dying speech began with the words, 'I was brought up in true, loyal, and anti-Revolution principles'. Several of the leading Jacobites who had fought in the campaign survived the war. Two French ships arrived at Borrodale a few weeks after the disaster at Culloden and took off many of the Prince's supporters, including the Duke of Perth, Lord John Drummond, Elcho, Sheridan and Hay. Over four months later another two French frigates entered Lochnanuagh and rescued about one hundred people, including the Prince himself, Lochiel, Lochgarry and Colonel Roy Stuart. But of those who escaped, almost all were unhappy and ruined men, and many did not live for long. Sheridan reached Rome in November 1746, and died only a few weeks later. Lochiel obtained a commission in the French army, but died in 1748. The Duke of Perth died at sea, only a few days after leaving Borrodale, worn out, it is said, by his unremitting efforts on behalf of the Prince. Lord John Drummond died in Holland in 1747. Lord Elcho lived much longer, to 1787, but he lived embittered and often in poor circumstances. Murray of Broughton, who could have escaped with the others in May, was taken prisoner a few weeks later, and turned King's evidence. He died in 1777. Only the dashing and youthful Lord Ogilvy found happier times. After hiding for several weeks in Glen Clova, he escaped to Norway and from there made his way to France. He became a general in the French army, was pardoned in 1782, and returned to Scotland where he died in 1803.

Among all those who escaped abroad, none can have lived with sadder thoughts than Lord George Murray. He was already forty-seven years of age when he reached the continent, having remained hidden in Glenartney for eight months, and he led the aimless life of an exile, principally in Germany, until his death in 1760. Like Lochiel, he had joined the Prince because he thought the cause was just, although the venture ill-timed. He was not a wealthy man, but he had much to lose, having recently been appointed Sheriff-Depute of the Regality of Atholl; and it is said that ever after the war his copy of 'The Office and Authority of a Justice of the Peace' opened at the page which dealt with the pains and penalties of high treason. He must often have reflected how different his fate might have been if the Prince had only trusted him. 'Had Prince Charles slept during the whole of the expedition, and allowed Lord George to act for him, according to his own judgment, there is every reason for supposing he would have found the crown of Great Britain on his head when he awoke.'[31] These words, by one who marched and fought from Prestonpans to Culloden, contain much truth although also some exaggeration. But Charles did not trust Lord George, and after Culloden they never met again.

The carnage at Culloden and the brutalities of Cumberland's raiding parties were only the beginning of the government's revenge. The men at Westminster had been very badly frightened, and they were resolved that never again would they be threatened by the supporters of the House of Stuart. So the campaign against the Jacobites continued, and as they were especially numerous and strong in the highlands, the government began a political war of extermination against the clans or at least against their ancient way of life. Government troops, having 'scoured' the country, were left in substantial numbers in the forts along the Great Glen, with a view to overawing the inhabitants. Strenuous efforts were made to confiscate all weapons in the possession of those living in the highlands. The wearing of tartan, which was a source of pride to the highlander and which helped to give him a sense of belonging, was forbidden. Numerous large estates owned by chiefs who had been 'out' in support of the Prince, were confiscated and managed for almost thirty years by Commissioners sitting in Edinburgh whose aim it was to modernise the estates and 'civilise' their inhabitants. The powers and status of all chiefs — Jacobite supporters or otherwise — were reduced by the abolition of their hereditary rights of jurisdiction over those living within their territories. The use of Gaelic was discouraged in education and church services. Young highlanders were recruited into the British army, often for service overseas.

But these measures, considerable as was their effect, were less important than the 'opening-up' of the highlands to commercial forces. There was money to be made in the highlands, by those who knew how to use the land for profit. So agricultural innovations were imported from the lowlands, and they spread north and west. Flocks of sheep began to cover the hillsides, fields and pastures were enclosed, the rotation of crops was introduced, manure was applied, and yields rose. Better crops meant better animals, and both meant increased sales beyond the highlands. Roads were improved and rents increased. The chiefs themselves, brought into increasing contact with the relatively prosperous lowland world and no longer living continually in an atmosphere of war, began to envy their richer counterparts farther south, and to seek to live like them. What this new style of life needed was money. And so the chiefs began to take advantage of the power which they had always possessed but never exercised, of doing with their land what they pleased, and renting it to the highest bidder. The customary rights of old retainers were disregarded, and in the course of time, the land available to them became less and less. Thus the clansmen became merely tenants, or were dispossessed altogether, and the chiefs, in the words of Dr Johnson, merely traffickers in land. We may call the process gradual, but it did not seem gradual to those who suffered by it. It was this collapse of established social and economic relations, rather than any laws passed at Westminster, which destroyed the old pattern of feudal or patriarchal life in the highlands and which brought about a state of apathy, misery and confusion which existed there, in varying degrees of intensity, for at least a hundred years. Celtic civilisation in the highlands was almost destroyed. This was what the Hanoverian victory achieved.

Notes and References

1. Chevalier de Johnstone, op. cit., p. 84.
2. Home, op. cit., p. 166.
3. Ibid., p. 172.
4. Ibid., p. 174.
5. Chevalier de Johnstone, op. cit., p. 92.
6. Ibid., p. 98.
7. Home, op. cit., p. 178.
8. Chevalier de Johnstone, op. cit., pp. 95-6.
9. Carlyle, op. cit., p. 163.
10. Chevalier de Johnstone, op. cit., p. 98.
11. Home, op. cit., Appendix 39.
12. John Hay's 'Account of the Retreat from Stirling', quoted in Home, op. cit., p. 355.
13. In Blaikie, *Itinerary*, p. 78.
14. Home, op. cit., p. 195.
15. Ibid., p. 211.
16. Ibid., Appendix 42.
17. Ibid., pp. 221-2.
18. Ibid., Appendix 42.
19. Ibid., p. 225.
20. Ibid., p. 231.
21. Quoted in K. Tomasson and F. Buist, *Battles of the '45* (London, 1978), p. 152.
22. Home, op. cit., p. 231.
23. Ibid., p. 233.
24. Quoted in Tomasson and Buist, op. cit., p. 165.
25. Elcho, op. cit., p. 434.
26. Ibid.
27. A. Henderson, *The History of the Rebellion* (Edinburgh, 1748), p. 200.
28. Home, op. cit., pp. 245-6.
29. Ibid., p. 251.
30. Quoted in Speck, op. cit., p. 169.
31. Chevalier de Johnstone, op. cit., p. 119 fn.

INDEX

Aberdeen 87, 97, 135, 136, 141, 211, 243, 245, 248
  Cope sails from 95, 198
  Cumberland marches from 140, 249
Aberfeldy 134
Agnew, Sir Andrew 140, 246-7
Anne, Queen 38, 42, 43, 160-1, 162
apocryphal stories 27
Argyll, Duke of 73, 74, 75, 78, 83, 88, 129, 139, 199, 261
  at Sheriffmuir 45, 165-6
Arisaig 81, 187, 188, 228
Association, the 61, 176-7
Atterbury, Francis 57, 58, 60
Atterbury plot 56, 80, 82
Austrian Succession, War of 35-6, 62, 100, 122, 137, 149
Avignon 40, 50, 57, 69, 148

Badenoch 48, 77, 141
Balhaldie, William Drummond of 61, 177, 183, 185
Balmerino, Lord 211, 262
Bartlett, Sir Frederick 4
Berwick, 2nd Duke of, (Duke of Liria) 80, 81, 105-6, 166, 211
  at Gaeta 55-6,174
Berwick-on-Tweed 109, 126, 209
Blakeney, General 128
Bland, General 249, 261
Bolingbroke, Viscount 160
Borrodale 28, 82, 187, 188, 189, 206
Boswell, James 169
Boulogne 104, 120, 121
Buchanan, Duncan 80
Byng, Amiral 43, 73, 99, 104, 108, 126

Cameron of Lochiel see Lochiel, Cameron of
Campbell, Lt-Col. 129
Carlisle 20, 74, 109, 118, 213, 216, 226-7, 262
  siege of 110-11, 214-15
Carlyle, Alexander 12-13
celtic civilisation 166-70
  government repression 146-7, 248, 259, 261-2, 263-5
Chamberlain, Neville 14, 16

Charles I 37, 153, 154-6
Charles II 37, 81, 156-9, 238
Chester 103, 108, 112, 218
Chevalier de Johnstone 8, 9, 10
China 17-18
Church of Scotland 114, 127, 155, 238
clan system see celtic civilisation
Clare, Lord 66, 121, 184
Clarendon, Earl of 153
Clementina Maria Sobieski 52-4, 171-3
Clifton 117-18, 224-6
Coldstream 98, 209
Cope, Sir John 21, 78-9, 80, 87, 90, 94, 105, 191, 198, 199, 200, 201, 213, 235
  at Corriearrack 24-5, 83-6, 192-4
  at Prestonpans 27, 95-8, 206-9
Corriearrack 24, 84-5, 95, 105, 190, 192-4, 200, 211
Crieff 84, 134, 191, 195, 196, 242
Cromarty, Earl of 125, 137, 200, 228, 245, 251, 262
Cromwell, Oliver 157
Culloden, battle of 6-8, 26, 27, 29, 141-5, 169, 226, 251-9
Culloden House 46, 74, 75, 123-4, 141, 199, 201, 254, 257
Cumberland, Duke of 42, 73, 103, 114, 129, 184, 220, 221, 230, 239, 243, 261
  and Derby 112, 116-17, 218-19
  at Clifton 117-18, 224-6
  at Culloden 142ff, 248-59
  early life 111
  reaches Edinburgh 134

Dalwhinnie 84, 85, 103, 105, 139, 193, 194
Derby 9, 22, 112-16, 128, 133, 219-23
Dettingen 36, 56, 162, 235
disarming of clans 78, 147
Dornoch 138
Doutelle, the 68-9, 185, 186, 189
Drummond, George 92fn
Drummond, Lord John 61, 104, 125, 226, 228, 229, 230, 243, 250, 253, 260

at Culloden 254, 255, 256
at Falkirk 133, 236
dies 147, 262-3
reaches Scotland 126, 220
Drummond, William of Balhaldie *see* Balhaldie, William Drummond of
Dunbar 90, 94, 206
Dunblane 47, 134
Dunkirk 43, 63, 64, 65, 104, 117, 119, 120, 121, 136, 180-1, 223

Edinburgh 25, 46, 73, 74, 78, 82, 93, 98, 102, 126, 127, 129, 192, 199, 209, 216, 236, 238, 239
Charles in 19, 105, 106, 107, 206, 210ff
leaves 108
Cope leaves 191
Cumberland at 134, 243
Lord Provost of 12-13, 22-3, 87, 89-90, 210-4
Porteous mob, 76, 163
taken by Charles 11-13, 86-91, 201-4
Eilean Donan 49-50
Elcho, Lord 6, 8, 9, 11, 21, 27, 107-8, 115, 184, 206, 211, 259, 262
at Culloden 257
death 148, 263
early life 60-1, 176, 198
Elizabeth, the 68, 69, 185, 186
English Jacobites
in 1715 46, 164-6
in 1745 101-2, 107, 113, 114, 115, 120, 122, 127, 216, 220, 222, 262
Eriskay 43, 71, 81, 186, 188

Falkirk 128, 129
battle of 130-3, 231-5, 258
Finchley 114-15, 219, 220
Fleury, Cardinal 58-9, 61, 62, 177
Florence 54, 175
Fontainebleau, Treaty of 100-1, 216
Fontenoy 42, 99, 235
Forbes, Duncan 71-2, 73, 80, 123-5, 139, 147, 191, 199-200, 228-9, 244, 245
character 25
early life 74-8
escapes to Skye 137-8, 246
Forfeited Estates 147, 264
Fort Augustus 82-3, 84, 125, 126, 137, 146, 190, 191-2, 259, 261
Fort George 82, 190

Fort William 82-3, 126, 137, 140, 141, 190, 191, 247-8, 251
Fortrose, Lord 125, 261
Fraser, Simon *see* Lord Lovat
Frederick the Great 35, 37, 149

Gaeta 55-6, 174-5, 179, 247
Gardiner, Colonel 88, 97
Garvemore 194
geopolitics 36
George I 37, 38-40, 43, 44, 56, 161, 162, 164
George II 24, 36, 40, 58, 74, 99, 102, 113-14, 135, 149, 162, 177, 180, 184, 223, 230
and Finchley 115
meets a Highland soldier 169
returns to London 103, 201
Glasgow 45, 128, 135, 140
Charles enters 126, 227
Charles leaves 229
Glenfinnan 82, 189, 190-1
Glengarry, MacDonald of 82
Glenshiel 50, 51, 52
Gordon, Duke of 44, 77, 123, 177
Gordon of Glenbucket 106, 213
Gordon, Lord Lewis 123, 228-9
Gortleck 9, 259
Guest, General 83, 88, 104

Hawley, Lt-General 27, 29, 134, 236, 248
at Culloden 257
at Falkirk 129-33, 230-5
Henry VIII 25, 39, 154
Henry, Prince Henry Stuart 53, 120-1, 172, 174, 179, 185
Hepburn of Keith 94
Heritable Jurisdictions 147, 264
Holyrood 93, 94, 98, 206, 210-12
Home, John 7, 10, 12, 28, 71, 88
Huntly, Marquis of 44, 47
Huske, General 230-1

Independent Companies 124-5
Inverness 63, 73, 75, 85, 86, 95, 125, 126, 127, 139, 141, 168, 192, 199, 229, 242, 249, 254, 260
Charles reaches 135, 244-5
Forbes leaves 137, 244
Forbes reaches 78, 191
Inverurie 229

James I and VI 37, 154, 168

James II and VII 37–8, 42, 56, 159
James Francis Edward (James III) 42,
    50, 57–8, 60, 65, 67, 75, 148, 165,
    177, 222
  and succession 161–2
  early life 39
  in 1708 43
  in Avignon 40
  in Scotland 47–8
  marriage 52–4, 171–3
  receives letter from Charles 68–9,
    185–6

Kelly, George 80, 99
Kelso 46, 108, 109, 214
Kenmure, Viscount 25
Keppoch, MacDonald of 82, 83, 239,
    251, 253
  at Glenfinnan 191
  joins the Prince 81, 189
  killed 256
  on the highlanders 208
Kilmarnock, Lord 211, 234, 262

Lancashire 46, 166
letter: chiefs to Charles 239–42
Leyden 60, 74, 176
Lichfield 111, 112, 117
Ligonier, Sir John 21, 103, 105, 108,
    109, 111, 117, 118–19, 218, 259
Linlithgow 88, 95, 132, 134
Lion HMS 43, 69, 186
Liria, 1st Duke of see Berwick, Duke of
Liverpool 109, 112
Lochgarry, MacDonald of 7, 194, 262
Lochiel, Donald Cameron of 28, 61,
    67, 77, 83, 85, 125, 128, 135, 141,
    178, 185, 195, 198, 210, 239, 251,
    252, 260
  at Culloden 257
  at Glenfinnan 191
  death 148, 262
  enters Edinburgh 91, 204
  joins the Prince 81–2, 189
Lochnanuagh 148, 186, 260, 262
Lord Provost of Edinburgh see Edin-
    burgh
Loudon, Earl of 78–9, 97, 124, 137–8,
    139, 229, 244–6, 261
Louis XIV 39, 40, 50, 75, 160
Louis XV 4, 18, 21, 67, 68, 101, 102,
    103, 104, 107, 114, 116, 118, 127,
    133, 182, 185, 222–3, 260
  1744 invasion plan 62–4, 178, 180–1

1746 invasion plan 136
  and invasion 119–22
  declares war on Great Britain 64–5
  Peace of Aix la Chapelle 149
  protector of James Edward 50
  sends aid to Charles 126, 128, 220
  sends envoy to Scotland 99, 216
Lovat, Master of 125, 126, 228
Lovat, Simon Fraser, Lord 61, 63, 77,
    123, 139, 176, 178, 192, 199, 200,
    211, 259
  early life and character 75, 195
  escapes arrest 125, 228
  executed 147, 262
Lumisden, Andrew 6, 10

MacDonald, Aeneas 55, 67, 68, 80,
    182, 188
MacDonald of Boisdale 81, 188
MacDonald of Clanranald 188, 189,
    191
MacDonald of Glengarry see Glengarry
MacDonald of Keppoch see Keppoch
MacDonald, Sir Alexander of Sleat 21,
    78, 177
  refuses to join the Jacobites 81,
    106–7, 189, 211
MacDonald, Sir John 80, 198
MacDonell of Lochgarry see Lochgarry
Macintosh (laird of) Borlum 45, 46,
    165
Macintosh, Lady 125, 139, 228, 243–4
MacLeod of MacLeod 21, 78, 184–5
  at Inverurie 229
  escapes to Skye 138, 246
  joins Forbes 124
  refuses to join the Prince 81, 106–7,
    189, 211
  writes to Forbes 71–2, 73, 191
MacPherson, Cluny 139, 141, 246–7,
    251, 260
  abducted 77–8, 199
  joins the Prince 211
Macclesfield 112, 217, 219
Manchester 112, 113, 118, 217,
    218–20, 224, 227
Mar, Earl of 43–8, 57, 59, 60, 165–6,
    213
Maria Theresa 35–6, 62, 100
Marischal, George Keith, 10th Earl 21,
    49, 63, 183, 223
Marlborough, Duke of 37, 43, 45, 129
Marx, Karl 13–14
Mersey 108, 112, 218–19

Milton, Lord 80, 137, 243
Mirabelle, M 8–9, 230, 239
Mollwitz, battle of 35, 58
Montague, Lady Mary Wortley 55
Montrose 48, 105
Moy 139, 243–4
Munro, Sir Robert 132
Murray, Lord George 108, 109, 128, 135, 211, 216, 227, 239–42, 243, 249
  and Derby 112–13, 218–19
  at Carlisle 110–11, 214–15
  at Clifton 118, 224–6
  at Culloden 142–6, 251–7
  at Derby 115–16, 221
  at Falkirk 131, 132, 231–4, 236
  at Prestonpans 207, 209–10
  at Ruthven 10, 260
  early life 196–7
  escapes 148, 263
  in Badenoch 139–40, 246–7
  joins Charles 105–6, 197–8
Murray of Broughton 24, 62, 64, 66, 67, 128, 177–8, 183–4, 194, 198, 211, 215, 242
  early life 60, 176
  escapes 263
  joins Charles 190

Nairn 142–3, 250, 251, 252–3
Newcastle 108, 109, 110, 111, 112, 213, 214, 215, 224
Newcastle, Duke of 79–80, 104, 115, 117, 137, 223
Newcastle-under-Lyme 112, 219
Nithsdale, Earl of 25
Norris, Admiral 180–1

Oakeshott, Michael 10, 15–16, 30
Ogilvy, Lord 44, 243
  at Culloden 257
  escapes 263
  joins Charles 106, 196
Oglethorpe, General 117
Oman, Sir Charles 25
opium trade 17–18
Ormonde, James Butler, Duke of 48, 56–7, 58
Ostend 79, 103, 104, 119, 125–6, 136, 184
O'Sullivan, John William 80, 142, 146, 198, 242
  at Culloden 251, 255, 256
  at Falkirk 236
  dies 148

escapes 259

Perth 73, 82, 128, 134, 198, 242
  Charles enters 88, 195
  Cumberland enters 243
  in 1719 45–7
  Jacobites' headquarters 126, 228
Perth, Duke of 61, 67, 108, 117–18, 130, 137, 184, 206, 209, 211, 245, 253
  at Carlisle 110–11, 215
  at Derby 221
  at River Spey 140–1, 250
  dies 147, 262
  early life 105, 176, 195–6
Piaget, Jean 5
Pitsligo, Lord Forbes of 44, 106, 184, 198, 211–12
Porteous mob 76, 163
Preston 46, 47, 112
Prestonpans 101, 103, 105, 123, 129, 131, 223, 226, 258,
  battle of 26–7, 95–8, 207–9
  slaughter at 145
privateering 66, 185
propaganda 17–19, 30

Richelieu, Duc de 119–21
Roman Catholicism 48, 81, 99, 100, 110, 114, 157, 158, 163, 164, 188, 215
  and Charles 53, 54, 127, 148, 149, 173, 238
  and succession 39, 42, 154, 159–62
Ruthven 9–10, 137, 146, 190, 260

Saxe, Marshal 64, 73, 103, 111, 178, 180–1, 184
Scott, Captain John 82, 190
Scott, Sir Walter 170
Seaforth, Earl of 77
Seven Men of Moidart 80, 99, 188
Shakespeare, William 16
Sheridan, Sir Thomas 80, 128, 174, 183, 184, 188, 211, 242, 251
  at Culloden 7–8, 146, 258
  dies 147, 262
  escapes 259
Sheriffmuir 47, 165–6
Skye 21, 72, 78, 138, 188, 229, 246, 259
Smith, Adam 161
Sobieski *see* Clementina Maria
Spain 36, 37, 40, 42, 52, 54, 55, 57, 58, 59, 106, 136, 172

in 1719   48–50
Spey, River   140–1, 229, 249–50
Stair, Lord   199
Stirling   44, 45, 46, 47, 79, 80, 83–4,
   88, 94, 165, 191, 201, 229
   castle   126
   siege of   8, 128, 130, 133–4, 229–30,
      238–9
Stornoway   49
Strickland, Sir John   80
Stuart Henry, *see* Henry, Prince Henry
   Stuart
Stuart, John Roy   106, 195
   at Clifton   224–5
   escapes   262
Sweden   48

Tongue, Kyle of   138
Traquhair, Earl of   61, 184
Tullibardine, Marquis of   44, 49, 80,
   188, 191, 195

Union, Act of   44, 94, 98–9, 100, 127,
   164, 237–8

Vernon, Admiral   104, 108, 119, 120–1,
   122, 149
Voltaire   120

Wade, Field Marshal   21, 108, 109–12,
   114–15, 117, 129, 134, 214, 215,
   217–18, 221, 224, 230
Wales   109, 112, 116, 166, 217, 218–19
Walkinshaw, Clementina   148–9
Walpole, Sir Robert   41, 57, 58, 74,
   162–3
Walsh, Antoine   67, 81, 104, 119–20,
   185
Wightman, Major-General   49–50, 85,
   102, 113, 191
William of Orange   38, 159–60
Wogan, Charles   171–2
Wolfe, James (General)   144, 256